Skepticism, Relativism, and Religious Knowledge

Skepticism, Relativism, and Religious Knowledge

A Kierkegaardian Perspective Informed by Wittgenstein's Philosophy

MICHAEL G. HARVEY

With a Foreword by Stanley Hauerwas

PICKWICK *Publications* • Eugene, Oregon

SKEPTICISM, RELATIVISM, AND RELIGIOUS KNOWLEDGE
A Kierkegaardian Perspective Informed by Wittgenstein's Philosophy

Pickwick Publications
An Imprint of Wipf and Stock Publishers
199 W. 8th Ave., Suite 3
Eugene, OR 97401

www.wipfandstock.com

ISBN 13: 978-1-4982-6406-8

Cataloging-in-Publication data:

Harvey, Michael G.

Skepticism, relativism, and religious knowledge : a Kierkegaardian perspective informed by Wittgenstein's philosophy / Michael G. Harvey ; foreword by Stanley Hauerwas.

xx + 196 pp. ; 23 cm—Includes bibliographical references and index(es).

ISBN 13: 978-1-4982-6406-8

1. Kierkegaard, Søren, 1813–1855. 2. Wittgenstein, Ludwig, 1889–1951. 3. Philosophy and religion. I. Hauerwas, Stanley, 1940–. II. Title.

B4378.R44 H26 2013

Manufactured in the USA

For Missy and Kaija

Contents

Foreword

I HAVE NO IDEA who Michael G. Harvey may be. All I know is I received a request from him to write a "Foreword" for a book he had written entitled, *Skepticism, Relativism, and Religious Knowledge*. He included with his request the "Introduction" to his book, which I read with great interest. I did so because Harvey was addressing questions about the veridical status of the attitudes and beliefs that make us Christian that have been at the heart of the way I have tried to do theological ethics. Reading his "Introduction" made it clear to me that Harvey was someone from whom I could learn.

I responded to his request indicating my willingness to write the "Foreword" but I also expressed a worry. By reading the "Introduction" I thought he might think Wittgenstein had tried to defeat skepticism. Influenced by Cavell, I was convinced that Wittgenstein thought that skepticism could not be defeated philosophically because any attempt to defeat skepticism philosophically could not help but reproduce the skepticism that was assumed to be the problem. Harvey responded to my worry acknowledging he shared my view that skepticism cannot be defeated because it is integral to our humanity. He explained that he is influenced by Hilary Putnam, who in turn was influenced by Cavell's arguments that help us see that skepticism has philosophical significance.

Harvey's response was a clear indication that he was a person of extraordinary philosophical and theological insight. Reading his book has only confirmed that judgment. In particular I urge readers to take seriously the subtitle of the book, "A Kierkegaardian Perspective Informed by Wittgenstein's Philosophy." That "perspective" is one he acknowledges he learned from the teacher we have in common—Paul Holmer. Thus Harvey, drawing on Holmer, argues that skepticism is often the result of the attempt to provide objective justification for beliefs that are properly groundless. That claim, or better, argument, is one that should stop you in your tracks or, in the very least, it ought to occasion the response, "I'll have to think about that."

Just to the degree that you think you will have to think about that is why you need to read Harvey's book. Drawing on the work of Wittgenstein and Kierkegaard, he has thought long and hard about what it means to be creatures who must trust the knowledge that trust makes possible. Accordingly he argues, an argument that makes him an appreciative critic of "reformed epistemology," that faith is a passion that reorients our will to the knowledge of God. He, moreover, rightly denies that this means that Christians have nothing to say about the rationality of our faith, but what cannot be forgotten is that truth for Christians is not just another object but a concrete person, Jesus of Nazareth.

For Harvey, therefore, what makes Christians Christian is not that they "believe in God." To be a Christian, which to be sure involves "believing," entails an ongoing transformation of the emotions. Such a transformation means to believe in God is to know how to do something. In particular it means knowing how to go on when you often do not know where you are or where you are going. The truth of what Christians believe cannot be separated from who they must be. I think Harvey is quite right, moreover, to attribute this perspective to how Paul Holmer taught him to read Kierkegaard and Wittgenstein.

Skepticism arises from our desire to know without the self being transformed. Ironically skepticism is but the result of our anxious desire to secure certainty by being "at home in the world." But we were not created to be at home in the world. We were created to glorify God, which means, as Harvey puts it, that the knowledge that comes from God cannot be possessed. Such knowledge is the work of patience that produces endurance that makes faith possible.

Harvey has written a book I feel sure Paul Holmer would have liked. I cannot imagine higher praise or a better reason to commend the book to anyone who seeks to better understand the status and character of what it means to be a Christian.

Stanley Hauerwas
Gilbert T. Rowe Professor of Theological Ethics
Duke Divinity School

Acknowledgments

I am grateful to several people who have influenced different parts of the book. These people include Reidar Thomte at Concordia College, Paul L. Holmer and John E. Smith at Yale University, and Ernest Sosa at Rutgers University, who taught previously at Brown University. I am especially grateful to the late Paul L. Holmer for comments he made on an earlier version of chapter 7 when I was his student. I have incorporated his comments into the chapter with full attribution, and bear full responsibility for their use. This book is written, in part, to discharge a debt to him for his many kindnesses over the years.

I would like to express my gratitude to Stanley Hauerwas for his generosity in writing the foreword. I have revised the introduction in light of comments he made about an earlier version in his foreword. I would also like to express my gratitude to my editor Charles Collier for giving me the opportunity to reach a wider audience with the book, and to the scholars who have taken the time to read the manuscript and offer endorsements. Thanks are also due to the editors at Cambridge University Press and The University of Chicago Press for allowing me to adapt the following material. Chapter 1 is a substantive revision of "Wittgenstein's Notion of 'Theology as Grammar,'" *Religious Studies* 25 (1989), 89-103. Chapter 5 is a light revision of "Science, Rationality, and Theology," *The Journal of Religion* 87 (2007), 225–47.

Most importantly, I am grateful to my wife, Melissa (Missy), and to our beloved Kaija. Without Missy's unwavering belief in me, I would not have amounted to much as a person. Without Kaija's smile, the sun would not have shone on cloudy days. Both are good and perfect gifts from above. I am especially grateful to Missy for her hard work in creating the indexes, reading drafts, and offering comments when my thoughts began to stray. Finally, I am grateful to the memory of my parents, Samuel R. Harvey and Bernice J. Stensland, who taught me to consider my creator in the days of my youth.

Introduction

Youth understands immediately that there is a God, because for the young person God's house is right next to his father's residence, and it is entirely natural for him to be there. But when one grows older, the way to the church is often very long.

—Søren Kierkegaard[1]

The skeptical spirit of modern criticism has cast suspicion on belief in God. It has eroded confidence in our capacity to know truth and in our ability to produce rational consensus. More fundamentally, it has undermined our trust in the authority of the Christian tradition. This book examines the challenges of skepticism and relativism to religious knowledge after the demise of classical foundationalism. In criticizing responses to these challenges, by Karl Barth and by Reformed epistemology, I hope to reconstruct their insights in a more robust response to skepticism and relativism that does not depend on making excessive claims about our epistemic capacities. The first part of the book examines how the disjunction of objectivism or relativism in philosophy has motivated the search for a more objective perspective in religion and theology to avoid relativism. The second part of the book outlines a hermeneutical model of rationality that involves a more nuanced conception of the relationship between trust, doubt, faith, and reason. This model is used in the last part of the book to develop a Kierkegaardian perspective on religious knowledge, which is illuminated by Wittgenstein's philosophy, that stresses the importance of the intellectual and theological virtues in religious knowledge.

One of the themes of the book is that doubt is part of our humanity. Whereas skepticism doubts whether we can know truth, relativism doubts whether we can find a sufficiently objective perspective to

1. "Three Upbuilding Discourses," 242.

adjudicate strong disagreement about truth. Thus, relativism involves skepticism about rationality or our ability to produce rational consensus. Although we cannot prevent these doubts from arising with a philosophical refutation of skepticism, we can learn to live with doubt through faith. Kierkegaard argues that doubt arises from the fundamental structure of human consciousness. Consciousness is a synthesis of the ideal and the real, the logical and the existential. This duality not only makes certainty and doubt possible, but the persistent incommensurability between these two discrete factors makes doubt an inescapable actuality. From this duality, all related dualities arise, including knowledge and its objective reference, truth and error, and faith and doubt. Because of this duality, time and space introduce fragmentariness and incompleteness in human experience. Through reason, we strive to complete the incomplete in a view of life that attains a certain wholeness, however imperfect and limited. That we can never attain this wholeness in actuality, however, is the mark of our finitude which prevents us from achieving the objective certainty we crave. The famous scientist Albert Einstein tells us that this search for meaning and intelligibility originates in a cosmic religious feeling. In this religious experience, "the individual feels the futility of human desires and aims and the sublimity and marvelous order which reveal themselves both in nature and in the world of thought. Individual existence impresses him as a sort of prison and he wants to experience the universe as a single significant whole."[2] Similarly, Wittgenstein describes the experience of the world as a limited whole as the mystical. The instinctive search for meaning and intelligibility corresponds to the desire to know, to the desire to transcend the limits of language and thought in order to view the meaning of the world *sub specie aeterni.*[3]

Thus, the cure for doubt, Kierkegaard tells us, is not more reflection, but an act of faith that moves the personality forward in response to the fundamental human need for meaning and intelligibility. Indeed, faith is not, nor can it ever be, the necessary outcome of reflection. Rather, it is the necessary presupposition for reflection. Einstein argues that this is as true for the scientist as it is for the believer. Kierkegaard argues that the fundamental human need for meaning and intelligibility identified by Einstein may even lead to the need for God, which is the

2. Einstein, *Ideas and Opinions*, 38.

3. Wittgenstein, *Tractatus*, 73.

human being's highest perfection. Without faith, the personality cannot constitute itself, any more than the scientist can discover the secrets of nature. The faith that is born of this human need is always struggling for its existence against objections and challenges, and is made strong through them. Here, as David F. Swenson argues, "strife and struggle, anxiety and hope, fear and trembling, despair and faith, are the disciplinarians that fashion the personality."[4] The decision of faith, therefore, is not a possession that can be objectively guaranteed; it is a subjective certainty that is acquired in patience through a gaining or doing in the face of an objective uncertainty.

In the complete absence of doubt, however, there can be no critical belief and a system of belief, which had been held quite critically for a time, tends to decay into a dogmatically held ideology. In religion and theology, this decay of critical belief is called fideism. Here we need to draw a distinction between appropriate and inappropriate forms of fideism. On one hand, as Michael Polanyi has argued, there can be no knowledge without faith, whether in science or in theology. To illuminate skepticism, on the other hand, we need to understand how ideology and fideism are skeptical attitudes or reactions to difference and diversity that lead to the decay of critical belief and ultimately to insularity. This requires a definition of fideism that is different from the one that has been shaped by the evidentialist model of rational inquiry in science. According to this definition, "a fideist is one who accepts or maintains religious belief in defiance of or contrary to reason. Fideism comes from the Latin *fide*, which means 'faith'. A fideist, therefore, affirms that one comes to belief in God as a matter of faith alone. Why is fideism considered odious and worth avoiding? In its antipathy for reason, it neglects or downplays a critical aspect of our nature."[5] This definition of fideism confuses the theological virtue of faith with an epistemic process that concerns whether our beliefs about God have warrant or justification. In contemporary philosophy of religion, faith is assumed to be an inferior form of knowledge that can be transmuted into a more rational form, perhaps due to the invisible influence of the Enlightenment. This assumption motivates the application of the analytic definition of knowledge, as justified true belief, to faith.

4. Swenson, "Objective Uncertainty and Human Faith," 120.

5. Clark, *Return to Reason*, 154.

Although the book probes the philosophical and theological details of this confusion, one observation needs to be made at the outset. The ideal that no one be fideistic in the manner they acquire beliefs of maximal concern, such as those found in ethics and religion, is connected to a foundationalist view of rationality. C. Stephen Evans and Merold Westphal rightly suggest that "perhaps Enlightenment critiques of the reasonableness of religious belief point to defects not so much in religious belief as in the conceptions of knowledge uncritically adopted as the basis of these critiques. Maybe religious knowledge looks dubious because we have the wrong idea about what it is to know something and how we know what we know."[6] Since the prevailing definition of fideism also depends on these conceptions of knowledge, it is not clear why the definition has not come under scrutiny with the conceptions of knowledge uncritically adopted as its basis. Maybe religious knowledge looks dubious because we also have the wrong idea about what it is to trust something and what the role of trust is in knowledge. Whichever definition of fideism we adopt after the demise of the classical picture of knowledge, fideism can no longer be simply defined as accepting religious belief in defiance of or contrary to reason when our very conception of reason has changed in light of fallibilist theories of knowledge.

Recent developments in epistemology, or the theory of knowledge, have questioned whether trust, or for that matter faith, can be defined as accepting belief in defiance of or contrary to reason. Some virtue epistemologists, for example, argue that trust and epistemic authority are normative belief-forming processes that are compatible with modern notions of egalitarianism and autonomy. In particular, trust has a crucial role in epistemic virtue because many of the intellectual virtues are enhancements of trust or restraints on it.[7] This suggests that a more nuanced conception of the relationship between trust, doubt, faith, and reason is needed. This conception, moreover, should include a definition of fideism that is more consistent with recent developments in epistemology. In a conversation about religious belief with M. O'C. Drury, Wittgenstein cautioned his friend that he should never allow himself to become too familiar with holy things. For, as Wittgenstein argues, "the essential fault of what has been called 'fideism' is that it

6. Evans and Westphal, "Introduction," 2.

7. See Zagzebski, *Epistemic Authority*, chapter 2.

dodges all difficulties by adopting a too familiar acquaintance with holy things."[8] This definition of fideism includes the crucial point of the prevailing definition of adhering to religious belief in defiance of or contrary to reason without confusing this decay of critical belief with faith. Although derived from the Latin root for faith, Wittgenstein suggests that fideism is quite different from faith. Whereas faith refers to a critical mode of acceptance by means of grace, fideism refers to an uncritical adherence to the deposit of faith in which we fail to transmute what is believed or accepted through faith into knowledge through the competent exercise of intellectual and theological virtues.

Wittgenstein argues that the child is naturally fideistic in trusting the veracity of what she is told by adults about the Christian tradition. Similarly, Kierkegaard argues that the child has a natural and immediate relationship with God undisturbed by reflection. But as the child matures in the Christian faith, she cannot remain fideistic about the system of belief she has inherited from the Christian tradition in the face of intellectual challenges. To do so, Kierkegaard argues, is to acquiesce in a state of natural religiousness or childish form of Christianity inappropriate for the adult. The notion of the responsible believer dates back to at least Augustine. As Eleonore Stump argues, "Augustine supposed that although we must accept this [Christian] worldview on faith, having accepted it on faith, we investigate it by reason in order to further our comprehension of it, to develop and deepen our grasp of religious truths."[9] Stump tells us that Anselm of Canterbury codified this epistemic disposition in the watchword, "faith seeking understanding." In the words of Anselm, "I do not seek to understand in order to believe, but I believe in order to understand. For this too I believe, that 'unless I believe, I shall not understand.'"[10] Thus, for both Augustine and Anselm, faith is a condition for religious knowledge rather than a form of religious knowledge. In contrast to faith, fideism is the failure to develop a rational faith or reasoned trust concerning the familiar elements of our religious knowledge and experience, in which the believer dodges all difficulties by adopting a too familiar acquaintance with holy things. Faith, the condition for religious knowledge, should not be confused with fideism, the failure to transmute what is believed or accepted

8. Drury, "Notes on Conversations," 94.

9. Stump, "Introduction," 4.

10. Anselm, "Proslogion," 73.

through faith into knowledge. For, as Anselm argues, in questioning what we already know through faith we seek by reasoning to learn what we do not know. This examination does not take place in advance of our acceptance of the deposit of faith, but only after we have already believed it to be true through the inward work of grace.

Although belief in God begins with faith, the responsible believer must reason about the beliefs whose veracity she has trusted in order to know what she believes. Faith seeking understanding requires knowledge. But knowledge requires more than mere true belief. Knowledge requires true belief that has been acquired through the competent exercise of intellectual virtues, in contrast to true belief that has been acquired by luck, or true belief that has been acquired immediately through immersion in the Christian tradition. In reflective knowledge, the exercise of these ground-level competences involves a second-order level competence, namely, determining when it is appropriate to trust or ascent to belief, and when it is appropriate to doubt or withhold belief when there is too much risk of error. In contrast to the excessive claims made about our epistemic capacities by Barth and Reformed epistemology, this view of our epistemic capacities is egalitarian; any normal adult human being can exercise these competences. The view of knowledge as a performance, as a matter of doing something rather than merely believing something, is rooted in the virtue tradition in Plato and Aristotle. Although religious belief may be acquired passively by trusting the authority of the Christian tradition, intellectual virtues such as open-mindedness, intellectual humility, and understanding are needed to transmute religious belief into knowledge. Alvin Plantinga and Nicholas Wolterstorff have rightly stressed the importance of the intellectual virtues in the Christian life.

Unlike Plantinga, however, Wolterstorff recognizes that religious knowledge requires more than the competent exercise of intellectual virtues. The transmutation of religious belief into knowledge also requires the competent exercise of moral or theological virtues such as faith, patience, and suffering. Indeed, another theme of the book is that the problem of religious knowledge is interconnected not only with the intellectual virtues, but more fundamentally, with the human will and the theological virtues. For Kierkegaard, faith is at once a theological virtue and an intellectual virtue. Contrary to the characterization of faith as something radically subjective, invidious, and irrational,

Kierkegaard argues that faith is a passion that has a dialectical nature. Unlike emotions, which are temporary and come and go, a passion is an emotional disposition that has duration. Thus, we may talk about the endurance of faith. Like other virtues such as courage, patience, or temperance, the believer needs faith not just once, but habitually to cope with what happens in the world. As such, faith is an acquired way of responding or reacting to God, to the world, and to other people without guarantees. Like any emotion, the passion of faith is transitive; its object is knowledge of God.

The dialectical nature of faith comes from its need to constantly mediate two extremes in Christian experience, absolute certainty and skeptical doubt, as it oscillates back and forth between them. Descartes argues that hope and anxiety are opposite, but necessary and complementary, passions of the soul. Whereas hope is convinced that what it desires will come about, anxiety is convinced that what it desires will not be fulfilled. When hope is so strong that it excludes anxiety, its nature changes into confidence or assurance. Conversely, when anxiety is so extreme that it leaves no room for hope, it changes its nature into despair which treats the object of passion as unattainable.[11] Thus, hope and anxiety are moderating factors in Christian experience. According to Descartes, this situation may lead to irresolution and inaction. An excess of irresolution results both from too great a desire to do our best in choosing the right and from a weakness of the will. The only cure for this situation, as Kierkegaard argues, is decisiveness. In the decision of faith, the dialectical nature of faith struggles to keep the soul balanced between the extremes of dogmatism and skepticism, by preventing hope from degenerating into dogmatism and by preventing anxiety from degenerating into skepticism. Faith must not only struggle against too little confidence, in which the believer is convinced that the object of her passion is beyond reach. It must also struggle against too much confidence, in which the believer dodges all difficulties by adopting a too familiar acquaintance with holy things.

According to the virtue tradition in ethics, moral and religious language assumes that there is already something there in the personality of the subject to talk about that needs to be given substance, definition, shape, and structure. Whereas Kierkegaard describes this identity as the self, Wittgenstein describes it as a form of life. In the absence of a

11. Descartes, *Passions of the Soul*, 389–91.

constellation of emotions, attitudes, and dispositions in a person that need to be corrected, the beliefs of the Christian tradition have little meaning. Plato and Aristotle understood that we need to learn to make sense with our lives as much as we need to learn to make sense with our thoughts. Paul L. Holmer argues that faith helps us do both. Persons themselves can be deprived of sense. Like thoughts, lives can also be invalid and need justification. In ethics and religion, we see that something besides language can be the bearer of sense, order, significance, and even truth, namely, the human being.[12]

But one must be careful here. Although Christianity assumes that there inheres in the subjectivity of the individual the possibility of its acceptance through faith, it does not assume that faith is a disposition that is already present in the personality. Barth has quite rightly criticized this tendency in liberal theology. The Christian identity, which is essentially characterized by faith, is not something that is ready-made. Rather, it is something that we have to make ourselves through the competent exercise of both the intellectual and theological virtues. When faith is included in the familiar elements of our religious knowledge or experience, one must be careful not to misrepresent faith as a disposition that already inheres in the subjectivity of the individual, independently of free will and moral virtue. One must also be careful not to misrepresent faith as an immediate disposition undisturbed by reflection, by situating it so deeply in our noetic structure that doubt cannot get at it there. Here, like Wittgenstein, Kierkegaard cautions that "anything offered as a belief, even if religious, which keeps the dialectical away, which stops doubt and inquiry, which causes the uncertain to appear certain, is a superstition, be it offered with religious purpose or not."[13]

12. Holmer, *Making Christian Sense*, 98.

13. Holmer, *Kierkegaard and the Truth*, 69–70.

Part One

The Exclusive Disjunction of Objectivism or Relativism

1

Religious Language, Reference, and Autonomy

Logical positivism emerged in the early 1920s when Moritz Schlick, around whom it centered, became professor of philosophy at the University of Vienna. The Vienna Circle included a group of philosophers, scientists, and mathematicians who shared a concern about problems in logic, the philosophy of mathematics, and the physical and social sciences. The group attempted to elucidate these problems by establishing an empirical foundation for knowledge in the principles of logic that did not depend on metaphysics. Although metaphysical utterances may have poetic merit or express an interesting attitude toward life, they do not state anything true or false. Consequently, metaphysics cannot contribute anything to empirical knowledge. As A. J. Ayer argues, "metaphysical utterances were condemned not for being emotive . . . but for pretending to be cognitive, for masquerading as something that they were not."[1] When the metaphysician talks about the absolute, transcendent entities, substance, the destiny of man, aesthetics, ethics, or religion, he breaks the rules that an utterance must satisfy in order to be literally significant.

In religion and theology, the restriction on what counts as an assertion raised the question of whether religious language can be cognitively meaningful if it does not make significant assertions about reality. This challenge precipitated an epistemological crisis that led to one of the most intense periods of critical mental activity in modern philosophy and theology. Disagreement over how to proceed in the face of this challenge polarized philosophers and theologians into two groups. One group, called the grammarians, attempted to reconstrue the meaning of religious language

1. Ayer, "Introduction," 10–11.

without making ontological commitments to a discourse-independent reality. Another group, called the Platonists, argued that religious language is meaningless without ontological commitments because it cannot otherwise be about anything objectively real. Religious language merely becomes an expression of emotion like poetry which can be neither true nor false. The disagreement in religion and theology about whether religious language is about something objectively real is part of a larger disagreement in philosophy about whether there is a ready-made world and whether there are determinate correspondences between this world and language. This disagreement has provoked a deep disquiet that is still with us today. I will argue that Ludwig Wittgenstein's notion of theology as grammar may help relieve the disquiet.

THE PLATONISTS VS. THE GRAMMARIANS

Philosophers have claimed that praying to God is like writing letters to a person with divine properties. If there is no person who answers to that definite description, then praying to God is meaningless. Peter Winch argues that philosophers often assume on the basis of this analogy that praying to God presupposes that there is a God in the philosophical sense of a metaphysical object that possesses divine properties.[2] Whether there must be such a metaphysical object corresponding to the practice of religion is the question that divides Winch from other philosophers and theologians in their interpretation of Wittgenstein's notion of theology as grammar.[3] In objecting to Winch and other grammarians such as Norman Malcolm and D. Z. Phillips, Renford Bambrough argues that "theology as grammar, insofar as grammar tells us what kind of object anything is, therefore presumably tells us what kind of object God is."[4]

Like Bambrough, Kai Nielsen argues that the question of whether God actually secures reference, standing for something objectively real, and whether we can resolve or even dissolve this question is of prior importance.[5] Although Nielsen agrees with the grammarians that religion can have no metaphysical foundation, he claims that such perplexities about

2. Winch, "Religious Language," 193–221.
3. Wittgenstein, *Investigations*, 1, ¶ 373.
4. Bambrough, "Introduction," 16.
5. Nielsen, "Groundless Believing," 98–99.

God and religion are not simply rooted in a second-order context where the engine is idling.[6] Nielsen takes the fact that some people doubt the existence of God as evidence for the validity of the philosophical question of whether God actually secures reference. The grammarians do not preclude the possibility of skepticism. Just because skepticism is possible, however, does not mean that the philosophical question of whether God actually secures reference is valid. In appealing to a non-philosophical context in which such a skeptical question seems to arise naturally, Nielsen assumes that the boundary line between philosophical and non-philosophical contexts is sharper than it is or needs to be in order to support his claim. It is doubtful whether anyone can be philosophically naïve in the sense required by Nielsen's argument. Skepticism about belief in God is influenced by philosophy more than Nielsen acknowledges. Religious skepticism does not presuppose any philosophical background, only immersion in a metaphysical tradition that is the subject of intense debate today among theists and secularists.

The disagreement between the Platonists and the grammarians is influenced by the exclusive disjunction of objectivism or relativism. Either religious language describes a metaphysical object, or language about God is meaningless and relativistic. This disjunction has acquired the status of what Hilary Putnam calls a cultural institution.[7] Regardless of the extent to which we are familiar with its philosophical details, the disjunction of objectivism or relativism is part of our shared world picture in the modern West. This undermines the sharp distinction between philosophical and non-philosophical contexts on which Nielsen's argument depends. When we claim that skeptical questions arise naturally, uninfluenced by philosophy, we must remember that the language game of doubt is played after the language game of belief.[8] Trusting what we apprehend other people as telling us as true occurs prior to doubting any part of it. Whereas trust is a natural reaction, doubt is something we must learn to do. Skepticism has become problematic because we have learned to doubt in a very sophisticated way in light of modern criticism. Thus, contrary to Nielsen, skepticism about belief in God cannot be resolved or even dissolved by clarifying the objective reference of religious language. The difficulty does not have to do with our capacity to know truth, but with the human will. If belief

6. Ibid., 104–5.

7. Putnam, *Reason, Truth, and History*, 127.

8. Wittgenstein, *On Certainty*, ¶ 160.

in God is more difficult for us, it is because we have proved unwilling to scrutinize the doubts that have gripped us intellectually, barring the way to belief.

Unlike Nielsen, Bambrough argues that the grammarian's notion of theology as grammar is anti-realist and therefore relativistic and heretical. For according to Bambrough, the denial of the classical realist position in theology was, until recently, set down as heresy.[9] The question of whether Christianity refers to an objective reality is never raised by the grammarians. Belief in God presupposes the existence of God in a sense independent of human thought and any linguistic and epistemic practices. To speak of God, however, as revealed in the person of Jesus of Nazareth through the historical event of the incarnation is one matter; to speak of God as a metaphysical object outside the context of this unique historical event is quite another. The Bible claims that God is a spirit, not a metaphysical object. Although it is heretical to reject the traditional belief in the incarnation, it is not heretical to reject the philosophical characterization of God as a metaphysical object with divine properties. Thus, the notion of theology as grammar raises two issues that must be addressed. The first issue concerns the question of whether religious language can be meaningful if there is no metaphysical object with divine properties that it describes. The second issue concerns Bambrough's charge of relativism. If we reject the classical realist or Platonist conception of the reference of religious language, the question is whether we are committed to a relativistic conception of religious language. I will address these issues in turn.

THE RELATION BETWEEN LANGUAGE AND REALITY

In his early philosophy, Wittgenstein argues that the possibility of comparing a proposition with reality is equivalent to the possibility of verifying it—the meaning of a proposition is the method of its verification. Malcolm notes the importance of this idea in making the verification principle emerge as a central doctrine of the Vienna Circle.[10] Wittgenstein's early views about the nature of language largely coincided with those of the Vienna Circle. Like the logical positivists, Wittgenstein argues that metaphysical assertions are nonsense. In general, a statement agrees with some

9. Bambrough, "Introduction," 15.

10. Malcolm, *Nothing Is Hidden*, 134–35.

truth distributions and disagrees with others. Among the possible states of affairs that a statement can describe, some would make it true and others would make it false. There are two extreme cases, however, where significant or meaningful language is degenerative. When a statement agrees with every truth distribution, it is called a tautology. Since tautologies agree with every possible state of affairs, they can be either true or false and therefore make no claim upon the facts. Suppose, for example, that we obtain information about the habits of lions. As Ayer argues, if I am told that lions are either carnivorous or not, I am told nothing about them at all. When a statement agrees with none of its truth distributions, on the other hand, it is called a contradiction. Since contradictions disagree with every possible state of affairs, they can be both true and false and therefore make no claim upon the facts. Thus, Ayer argues that if I am told that lions are and are not carnivorous, I am told nothing about them at all. Thus, tautologies and contradictions are degenerative cases of factual statements.[11]

On this literal view of language, significant propositions can be divided into two classes. One class consists of formal propositions such as those found in logic and pure mathematics. Wittgenstein argues that these propositions are tautologies because they do not give us any information or knowledge about the world. They add to our knowledge only in the sense that we are able to derive one statement from another, thereby making explicit the implications of what we already in a sense knew. The other class consists of factual propositions that are empirically verifiable in principle. Like the logical positivists, Wittgenstein considered these two classes exhaustive. Thus, if a statement does not express something that is formally true or false or something that can be empirically tested, it does not express any proposition at all. Consequently, since metaphysical assertions are neither formal statements nor made up of elementary propositions that bear a relation to facts, they are literally nonsensical or cognitively meaningless.

Because religious language refers in some sense to a transcendent reality, it is open to the criticism of metaphysics. One of the ways in which the metaphysical claims of religion have been attacked in the past is by questioning whether religious propositions can be deduced from premises that are self-evident to the senses. This line of attack is illustrated in the evidentialist challenge to religious belief embedded in classical foundationalism. Contrary to Kant's conclusions about the limits of theoretical reason, many philosophers and theologians have responded to this attack

11. Ayer, "Introduction," 10–12. See Wittgenstein, *Tractatus*, 34-35.

by postulating a special faculty of intellectual intuition that enables them to know facts that could not be known through sense experience. They attempt to ground such intuition or perception in the empirical premises of religious experience. As Ayer argues, "they say that it is logically possible for men to be immediately acquainted with God, as they are immediately acquainted with a sense-content, and that there is no reason why we should be prepared to believe a man when he says that he is seeing a yellow patch, and refuse to believe him when he says that he is seeing God."[12] If the meaning of religious propositions could be shown to rely on empirical premises, even though the venture into a non-empirical world would be unjustified, it would still not follow that the assertions that religious language makes about this non-empirical world could not be true. For, as Ayer argues, the fact that a conclusion does not follow from its premise is not sufficient to show that it is false. Consequently, one cannot overthrow metaphysics or the metaphysical assertions of religious language by criticizing the way in which they come into being.[13]

What is required instead, Ayer argues, is a criticism of the nature of the actual statements that comprise metaphysics. Unlike Hume and Kant, who grounded the impossibility of metaphysics in the nature of what can be known, the logical positivists grounded its impossibility in the nature of what can be said. No statement that refers to a reality transcending the limits of all possible sense experience can have literal significance. Thus, the logical positivists argued that the Platonist's notion of a person whose essential attributes are non-empirical is unintelligible. Although we may ascribe the name "God" to this person, it cannot symbolize anything unless the sentences in which the name occurs express propositions that are empirically verifiable. For, as Ayer argues, "the mere existence of the noun is enough to foster the illusion that there is a real, or at any rate a possible entity corresponding to it. It is only when we enquire what God's attributes are that we discover that 'God,' in this usage, is not a genuine name."[14]

Ayer argues that the argument from religious experience is open to the same criticism as metaphysics. Although the mystic may claim that intuition reveals synthetic propositions, and we cannot maintain *a priori* that there are no ways of discovering true propositions except those that we employ, Ayer argues that those propositions must ultimately be subject to

12. Ayer, *Language, Truth, and Logic*, 119.

13. Ibid., 34.

14. Ibid., 116.

the test of actual experience. When the mystic's discoveries are expressed as propositions, we can determine whether they are verified or confuted by empirical observation. That the mystic cannot express intuition as facts that can be tested, however, shows that the state of mystical intuition is not a genuine cognitive state. For, in describing his vision, the mystic does not give us any information about the world, but only indirect information about the conditions of his or her own mind.[15] The only meaningful defense of belief in God allowed by logical positivism is some version of pantheism in which deities are identified with natural objects.

Although several issues distanced Wittgenstein from the Vienna Circle, perhaps the most important is the mystical. Whereas the logical positivists sought to emancipate philosophy from metaphysics, Wittgenstein included metaphysics in his philosophy by designating a special sphere called the mystical. The mystical includes, among other things, the most important problems of life addressed in ethics and religion, which the Danish philosopher Søren Kierkegaard called essential truth in contrast to scientific truth. These areas of knowledge make cognitively meaningful assertions that cannot be expressed as facts and thereby reduced to the sphere of science. As Wittgenstein argues, "ethics, if it is anything, is supernatural and our words will only express facts."[16] As such, ethics and religion violate the literal sense of a proposition as defined by logical positivism. The metaphysical or transcendent nature of ethics and religion is not related literally and directly to moral and religious language in the way facts are related to empirical and scientific language. The relation between language and reality in the sphere of the mystical must be communicated indirectly. In revising the picture theory of meaning in his early thought to include ethical and religious language, Wittgenstein argues that the meaning of this language is not to be found in the object or referent that it is alleged to describe, but in the way that it is used to form a way of living that corresponds with this transcendent reality. The purpose of religious language is not to make metaphysical claims about the universe, but to shape the emotions, attitudes, and dispositions of a human being into a religious form of life. This form of life or subjectivity has a logic that can be objectively described by religious language. Thus, the existence of God is shown *indirectly* in the application of religious language in the life of the believer rather than described directly by it. This reconception of the relation between language

15. Ibid., 119.

16. Wittgenstein, "Lecture on Ethics," 7.

and reality still involves the notion of "correspondence with reality" found in the *Tractatus*. But the nature of the correspondence is passional and indirect rather than literal and direct, and the reality is a concrete way of living rather than an abstract metaphysical object. In the case of ethics and religion, it is not language itself that corresponds with reality, but rather a way of living that is shaped by this language.

But if the primary purpose of religious language is to make statements about a discourse-independent reality, the more ordinary usage appears inferior. Like Kierkegaard, Wittgenstein argues that religious language has a limited degree of cognitive, literal, or propositional significance. As Paul L. Holmer explains, ordinary religious language has passional significance in providing a cognitively meaningful description of a constellation of passions, attitudes, and dispositions that give a religious form of life its logical shape.[17] This passional significance is essential for understanding *what* is meant by God rather than whom is meant. Thus, when Wittgenstein argues that grammar tells us what kind of object anything is, he points out that "the great difficulty here is not to represent the matter as if there were something one *couldn't* do. As if there really were an object, from which I derive its description, but I were unable to shew it to anyone. —And the best that I can propose is that we should yield to the temptation to use this picture, but then investigate how the *application* of the picture goes."[18] Because the referent of religious language cannot be expressed in language, it shows itself in the application of religious language in the life of the believer. Thus, Wittgenstein tells us that "the word 'God' is amongst the earliest learnt—pictures and catechisms, etc. But not the same consequences as with pictures of aunts. I wasn't shown [that which the picture represented]."[19]

Contrary to the logical positivists and the Platonists, Wittgenstein argues that the word "God" is not a proper name or definite description. As Wittgenstein explains, "if the question arises as to the existence of a god or God, it plays an entirely different role to that of the existence of any person or object I ever heard of. One said, had to say, that one *believed* in the existence, and if one did not believe, this was regarded as something bad. Normally, if I did not believe in the existence of something no one would think there was anything wrong in this."[20] In a non-philosophical context,

17. Holmer, *Kierkegaard and the Truth*, 8; and "Religious Propositions."

18. Wittgenstein, *Investigations*, 1, ¶ 374.

19. Wittgenstein, *Lectures & Conversations*, 59.

20. Ibid.

Wittgenstein argues that we would never think that Michelangelo's picture, "God created man," represented the Deity: "the picture has to be used in an entirely different way if we are to call the man in that strange blanket God. If I showed someone Michelangelo's picture and said I cannot show you the real thing, only the picture, the absurdity is that I've never taught her the technique of using this picture. If you asked Michelangelo if he thought God creating Adam looked like this, he wouldn't have said that God or Adam looked as they do in his picture."[21]

Since God is neither an object of sense experience nor an object of theoretical reason according to Kant's theory of knowledge, we cannot compare Michelangelo's picture with its referent. Unlike the case of an ordinary object, there is no technique of comparison here. There is no determinate "correspondence with reality" as required by the literal view of language in the *Tractatus*. Thus, unlike the philosophical use of the word "God," Wittgenstein argues that the ordinary use of the word does not require a correspondence theory of truth. In the words of Malcolm, what is important to see is open to everyone's view: look at how this picture, "God created man," is used in the religious life. As Winch explains, "the point of Michelangelo's representation has to be seen in relation to the way in which worship and love are connected in the life of the believer. It is here that the picture is 'confronted with reality.' The form of representation, the sort of connection with reality, involved are totally different from that in a diagram of an accident presented with a claim on an insurance company."[22] Kierkegaard, for example, tells us that the concept of sin as it is used in Christian discourse does not correspond to an objective fact in the world, but to the mood of seriousness which may or may not be part of the subjectivity of the individual.[23]

The philosophical question of whom the picture represents disregards the more ordinary question of what the picture means in the religious life. As Wittgenstein tells us, "the way you use the word 'God' does not show whom you mean—but, rather, what you mean."[24] Thus, Winch argues that "how a term refers has to be understood in the light of its *actual* application with its surrounding context in the lives of its users. I italicize 'actual' by way of contrasting what I am talking about both with some 'ideal' application

21. Ibid., 63.
22. Winch, "Religious Language," 208–9.
23. See Holmer, *Kierkegaard and the Truth*, 75.
24. Wittgenstein, *Culture and Value*, 50.

imagined by philosophers and also with what users of the term may be inclined to say about their application of it if asked."[25] The logic of God is different from the logic of a proper name or definite description. In the case of God, what appears to be a proper name that represents a fact turns out to have an irreducible metaphysical nature that cannot be described or expressed directly. When believers talk about God in a non-philosophical context, they do not refer to an abstract metaphysical object. If asked what they are referring to, however, believers may substitute an ideal application of the word "God" in place of its actual application. Consequently, Winch argues that when the question is posed in a philosophical context ordinary believers may respond just like the philosopher.

Winch argues that the reference of religious language is a special case of the more general problem of objective reference. Like Wittgenstein's criticism of his early philosophy, we must scrutinize the idealized conception of language in which reference is conceived as hidden intentional relations in the mind that somehow latch onto ontological properties in the world, as when a thought or proposition reaches out to reality. Like Wittgenstein's later philosophy, Winch urges us to think of the relation between language and reality in terms of a person's ability to apply ordinary language in a referring way. Contrary to Bambrough, this reconception does not reduce God to a grammatical convention. Rather, the form of representation or sort of relation between language and reality proposed by a metaphysical theory of reference must be changed. Winch makes this point clear when he says that "I am not saying the 'existence' of what is spoken of simply consists in the fact that people talk in a certain way; I am saying that what the 'existence' of whatever it is amounts to is expressed (shows itself) in the way people apply the language they speak."[26]

Despite the obscure nature of the alleged "correspondence with reality," the Platonists argue that one cannot maintain the objective truth-claims of the Christian tradition without a metaphysical theory of reference. To avoid this obscurity, we must find another way to express the traditional realist claim that God exists in a sense independent of human thought without conceiving of God as a metaphysical object and thereby falling into the conundrums of objectivism. If Winch is right, classical realism depends on a literal view of language that makes the ordinary language of the Bible look imprecise because it does not conform to the paradigmatic usage of

25. Winch, "Religious Language," 200.

26. Ibid.

picturing facts. When we try to describe the existence of God directly in language, we become perplexed by the relation between language and reality, by the relation of our God-talk to the existence of what is spoken about. Here, as Winch argues, "the temptation in philosophizing about religion and theology is similar to temptations in other areas of philosophy. For we seem to see a different and more direct sort of relation between language and reality by disregarding the complexities of the actual application of that language. Thus, we are led to the view that using religious language commits us to a theory about the nature of the world that language somehow enshrines."[27] What is at issue is not the commonsense realist conviction, but the philosophical theory about the relation between language and reality that attempts to express this conviction. Here, as Wittgenstein argues, we bump up against the limits of language and thought when we try to express the mystical.

The Autonomy of Religious Language

The Platonists argue that the adoption of a more pragmatic account of the relation between language and reality in place of the classical realist account is tantamount to anti-realism. This argument seemed plausible at the time, given the mutually exclusive dichotomy between realism and pragmatism.[28] Today, in light of developments in the theory of knowledge, it is argued that one can be realist with respect to truth and pragmatist with respect to knowledge. Despite these developments, however, the charge of relativism still stands because it is supported by the exclusive disjunction of objectivism or relativism that motivated the dichotomy between realism and pragmatism in the first place. Thus, it is argued that if we adopt the more epistemically humble perspective of theology as grammar in place of the objectivist perspective in classical realism we are committed to relativism. I will argue that this skeptical conclusion does not follow.

Nielsen claims that the autonomy of language games in Wittgenstein's philosophy of language raises the problem of relativism. In particular, since the grammarians argue that religious language is distinctive, the autonomy of religious language raises the problem of relativism in religion and theology. If language games are autonomous, how can we criticize one language

27. Ibid., 203.

28. See, e.g., Jackson, "Against Grammar," 240–45.

game from the standpoint of another? In religion and theology, how can we claim that one religion is more valid or that one theology is more truth-preserving than another if we lack common criteria of meaning and intelligibility? If common criteria do not exist, the form of life enshrined in religious language appears fideistic and immune from public scrutiny. The grammarians, however, do not argue that religious language is autonomous in the sense of Cartesian internalism. Quite the opposite, they argue that the distinctiveness or intramural character of religious language depends on its external or extramural relations to other language games.[29]

The question, therefore, is not whether there are common criteria of meaning and intelligibility, but what sort of status they have in language. In the history of philosophy and theology, they have been given either ontological or nominal status. In both cases, Winch argues that philosophers and theologians imagine an ideal set of universal concepts whose criteria of meaning and intelligibility are independent of any language game or conceptualization. For Wittgenstein, the question of whether these criteria of meaning and intelligibility have ontological or nominal status is eclipsed by the more illuminating question of why we feel compelled to search for a neutral language that can replace the concepts of ordinary language with conceptually uncontaminated concepts. In his early philosophy, Wittgenstein argues that this compulsion is related to the experience of the mystical, to the desire to transcend the limits of language and the world in order to view the meaning of the world *sub specie aeterni*.[30] In his later philosophy, Wittgenstein argues that although this compulsion is worthy of deep respect in the case of ethics and religion, the criteria of meaning and intelligibility established within the practice of ordinary language are valid as they stand without a metaphysical backing.

Although every language game has distinctive concepts whose criteria of meaning and intelligibility are determined by their application within that language, the concepts within one language game are related externally to concepts within other language games by family resemblances. These resemblances may disguise important differences in the actual application of concepts in various regions of language. Thus, when we place too much emphasis on family resemblances alone, we are led to an idealized conception of the universal nature of language in which these differences are disregarded. These family resemblances, however, are continually changing

29. See, e.g., Phillips, "Externalism and Internalism," 60–92.

30. Wittgenstein, *Tractatus*, 73.

with the development of language and the emergence of new applications of language. Although we may take a snapshot of the dynamically unfolding landscape of ordinary language, we cannot pin it down in a static description. Thus, Wittgenstein argues that we cannot appeal to a set of fixed and stable criteria of meaning and intelligibility that overarch all language games. The logic of ordinary language does not permit such a meta-linguistic perspective.

More fundamental is the assumption that we can only criticize a language game from a meta-linguistic perspective. As Hans-Georg Gadamer suggests, the Enlightenment's prejudice against prejudice has blinded us to the fact that the concepts of ordinary language provide a sufficiently objective perspective for criticism within a language game.[31] For example, the language games of science and theology are two systems of thought and action within which there is controversy and argument. As Malcolm writes, "within each there are advances and recessions of insight into the secrets of nature or the spiritual condition of humankind and the demands of the Creator, Savior, Judge, Source. Within the framework of each system there is criticism, explanation, justification. But we should not expect that there might be some sort of rational justification of the framework itself."[32]

The relativist thesis that there is no sufficiently objective perspective within a language game that enables us to criticize a system of belief grips us when we disregard the actual application of language. We cannot invent an ideal set of criteria of meaning and intelligibility from scratch, apart from their application within a language game or system of belief. Such criteria emerge naturally from the application of the concepts of ordinary language. Thus, there is an intelligible notion of objective fit between our God-talk and the God of Abraham, Isaac, and Jacob within the language game of theology. For there are clear and unambiguous criteria of meaning and intelligibility established by the Christian tradition. These criteria enable us to draw a distinction between orthodox beliefs and unorthodox beliefs. The history of Christian doctrine is the story of how this dogmatic norm has evolved naturally through the application of theological concepts in the face of strong disagreement about the deposit of faith. Without these criteria, the notions of conforming to and deviating from the practice of faith are unintelligible. These criteria enable us to distinguish between "being right" and "believing one is right" within the language game of theology.

31. Gadamer, *Truth and Method*, 270.

32. Malcolm, *Thought and Knowledge*, 208–9.

Relativism, however, rejects such a distinction. It claims that one point of view is just as valid as another point of view. But, as Hilary Putnam argues, it is contradictory to hold this particular point of view while holding that no point of view is better than another. If all points of view are equally valid, why isn't the point of view that relativism is false just as valid as the point of view that it is true? One takes it for granted, like Bambrough and Nielsen, that the question of whether a belief is true relative to a particular language game is itself something absolute. But, as Putnam argues, a total relativist would have to claim that this question is also relative.[33] Clearly, the grammarians make no such claim. Thus, relativism, given its skeptical conclusion that no point of view is better than another, is incompatible with any intelligible notion of objective fit between our God-talk and the God of Abraham, Isaac, and Jacob. Relativism rejects what Wittgenstein and the grammarians both accept, namely, that there is a valid distinction between "being right" and "believing one is right" within a language game.

Relativism is based on the internalist Cartesian assumption that language games are autonomous, isolated atoms of discourse. The criteria of meaning and intelligibility that govern one discourse are cut off from the criteria that govern another discourse in a dramatic sense. Wittgenstein challenges this assumption with counterexamples that show how the application of words in one language game is related to their application in other language games. When we emphasize family resemblances or what is common to language games while disregarding important differences in the application of language, we are led to a universalist or objectivist perspective that is distortive of ordinary language. Conversely, when we emphasize important differences in the application of language while disregarding family resemblances, we are led to a relativist perspective that is equally distortive of ordinary language. Thus, Wittgenstein suggests that the exclusive disjunction of objectivism or relativism arises from the failure to take into account both the similarities and differences in the actual application of language. In particular, the failure to recognize how language games are related externally has led to a dissatisfaction with ordinary language in its ability to supply sufficiently objective norms for rational inquiry.[34] We no longer trust the criteria of meaning and intelligibility established within the practice of ordinary language as providing a reliable foundation for conducting further rational inquiry. The search for a neutral language that

33. Putnam, *Reason, Truth, and History*, 119–24.

34. Wittgenstein, *Investigations*, 1, ¶¶ 65–67.

could provide a more reliable foundation and objective perspective is the result of our *unwillingness* to trust ordinary language as it stands.[35] Whereas skepticism doubts our capacity to know truth, relativism doubts whether we can find a sufficiently objective perspective within a language game to adjudicate strong disagreement about truth. Thus, relativism involves skepticism about rationality rather than truth.

The question of whether there are universal criteria of meaning and intelligibility that can provide a meta-linguistic perspective that overarches all language games is forced on us by the internalist Cartesian assumption of the autonomy of language games. If this assumption is correct, it follows that there is no sufficiently objective perspective within a language game according to which we can adjudicate the objective fit between our God-talk and the God of Abraham, Isaac, and Jacob. To avoid relativism, we feel compelled to search for a more objective perspective in order to make up our minds with confidence about questions of maximal concern. In ethics and religion, however, Wittgenstein argues that the quest for objectivity distracts us from the ethical task of becoming a self. If belief in God is more difficult today, it is not because it was easier in the past, but because we have no use for old fashioned concepts like sin, repentance, and salvation. These concepts have meaning only within the context of a way of living in which one perceives Christianity to be the remedy for consciousness of sin. Abstracted from this context, the ordinary language of the Bible is meaningless. An objectivist perspective in religion and theology assumes that we can sever the ordinary language of the Bible from the very way of living or practice that instantiates it with meaning. It assumes that we can understand the words of faith cheaply without acquiring the substantial concepts that make the words meaningful.

Objectivism assumes that we can criticize a language game, form of life, or mode of subjectivity independent of all conceptual choices. But, as Putnam argues, there just are no inputs to knowledge that are not to some extent shaped by our concepts and which admit of only one description.[36] That we make conceptual choices in the way we apply religious language shifts the focus of the discussion from the reference of religious language to the ability to use this language to form a way of living that corresponds with this referent. The existence of God does not thereby drop out of the discussion as an idling piece of discourse, only the philosophical characterization

35. Ibid., 1, ¶ 105; 2, ¶ 200.

36. Putnam, *Reason, Truth, and History*, 54.

of a person's relation to his existence in terms of a metaphysical theory of reference. As a person's life grows into the demanding usages of religious language, one becomes more like the reality of which it speaks. Thus, the mature Christian life is a picture of the reality of God. Through the application of religious language in the life of the believer, the human being bears the potential to manifest the existence of what is spoken about. But, as Wittgenstein argues, "what *can* be shown, *cannot* be said."[37]

If God's reality cannot be expressed directly in language, but only shown indirectly by the application of religious language in the life of the believer, the question about the objective reference of God is moot. As Wittgenstein writes, "conflict is dissipated in much the same way as is the tension of a spring when you melt the mechanism (or dissolve it in nitric acid). This dissolution eliminates all tensions."[38] If we eliminate the philosophical mechanism of a literal relation between religious language and the existence of what is spoken about, disagreements about the objective reference of God are dissolved with the mechanism that held them in place. Instead, we may develop the emotional capacities needed to understand the ordinary language of the Bible such as despair, the consciousness of sin, and suffering. Then the Christian concepts of faith, repentance, and hope have something meaningful to say to these realities. It is here that religious language is confronted with reality, not in the philosophical sense of a religious proposition that corresponds with a metaphysical object, but in the ordinary sense of an ethical form of life that is shaped by the words of faith such that it corresponds with (shows) the invisible God of the Bible.

37. Wittgenstein, *Tractatus*, 26.

38. Wittgenstein, *Culture and Value*, 9.

2

Revelation, Imagination, and Arbitrariness

THE REFORMED THEOLOGIAN KARL Barth posed the question of whether the believer can escape the accursed relativity of every merely human possibility. Barth argues that we cannot escape because even our thinking is conducted within the sphere of relativity.[1] In casting suspicion on our capacity to know truth, Barth attempts to formulate a more rigorous religious epistemology in its place. This epistemology allegedly avoids arbitrary or relativistic theological interpretations with a Christocentric method. The problem of method in theology looms large today. Where do we begin and how do we proceed with the constructive task of theological understanding? What is the relation between divine revelation and human imagination? What constraints should be placed on imagination in understanding revelation in order to avoid arbitrariness? Can we avoid arbitrariness, either in our choice of a dogmatic method or starting point for theology, or in our choice of a dogmatic norm that provides criteria of meaning and intelligibility for adjudicating disagreement in religion and theology?

I will argue that these questions are shaped by the exclusive disjunction of objectivism or relativism that distorts the hermeneutical issues raised by the problem of theological method. So long as the debate about method remains polarized by this exclusive disjunction, we cannot advance the discussion beyond the current impasse. Nowhere perhaps is this impasse better illustrated than in Gordon Kaufman's criticism of Barth. Kaufman argues that Barth's Christocentric method is arbitrary, fideistic, and idolatrous. This criticism has elicited a strong backlash from Barth's apologists,

1. Barth, *Epistle to the Romans*, 436.

such as Bruce L. McCormack.[2] Unfortunately, the polemical nature of the backlash has reinforced rather than questioned the mutually exclusive nature of the disagreement. Once the exclusive disjunction of objectivism or relativism is imposed on the debate, it becomes all too easy to read Barth as the "objectivist" and Kaufman as the "relativist." Although this characterization may be true to a certain extent, it creates a lens that may lead us to see only what is valid in Barth's position while ignoring its weaknesses. Conversely, we may see only what is problematic in Kaufman's position while ignoring its strengths. Consequently, we may not find a substantial common ground for a critical assessment of the hermeneutical issues at stake in the disagreement. By exposing the common framework beliefs in the arguments of both theologians, however, we may move beyond the impasse to a better grasp of the hermeneutical relation between divine revelation and human imagination ignored by both theologians.

THE COMMON FRAMEWORK BELIEFS OF THE DEBATE

The debate about theological method arises from an anxiety to place appropriate constraints on the use of imagination in understanding the Bible, such that we do not find ourselves mirrored back in something we have made. As Richard J. Bernstein argues, "either there is a fixed foundation for knowledge, or we cannot escape intellectual and moral chaos . . . either there are or must be some fixed, permanent constraints to which we can appeal and which are secure and stable . . . [or] there are no such basic constraints except those that we invent or temporally (and temporarily) accept."[3] The exclusive disjunction of objectivism or relativism has influenced both the question of whether a given dogmatic method is arbitrary and the question of whether a given dogmatic norm is arbitrary. Barth and Kaufman both accept this exclusive disjunction. This may be seen in Barth's claim that "there is no relativity which does not reflect a vanished absolute which can never be wholly obliterated, since it is this absolute which makes relativity relative."[4] Similarly, it may be seen in Kaufman's claim that the idea of the absolute derives its sense from the traditional concept of God and that the idea of the relative derives its sense only in relation to this ab-

2. See McCormack, "Revelation and Imagination," 431–55.

3. Bernstein, *Objectivism and Relativism*, 19.

4. Barth, *Epistle to the Romans*, 170.

solute. Thus, Kaufman tells us that "the idea of universal or absolute truth, with which the notion of relative truth is always (implicitly or explicitly) being contrasted, is nothing other than a secularized version of the old theological idea of 'God's truth.'"[5]

Kaufman argues that the disagreement between objectivists and relativists is "difficult to resolve so long as its theological roots remain unrecognized. For, without realizing it, the opponents are passing each other in the dark. Each has seized one side of the creature/creator polarity and has (rightly) defended its importance; but since, with the secularization of modern philosophical thought, the polarity itself has dropped out of view, neither side recognizes its actual interdependence with the other."[6] Although the disagreement between objectivists and relativists is related to the theological tradition, the disagreement is not rooted in that tradition. Contrary to Kaufman's analysis, the roots of the disagreement are distinctly modern and Cartesian. Thus, like Barth, Kaufman fails to recognize how the disagreement is influenced by the modern philosophical tradition beginning with Descartes. As Bernstein argues, the exclusive disjunction of objectivism or relativism is "itself parasitic upon an acceptance of the Cartesian persuasion that needs to be questioned, exposed, and overcome . . . Only if we implicitly accept some version of Cartesianism does the exclusive disjunction of objectivism or relativism become intelligible."[7]

The arguments of Barth and Kaufman both depend on an implicit acceptance of the Cartesian persuasion. In the language of Charles Taylor, this persuasion is ontologically basic to the debate about theological method. It involves an inescapable framework or outlook that is not consciously chosen by either theologian, but is unconsciously inherited from the modern philosophical tradition as a formative belief. As such, it is constitutive of the modern identity in the West. As Taylor explains, "to understand our predicament in terms of finding or losing orientation in moral [or theological] space is to take the space which our frameworks seek to define as ontologically basic. The issue is, through what framework-definitions can I find my bearings in it? In other words, we take as basic that the human agent exists in a space of questions. And these are the questions to which our framework-definitions are answers, providing the horizon within which we know where we stand, and what meanings things have for us."[8]

5. Kaufman, *Theological Imagination*, 88.
6. Ibid., 89–90.
7. Bernstein, *Objectivism and Relativism*, 19.
8. Taylor, *Sources of the Self*, 29.

This suggests that Barth's Christocentric method and Kaufman's anthropocentric method may best be understood as alternative framework-definitions that orient us in a space of common theological questions. But which framework-definition do we choose in finding our bearing in this space? In answering this question, the common framework beliefs of the disagreement must be kept in view. We must bear in mind that both theologians exist in the same space of theological questions shaped by the Cartesian persuasion. It is this space of questions, which their framework-definitions or theological methods seek to answer in opposite ways, that I take to be ontologically basic for both theologians. This space of questions determines the common framework beliefs of the debate.

The Justification of a Theological Orientation

Kaufman argues that Barth's Christocentric procedure, which attempts to ground the knowledge of God and of humanity in Christ's revelation in the Bible, is arbitrary because it presupposes the traditional Christian myth and then proceeds to imaginatively elaborate its meaning:

> Such a procedure, however, forces us to ground our theological work in an arbitrary starting point which must be accepted fideistically. In contrast, the theological stance which I have been urging . . . calls for different moves. Once it is recognized that theology is . . . an activity of human imaginative construction, it is no longer acceptable to begin our theological work with an authoritarian starting point, however venerable and revered that foundation may be. For that is simply building on the imaginative work of earlier generations, accepted more or less uncritically, instead of carefully, critically, and deliberately doing our own constructive work, thus taking full responsibility for ourselves and our theology.[9]

In sharp contrast to Barth's Christocentric method, Kaufman argues that the only tenable and rational starting point for theology is human experience. Our understanding of the Bible is based on human experience as it is mediated through a common language and culture. As Kaufman argues, "the language of the church and of scripture . . . is common language in the societies and cultures where church and scripture are found. It is with this common language and these ordinary uses that theology actually begins, not with special or technical meanings alleged to be authoritative

9. Kaufman, *Theological Imagination*, 138.

because 'revealed' by God. All special and technical meanings are variations or developments of the ordinary language, building upon it, refining it, transforming it."[10] Because the special meaning of revelation is parasitic on common language, the Bible cannot be understood apart from human experience. It is a delusion, Kaufman tells us, to suppose that we have reached the infallible and indefeasible foundations of theology when we turn to these special meanings. The foundations of theology are public, not private and parochial. Thus, we can understand the meaning of God and humanity only on the basis of the meaning of the world as it is mediated in human experience.

In his later work, Kaufman clarifies the complexity of his theological point of departure in human experience relative to Barth. Although Kaufman concedes that Barth may be right in arguing that theology in some sense has its foundations in revelation, he argues that Barth's Christocentric method makes epistemological claims that exceed the limits of what we are capable of in relation to God. In particular, Kaufman does not take it for granted as Barth does that Christ is the definitive revelation of God and the normative human being.[11] Today, Kaufman is not alone in his assessment. In theology, we see a movement away from a narrow Christocentric understanding of the relation between God, humanity, and the world to a broader Trinitarian understanding.[12] Kaufman argues that no one has succeeded in defining and developing the notions of God and the human person entirely in terms of Christ.[13] Barth attempted to follow a Christocentric procedure rigorously in response to the anthropocentric relativism of nineteenth-century liberal Protestant theology, but without success. Barth succeeded only in demonstrating that this procedure is an impossible project. Kaufman argues that the project is untenable because in order to fill out the notions of God and of humanity, much extra-Christic material must be put together from experience, from reflection, and from a whole range of traditions. Further, there is no agreement or certainty on just what content the symbol "Christ" should be given. For many alternative possibilities are plausible. Because the terms God, Christ, and humanity have always stood in complex dialectical relation with each other, Kaufman argues that it remains an open question to what extent the concept of God

10. Kaufman, *Theological Method*, 8.

11. Kaufman, *In Face of Mystery*, 88.

12. See, e.g., Peters, *God as Trinity*; and Marshall, *Trinity and Truth.*

13. Kaufman, *In Face of Mystery*, 412–25.

is to be defined with reference to Christ, and to what extent it is to be defined on the basis of other considerations. It is also an open question to what extent the human is to be defined by Christ, and to what extent in terms of general human experience.[14]

Like Kaufman, Jaroslav Pelikan argues that the meanings attributed to Christ have changed through the centuries. In the history of images of Jesus, Pelikan argues that "it is not sameness but kaleidoscopic variety that is its most conspicuous feature."[15] Each period of history brings something new to its portrayal of Jesus. Although our theological interpretations of Christ depend on the imaginative reconstructions of earlier generations, they also reflect the character and preoccupations of the present culture. In sharp contrast to Kaufman and Pelikan, however, Barth argues that "we can never expect to know generally what event or act or life is, in order from that point to conclude and assert that God is He to whom this is all proper in an unimaginable and incomprehensible fullness and completeness. When we know God as event, act and life [Christ], we have to admit that generally and apart from Him we do not know what this is."[16]

McCormack has pointed out that Barth and Kaufman agree that scripture is a work of human imagination that possesses a divinely invested normativity. But there is another important area of agreement between Barth and Kaufman that McCormack has overlooked. Both theologians agree that our dogmatic method or starting point for theology is arbitrary if it cannot be grounded in human experience or the Bible. This conclusion follows from their shared belief in the exclusive disjunction of objectivism or relativism. Either there is an absolute starting point for theology in human experience or in revelation, or we cannot avoid arbitrariness in our theological interpretations. For, according to McCormack's interpretation of Barth, if we cannot agree on what constraints should be placed on the use of imagination in understanding revelation before we begin the practice of theological inquiry, there is nothing to prevent a person from giving a word any meaning he chooses. Similarly, in defending his starting point in human experience, Kaufman argues that "such a humanistic and this-worldly criterion for theological work will seem much too nearsighted and restrictive to many . . . Have we not lost the ultimate reference point for deciding what we shall do here and now? Are we not left in the flux and

14. Ibid., 88.

15. Pelikan, *Jesus through the Centuries*, 2.

16. Barth, *Church Dogmatics* 2/1, 264.

turmoil of conflicting relativities in which there is no ultimately guiding beacon? Yes, that is indeed the case. But is not that just our actual present situation?"[17] Thus, for both theologians, if we cannot justify the choice of a theological orientation absolutely and finally, anything goes.

The language game of theology, however, is possible only if one trusts something as a foundation. Here, as Ludwig Wittgenstein argues, giving grounds and justifying the evidence comes to an end. But the end is not certain propositions or a theological orientation striking us immediately as true. It is not a kind of seeing on our part that lies at the bottom of the language game of theology, but our acting.[18] After the demise of classical foundationalism, we must admit that there are no raw data or facts of revelation that could provide an absolute starting point for Barth's criterion of Scripture as the Word of God. Revelation is not "given" to us directly, but is mediated to us through the common language and culture of the Christian tradition. Likewise, we must admit that there are no raw data or facts of human experience that could provide an absolute starting point for Kaufman's criterion of humanization. Experience is given to us already in the form of the imaginative reconstructions of earlier generations. Experience is not directly accessible to us in the sense of Cartesian internalism. Rather, it is accessible through the external traditions of rational inquiry. Thus, in defense of Barth, if we presuppose the authority of the imaginative reconstructions of earlier generations as our starting point for theology, it does not follow that we are being arbitrary as Kaufman claims. For both theologians, there are no neutral facts of the matter to which we can appeal in order to justify the choice of a starting point.

Like Barth, Kaufman argues that we need "criteria [a dogmatic norm] for distinguishing God from all idols, criteria that will enable us to recognize which claims to deity are false and deceitful and misleading, and which are true."[19] Unlike Barth, however, Kaufman argues that "we can never jump out of our concept of the world, or of God, in order to see if the 'real world' and the 'real God' correspond to those concepts; we have no independent source of information about them which can provide a check on our ideas."[20] Despite his criticism of Barth's objectivism, Kaufman argues that we must still justify our starting point for theology in human

17. Kaufman, *Theological Imagination*, 183.

18. Wittgenstein, *On Certainty*, ¶¶ 204, 509.

19. Kaufman, *In Face of Mystery*, 10.

20. Kaufman, *Theological Method*, 76.

experience. The exclusive disjunction of objectivism or relativism presupposed by both theologians compels them to search for a fixed and stable foundation, starting point, or dogmatic method for theology. Both attempt to justify a theological orientation by claiming special access to the raw data of human experience or the raw data of revelation. But in practice there is no authoritative starting point that can provide an apodictic certainty of the connection between rationality and truth. As Wittgenstein argues, "nothing we do can be defended absolutely and finally, but only by reference to something else that is not questioned."[21]

For both Barth and Kaufman, what is not questioned is the space of common theological questions influenced by the Cartesian persuasion. This space of questions includes what Hans-Georg Gadamer calls the prejudices or fore-meanings inherited from tradition. Thus, in contrast to both Barth and Kaufman, Gadamer argues that "a person who is trying to understand is exposed to distractions from fore-meanings that are not borne out by the things themselves. Working out appropriate projections, anticipatory in nature, to be confirmed 'by the things' themselves, is the constant task of understanding. The only 'objectivity' here is the confirmation of a fore-meaning in its being worked out. Indeed, what characterizes the arbitrariness of inappropriate fore-meanings if not that they come to nothing in being worked out? But understanding realizes its full potential only when the fore-meanings that it begins with are not arbitrary."[22] Although we are forced to begin the task of theological understanding with prejudices inherited from the Christian tradition, it does not follow that these prejudices are arbitrary as both Barth and Kaufman claim. Although we cannot defend our theological interpretations absolutely and finally, it does not follow that there are no better or worse interpretations, or that we are left in the flux and turmoil of conflicting relativities in which there is no ultimately guiding beacon as Kaufman claims. If Gadamer is right, disagreement in interpretations can be worked out only by engaging our prejudices with differing points of view that call them into question. By bringing our own theological interpretations into genuine conversation with alternative interpretations, we do not end up in a relativistic standoff. Rather, we risk our interpretations by putting their veracity to the test.

When we attempt to justify the starting point for theological interpretation in the indefeasible and incorrigible foundations of divine revelation

21. Wittgenstein, *Culture and Value*, 16.

22. Gadamer, *Truth and Method*, 267.

or human experience, we recoil to the relativistic point of view that anything goes when this project of rational justification fails. In this way, dogmatism about our capacity to know truth leads to skepticism about rationality. The failure to find a more objective starting point for knowledge which everyone can agree on casts suspicion on our ability to produce rational consensus in the face of strong disagreement. What we find difficult to accept is that we cannot begin the task of theological understanding without having already accepted a whole system of belief full of prejudices. As Gadamer argues, whereas some prejudices enable understanding, others present obstacles to understanding. This inherited system of belief determines our common framework beliefs. As Wittgenstein remarks, "the questions that we raise and our doubts depend on the fact that some propositions are exempt from doubt, are as it were like hinges on which they turn."[23] Whereas Gadamer argues that these propositions are prejudices that open us to the world of tradition, Wittgenstein argues that they comprise a shared world picture. These propositions are initially exempt from skepticism, not because they are self-evident or intrinsically obvious and convincing, but because we cannot perform the tasks of living life in the everyday without them.

This system of belief provides a nonarbitrary starting point for rational inquiry. We cannot stand outside this system of belief, however, in order to attain a more objective or neutral point of view free of bias. Wittgenstein and Gadamer both claim that we are already immersed in this system of belief before we are conscious agents. Thus, Bernstein argues that, "as Gadamer sees it, we belong to a tradition before it belongs to us: tradition, through its sedimentations, has a power which is constantly determining what we are in the process of becoming. We are *always already* 'thrown' into a tradition."[24] According to Wittgenstein, this shared world picture is inescapable because we cannot choose whether to accept it. It is there like our lives, embodied within the traditions of rational inquiry that form our lives from the very beginning.[25] Similarly, Taylor argues that we are not born into a world free of bias, but into a world deeply infused with meanings or horizons of significance, at least some of which we all share.[26] This inescapable framework makes the foundationalist project of grounding theological understanding in an absolute starting point both unnecessary

23. Wittgenstein, *On Certainty*, ¶ 341.

24. Bernstein, *Objectivism and Relativism*, 142.

25. Wittgenstein, *On Certainty*, ¶ 559.

26. Taylor, *Ethics of Authenticity*, 52.

and impossible. As Wittgenstein argues, "from the very beginning our lives consist in being content to accept many things because at the foundations of well founded belief lies belief that is not founded."[27]

This inescapable framework includes the language game of theology. The question of which starting point is more objective or truth-preserving, the Bible or human experience, cannot be answered outside this framework. Thus, when Barth claims that the Christocentric method is the true way of unfolding the Word of God, he is not playing the language game of theology. For, as Hilary Putnam argues, to say something is true in a language game is to stand outside of that language game and make a comment, but that is not what it is to play a language game.[28] Playing the language game of theology requires that something be taught as a foundation or starting point, but not the sort of foundation sought by the foundationalist.[29] We simply have no other place to stand except within the language game of theology. The question of whether a given interpretation of God or humanity is more or less truth-preserving is meaningful. For it can be answered within the language game of theology as one theological interpretation competes with another for our rational allegiance. But the question of whether a theological orientation as a whole is more or less truth-preserving is nonsense. For, as Wittgenstein argues, "it is like saying it tallies with the facts or it doesn't when the very thing that is in question is what tallying is here."[30] All correspondence theories of truth, including Kant's internal realism that guides Kaufman's theological work, suffer from this problem. The nature of the alleged "correspondence with reality" remains obscure.

Barth draws a very helpful distinction between Socratic doubt and skeptical doubt. Socratic doubt is a form of responsible doubt that springs from the necessity of treating the quest for theological truth as a task that is never completed, a task that is set before the theologian time and again. As such, it is the painstaking but necessary openness of theological questioning. In contrast, skeptical doubt is a form of irresponsible doubt that calls into question God's Word as a whole before it has been examined for its truth. Thus, whereas Socratic doubt is justified, Barth correctly argues that skeptical doubt is never justified.[31] Barth develops the notion of Socratic

27. Wittgenstein, *On Certainty*, ¶¶ 253, 344.

28. Putnam, *Renewing Philosophy*, 176.

29. Wittgenstein, *On Certainty*, ¶ 449.

30. Ibid., ¶ 199.

31. Barth, *Evangelical Theology*, 121–32.

doubt into an ethics of belief that goads the dogmatician in his quest for theological truth. Although this notion provides a helpful account of the normative process of theological understanding, it becomes problematic when the process is described within a critically realistic theory of knowledge that places our theological interpretations at the bottom and theological truth at the top.

In explaining Barth's critical realism, George Hunsinger argues that Barth's view of theological truth is based on the notion of sufficient certainty or "the view from below": "although not neutral it was objective, and although not discretionary it was provisional."[32] Although Barth acknowledges that our theological interpretations are never indefeasible or incorrigible, he argues that we must nevertheless justify them with reference to a Christocentric perspective that is indefeasible and incorrigible. According to Hunsinger's explanation of Barth on this point, our theological interpretations are validated to the extent that they approximate in practice the ideal of such a perspective, which is alleged to provide access to a higher mode of knowledge and certainty called "the view from above." Like Kaufman, Barth acknowledges the fallible character of the process of theological understanding, and that our truth-ascertainings and theological interpretations are always provisional. Unlike Kaufman, however, Barth argues that "the view from below" or sufficient certainty is epistemically below par. For Barth, the dogmatician must achieve a higher pitch of certainty by grounding his theological interpretations in a method that yields determinate knowledge in the sense of the Enlightenment's conception of the eternal truths of reason. But, as Wittgenstein argues, this sort of certainty is unattainable: "with the word 'certain' we express complete conviction, the total absence of doubt, and thereby we seek to convince other people. That is subjective certainty. But when is something objectively certain? When a mistake is not possible. But what kind of possibility is that? Mustn't mistake be logically excluded?"[33]

When Barth takes the Bible as his starting point for theology, he expresses complete conviction or the total absence of doubt, and thereby seeks to persuade others of his conviction. This is subjective certainty, sufficient certainty, or "the view from below." Subjective certainty expresses Barth's readiness to believe that the Bible is the Word of God.[34] Barth argues,

32. Hunsinger, *Karl Barth*, 93.

33. Wittgenstein, *On Certainty*, ¶ 194.

34. Ibid., ¶ 330.

however, that it is necessary to secure objective certainty for our theological interpretations. Thus, it is alleged that the Christocentric method gives us access to a higher mode of knowledge and certainty in "the view from above." The "view from above" functions as an epistemic filter in minimizing the noise or distractions of erroneous theological interpretations acquired in "the view from below." This epistemic filter, as we will see, is based on a special and technical meaning of obedience that is different from the ordinary meaning of trust.

Hunsinger defends Barth's critical realism with a coherence theory of knowledge. Although coherentism is compatible with Barth's realism and "the view from below," it is incompatible with "the view from above." Here coherentism offers no help in melding together these two modes of knowledge and certainty in a coherent view of religious knowledge. For, according to "the view from below," bias in our theological interpretations is inescapable. But according to "the view from above," there is no bias whatsoever. This troubling incoherence also motivates McCormack's revisionist interpretation of Barth as a critical realist.[35] On the contrary, there is a striking similarity between Barth's Christocentric project and the project of classical foundationalism. In both cases, what is sought is an authoritative starting point or foundation for knowledge. In both of these revisionist interpretations of Barth's theology, it is difficult to see how critical realism is compatible with a Christocentric perspective that is alleged to be free of bias. This objectivist thesis is incompatible with critical realism, which maintains that mind-independent realities can be grasped only in a mind-dependent manner. A critical realist position implies that although the noise or distractions from erroneous theological interpretations may be minimized to some extent, it can never be suppressed to the degree required by "the view from above." For both Hunsinger and McCormack, our mind-dependent contributions in understanding the mind-independent realities of theology are mere distractions that must be eliminated as we approximate theological truth.

Barth's apologists conceal a troubling aspect of his theology with clever arguments designed to distract more than illuminate. If Barth is not content to accept the Bible as an authoritative starting point for theology in the ordinary sense of relying on it as a nonarbitrary foundation for further theological interpretation, then he ought to admit that something more is required for a foundation. For the type of foundation sought by the

35. See McCormack, *Karl Barth's Critically Realistic Dialectical Theology*.

foundationalist is not trust. The objective certainty characteristic of "the view from above" is incompatible with the subjective certainty characteristic of "the view from below." Although the notion of objective certainty may serve a pragmatic purpose in directing our quest for theological truth, it is an unattainable ideal in practice given that theological truth must be approached in an endless approximation process of truth-ascertainings. Instead of putting us in touch with theological truth therefore, this endless approximation process of truth-ascertainings leads to skepticism about the connection between rationality and truth. Perhaps most importantly, the ideal of objective certainty depreciates the value of subjective certainty in trusting God's promise to lead us into truth and keep us from error through the ultimately guiding beacon of the Holy Spirit.

Given Barth's argument that the starting point for theology is arbitrary if it is not grounded in a Christocentric orientation, one may well ask how Barth himself acquired belief in God or the belief that the Bible is the Word of God. This question is fitting in light of McCormack's claim to have reconstructed the genesis and development of Barth's theology. Perhaps McCormack would admit that Barth did not first convince himself of the correctness of his theological orientation, that it was not a kind of seeing on his part in which the single axioms of revelation struck him as obvious, self-evident, or self-authenticating. Rather, as Wittgenstein suggests, the genesis and development of Barth's theology has to do with being taught a foundation and then reflecting on that foundation at a later stage.[36] The only possible starting point for theology is the acquisition of a system of religious belief by trusting the authority of the Christian tradition. Wittgenstein suggests that the Bible stands unshakably fast for the believer, not because its truth-claims are intrinsically obvious or convincing, but because of the human activity that lies around it.[37] This human activity consists of the ongoing task of reflection and interpretation within a tradition of theological inquiry. The Bible stands unshakably fast within the hermeneutical circle of revelation and imagination or tradition and interpretation. This hermeneutical circle is comprised of a system of religious belief in which consequences (our present theological interpretations) and premises (the theological interpretations of earlier generations) give each other mutual support.[38] Thus, like Hunsinger's claim about the structure of

36. Wittgenstein, *Culture and Value*, 85.

37. Wittgenstein, *On Certainty*, ¶ 144.

38. Ibid., ¶ 142.

Barth's theology, the hermeneutical circle exhibits the structure of a coherence theory of knowledge.

Like a system of empirical belief, we acquire a system of religious belief unconsciously through a credulity disposition or readiness to believe. A system of belief, whether religious or empirical, is not acquired because we first satisfied ourselves of its correctness. The system of religious belief that is constitutive of the Christian tradition is the inherited background against which we distinguish between true and false theological interpretations, or better and worse interpretations of God and humanity. But the question of whether the system itself is more or less truth-preserving, whether it is based on a more or less arbitrary starting point, calls into question the very substratum of all our inquiring and asserting. If we call the very starting point for belief in God into question through skeptical doubt, Socratic doubt is precluded because the language game of doubt presupposes certainty.[39]

Trusting what we apprehend other people as telling us as true and then doubting it as the evidence demands are complementary epistemic processes. These processes form more truth-preserving interpretations within the hermeneutical circle of tradition and interpretation. But the circle itself—the inherited system of belief in which we conduct such a rational inquiry—is neither true nor false, neither rational nor irrational.[40] Theological understanding cannot be grounded in a fixed and stable starting point because the interplay between the theological interpretations of earlier generations and our refinements of those interpretations is an ongoing process of theological inquiry. As Gadamer argues, "the anticipations of meaning that govern our understanding of a text is not an act of subjectivity, but proceeds from the commonality that binds us to the tradition. But this commonality is constantly being formed in our relation to tradition. Tradition is not simply a permanent precondition; rather, we produce it ourselves inasmuch as we understand, participate in the evolution of tradition, and hence further determine it ourselves."[41]

Like the shared world picture we inherit from any tradition of rational inquiry, the shared world picture we inherit from the Christian tradition provides a foundation for theological inquiry. But this foundation is not a permanent precondition. For it is constantly changing as the meanings we

39. Ibid., ¶¶ 94, 115, 162.

40. Ibid., ¶ 559.

41. Gadamer, *Truth and Method*, 293.

give to theological concepts change, and as we use these concepts to purify the tradition of anomalies and enlarge it in response to the character and preoccupations of the present. Thus, analogous to Wittgenstein's argument about the dynamically unfolding landscape of ordinary language in the previous chapter, an objectivist perspective is impossible. For, as Gadamer argues, "the historical movement of life consists in the fact that it is never absolutely bound to any one standpoint, and hence can never have a truly closed horizon. The horizon is, rather, something into which we move and that moves with us. Horizons change for a person who is moving. Thus, the horizon of the past, out of which all human life lives and which exists in the form of tradition, is always in motion."[42]

The Relation between Revelation and Imagination

Like Gadamer, Wittgenstein attempts to overcome the dominant subject-object scheme in modern philosophy that has polarized the relation between tradition and interpretation or revelation and imagination. In place of the metaphor of a fixed and permanent foundation, Wittgenstein suggests that we adopt a more dynamic metaphor that describes the hermeneutical relation between tradition and interpretation: "it might be imagined that some propositions, of the form of empirical propositions, were hardened and functioned as channels for such empirical propositions as were not hardened but fluid; and that this relation altered with time, in that fluid propositions hardened, and hard ones became fluid. The mythology may change back into a state of flux, the river-bed of thoughts may shift. But I distinguish between the movement of the waters on the river-bed and the shift of the bed itself; though there is not a sharp division of the one from the other."[43] Whereas the movement of the waters on the riverbed corresponds to the present task of theological interpretation, the riverbed itself corresponds to the theological interpretations of earlier generations deposited in the Christian tradition.

Given the unpredictable interplay between the riverbed and the movement of the waters on the riverbed, the theological meanings of God and humanity can never be determinate. As Pelikan has shown with the

42. Ibid., 304.

43. Wittgenstein, *On Certainty*, ¶¶ 96–97.

kaleidoscopic variety of images of Jesus through the centuries, our theological meanings change as we engage the theological interpretations of the past with the character and preoccupations of the present. Due to the interplay between the theological meanings of the past and our present interpretations or refinements of those meanings, we cannot appeal to the raw data or facts of religious knowledge or experience in order to adjudicate conflicting theological interpretations. Because such facts are unavailable, we cannot settle strong disagreement in religion and theology by reference to a more objective and less arbitrary perspective that stands outside the practice of theological inquiry. Although the present task of theological interpretation depends on the Christian tradition as a foundation, the foundation itself is always in motion as new interpretations take the place of the interpretations of earlier generations.

Like Gadamer and Wittgenstein, Kaufman stresses the interdependence of the creature/creator polarity: "the idea of the finite and the idea of God are correlative and interdependent parts of a conceptual whole which for many centuries in the West provided the context within which all experience and reality were grasped, and it is questionable, therefore, whether the full significance of either of these ideas can be grasped apart from the other."[44] Also like Gadamer and Wittgenstein, Kaufman argues that there is no perspective apart from our conceptualizations and theological interpretations of the world and God, according to which we can determine whether they correspond.[45] Like Barth, however, Kaufman ultimately fails to replace the subject-object scheme in the form of the creature/creator polarity with the more dynamic metaphor of the hermeneutical circle of divine revelation and human imagination.

Barth argues that dogmatic method is a way of unfolding the content of the Word of God in a way that is not determined by an external law, but is chosen freely by the interpreter. Because there is no external law that prescribes the method of dogmatics, the interpreter cannot know with unfailing certainty the way prescribed by the Word of God. Similarly, Kaufman argues that it is not false to claim that theology in some sense may have its foundations in God's revelation, only that it is a mistake to suppose that this claim tells us how to begin our theological work.[46] Thus, both theologians acknowledge a certain degree of autonomy in the task

44. Kaufman, *Theological Imagination*, 88.

45. Kaufman, *Theological Method*, 75.

46. Ibid., 3.

of theological interpretation. Unlike Kaufman, however, Barth argues that we must discover the way of unfolding the content of the Word of God prescribed by the Bible in an act of obedient listening. This is the epistemic filter mentioned previously. As Barth explains:

> The path that dogmatics has to tread in unfolding and presenting the contents of the Word of God, cannot possibly be based upon the arbitrary will of the human subject concerned, but solely upon his encounter with the work and activity of God . . . it does not rest upon a demand laid upon it from outside, but upon the relative and concrete demand which the human subject must address to himself in full and free obedience to the Word of God . . . This does not mean that it will have to be examined any the less seriously, or be any the less seriously justified to others . . . If dogmatics can be flippant with regard to the choice of its method, it is open to serious question whether, after all, in its most intimate personal character where its entire inward obedience is demanded, it does not finally rest upon arbitrariness, and how far under these circumstances, on the basis of the method it chooses and follows, it is really in a position to make an offer that can be taken seriously.[47]

Notice the exclusive disjunction of objectivism or relativism in Barth's argument. Either we must listen obediently to the Word of God, or our theological interpretations are arbitrary. Barth claims that the choice of dogmatic method cannot be based on the arbitrary will of the human subject. Yet the act of full and free obedience to the Word of God is surely an act of the will. Otherwise it is not free and, contrary to the Christian tradition, we are determined in a way that does not respect our freedom and autonomy. Since obedience itself depends on an act of the human will therefore, it cannot exclude arbitrariness in our theological interpretations by minimizing the critical role of the will in interpretation.

Like Barth, Kaufman argues that the Bible and human experience constitute different sources for theological understanding. Further, both theologians agree that these sources are ultimately compatible. Otherwise the Bible could not say anything meaningful to human experience. Although McCormack acknowledges these important areas of agreement, he changes the terms of the discussion about the relation between revelation and imagination in a subtle way by invoking Barth's notion of "obedience." This notion shifts the discussion about the relation between revelation and imagination or the Bible and human experience as compatible sources for

47. Barth, *Church Dogmatics* 1/2, 860.

theology back to a discussion about whether they are compatible theological orientations. Whereas the question of how and in what sense revelation and imagination are compatible sources for theology could lead to progress, the question of whether they are compatible theological orientations arises only if we accept the exclusive disjunction of objectivism or relativism. Either we must listen obediently to the Word of God in a direct and divinatory sense, or we cannot escape the arbitrariness of our way of unfolding the content of the Word of God. At least according to McCormack's interpretation therefore, Barth never addresses the issues raised by and possibly solved through a hermeneutical approach to the relation between revelation and imagination. Like Barth, McCormack remains stuck on the question of theological orientation.

McCormack's invocation of Barth's notion of obedience illuminates the objectivist character of Barth's theology. To avoid arbitrariness or relativism in our theological interpretations, Barth invents a special and technical meaning of obedience that is compatible with objectivism, but incompatible with the ordinary meaning of obedience as it is used in the Bible and in the Christian tradition. The ordinary sense of "obedience" means trusting, accepting, or submitting to an authority. If the human will is reoriented to God through grace, the believer is open to the claim that the Bible has something meaningful to say to him. Contrary to Barth, Gadamer argues that this openness refers to an obedient disposition to what we are trying to understand rather than a single act of obedience: "for the interpreter to let himself be guided by the things themselves is obviously not a matter of a single, 'conscientious' decision, but is 'the first, last, and constant task.' For it is necessary to keep one's gaze fixed on the thing throughout all the constant distractions that originate in the interpreter himself."[48] In conformity with the Christian tradition, Barth correctly claims that the will is closed to God in its natural state.[49] Contrary to Gadamer, however, Barth argues that we are *completely* closed to revelation in our natural state. As Hunsinger explains, "in and of ourselves, Barth argues, we have no readiness at all to know God. Openness for grace is the concept by which the idea of human readiness is explicated. This openness would involve at least three things on our part [which we do not possess]: neediness, knowledge, and willingness."[50] Because the will is closed to God in its natural state, it must

48. Gadamer, *Truth and Method*, 267.

49. Barth, *Church Dogmatics* 2/1, 130.

50. Hunsinger, *Karl Barth*, 92.

be reoriented to God through grace. Thus, there is an incommensurability between the creature and the creator that only grace may bridge. Barth, however, overstresses this incommensurability in light of the creature/creator polarity influenced by the exclusive disjunction of objectivism or relativism.

It is a mistake to suppose that this incommensurability implies a type of closure in which we remain imprisoned within the well of our own prejudices. Our prejudices are not arbitrary judgments or mere distractions, but connect us to a human community bound together by a common language and tradition. They are necessary conditions for our participation in this community. As Gadamer argues, "prejudices are biases of our openness to the world. They are simply conditions whereby we experience something—whereby what we encounter says something to us."[51] If we place too much emphasis on the incommensurability between the creature and the creator, we cannot make sense of the traditional theological claim that the creature in some sense bears the image of God, however distorted the image may be through disobedience. If we are completely closed to revelation as Barth claims, it follows that we are completely closed to grace. For the revelation of God in Jesus of Nazareth is the grace of God. And if we are completely closed to grace, the Bible can never have anything meaningful to say to human experience.

Despite sharing a common language and culture with the believer, the unbeliever can never understand theological truth because she remains imprisoned within the well of her own prejudices. This places grace and nature in a mutually exclusive opposition that makes a new relationship between the creature and the creator through faith impossible. Such a sharp contrast overlooks the fact that the believer and unbeliever share the same prejudices or background knowledge inherited from tradition. That we belong to a shared world picture means that our common experiences can educate one to belief in God. Thus, Wittgenstein argues that "*experiences* too are what bring this about; but I don't mean visions and other forms of sense experience which show us the 'existence of this being', but, e.g., sufferings of various sorts. These neither show us God in the way a sense impression shows us an object, nor do they give rise to *conjectures* about him. Experiences, thoughts, —life can force this concept on us."[52] As Kaufman correctly points out, before we are believers or unbelievers, we belong to

51. Gadamer, *Philosophical Hermeneutics*, 9.

52. Wittgenstein, *Culture and Value*, 86.

a common tradition that consists of a complex of language games. This complex includes the language game of religious belief. Although nature and human experience cannot create the willingness to believe in God or give us an intimate knowledge of God beyond what is revealed in nature, it can create a *neediness* for a moral source outside the self that only grace may satisfy.

In sharp contrast, Barth's notion of obedience creates private and parochial foundations for theology within an internalist Cartesian framework that fragments the public character of our common experience. Access to these foundations depends on a special and technical meaning of obedience that is cut off from the ordinary usage of the word. Barth argues that although the way taken by dogmatics ought to be the way claimed by its object, the object does not impose any external law that tells us how to begin. Rather, the object *speaks* to the dogmatician or presents itself as he listens in obedience. Barth's notion of allowing the object to "speak to us," however, is quite different from Gadamer's notion. Whereas for Gadamer such receptiveness is possible only by virtue of those "justified prejudices" that open us to experience, for Barth it is possible only by virtue of bracketing and minimizing their influence on the process of interpretation.[53] Although the dogmatician can never be absolutely certain that he has found the objective way prescribed by the Word of God, he can approximate it through an act of obedient listening. This argument presupposes that the Bible has a predeterminate meaning that may be discovered only in a divinatory way, which leads to the idea of arbitrariness. For, as Bernstein argues, "the ongoing and open character of all understanding and interpretation can be construed as distortive [arbitrary] only if we assume that a text possesses some meaning in itself that can be isolated from our prejudgments."[54]

Barth's notion of obedience is influenced by what Gadamer calls the Enlightenment's prejudice against prejudice.[55] For Barth argues that "the obscurities and ambiguities of our way were illuminated in the measure that we held fast to that name and in that measure that we let Him as the first and the last, according to the testimony of Holy Scripture. Against all the imaginations and errors in which we seem to be so hopelessly entangled when we try to speak of God, God will indeed maintain Himself if we will only allow the name of Jesus Christ to be maintained in our thinking as

53. Bernstein, *Objectivism and Relativism*, 137.

54. Ibid., 139.

55. Gadamer, *Truth and Method*, 270.

the beginning and the end of all our thoughts."[56] This special and technical meaning of obedience is not based on the Bible or the Christian tradition, but on the Cartesian ideal of objectivity. Barth argues that in the act of obedient listening the dogmatician can bracket his "subjective prejudices" so that he can understand the "objective way of dogmatics" prescribed by the Word of God. With the aid of grace, the dogmatician can free his understanding from the distractions and prejudices that blind him to the predeterminate meaning of the Word of God. Thus, the critical realist interpretation of Barth's theology appears to disguise a correspondence theory of truth that cannot be defended. The objective way of dogmatics provides access to "the view from above" which allows us to compare the theological interpretations acquired in "the view from below" with the predeterminate meaning of the Word of God.

Contrary to Gadamer, Barth regards our prejudices as obstacles to understanding theological truth that must be overcome rather than as necessary conditions for understanding theological truth. As a result, Barth fails to draw a distinction between prejudices that enable theological understanding and prejudices that impede it. Instead, Barth draws a distinction between the formal and material tasks of dogmatics. Whereas the formal task of dogmatics consists of hearing or listening to the Word of God in obedience, the material task of dogmatics consists of the teaching of the church. Barth argues that dogmatic method or theological interpretation arises only in consideration of the material task. At the same time, he claims that imagination is involved in both listening and teaching. Apparently, although imagination is involved in both tasks, it is not involved in the same way. The dogmatic task of listening in obedience provides a more direct and divinatory access to the predeterminate meaning of the Word of God because it is alleged to be free of the bias of theological interpretations of earlier generations. Kaufman, incidentally, overlooks this argument when he claims that Barth's Christocentric method is arbitrary because it is based on the imaginative work of earlier generations. Here Barth's argument presupposes a further distinction between theological understanding and theological interpretation. Whereas we "understand" only when we listen in obedience, we "interpret" what we understand only when we teach. When we listen in obedience, however, interpretation is also involved. For according to the hermeneutical relation between revelation and imagination or tradition and interpretation, the present task of

56. Barth, *Church Dogmatics* 2/2, 4–5.

theological understanding depends as much on interpretation as interpretation depends on the theological understanding of earlier generations.

Contrary to Barth's suspicion of the rational aspect of our nature, we do not need to build an epistemic filter between the "subjective act of listening" to the Word of God and the "objective way of dogmatics" prescribed by the Bible by inventing a special and technical meaning of obedience. As Heidegger argues, we do not have to get out of an inner sphere in which our thinking has become encapsulated or imprisoned. Rather, our primary relation to the world, other people, and God is such that our thinking is already outside *alongside* the external realities we encounter.[57] Similarly, as John E. Smith argues, "breaking 'out' of subjectivity is not the problem because we were never confined to the 'inside' in the first place."[58] If Heidegger and Smith are right, this implies that the debate about theological method must be shifted from its internalist Cartesian framework to an externalist framework. For it is only against the objective background of a shared world picture that we can distinguish between better and worse subjective interpretations. The hermeneutical circle of tradition and interpretation or revelation and imagination undercuts the sharp contrasts we are inclined to draw under the Cartesian persuasion between subject and object, creature and creator, inner and outer, human experience and the Bible, and human imagination and divine revelation.

Despite Barth's attempt to reconcile these contrasts, he proposes an untenable ideal of theological objectivity in his religious epistemology that is incompatible with critical realism. Despite Kaufman's insight into the interdependence of the creature/creator polarity, he never develops this insight into a hermeneutical description of the relation between revelation and imagination. So can we, after all, escape the accursed relativity or arbitrariness of every merely human possibility? Contrary to both Barth and Kaufman, our thinking does not have to remain imprisoned within the sphere of relativity that alienates us from the world, from the community, and from God. To open ourselves to these external realities, we must risk our theological interpretations by putting their veracity to the test. As we engage our theological interpretations with those of others, past and present, we must draw a distinction between prejudices that enable theological understanding and prejudices that impede it. But we cannot determine which prejudices enable theological understanding and which impede it

57. Heidegger, *Being and Time*, 89.

58. Smith, *Experience and God*, 36.

in advance of a theological conversation. Thus, contrary to both Barth and Kaufman, we cannot foreground our prejudices in a theological orientation before we begin our theological work.

In particular, any project that attempts to justify a theological orientation with reference to a perspective that is alleged to be indefeasible and incorrigible such as "the view from above" must ultimately fail. For it dodges the problem of interpretation by grounding our reading of the Bible in a direct and divinatory process that seeks to eliminate the influences of the will. Barth's insistence on following a Christocentric procedure rigorously and his special and technical meaning of obedience do not make the task of theological understanding any clearer. As Wittgenstein argues, "a theology which insists on the use of certain particular words and phrases, and outlaws others, does not make anything clearer (Karl Barth). It gesticulates with words, as one might say, because it wants to say something and does not know how to express it. Practice gives the words their sense."[59] The task of theology is not to translate the ordinary language of the Bible into a technical vocabulary that only theologians can understand, but to describe how the ordinary language of the Bible is used in practice to reorient a person to God.

What is required in the quest for theological truth is freedom from illusion, not in the Cartesian sense of bracketing and foregrounding our prejudices in a theological orientation, but in the sense of error that is rooted in and expressed in one's way of living. Contrary to Barth, our incapacity for revelation is not due to our being closed to what the Bible has to say to us in an epistemic sense. Rather, our incapacity for revelation has to do with our being unprepared to hear what the Bible has to say to us because of disobedience. The orientation of the will in relation to the one who created us must be changed, not the orientation of our theological method. The influences of the will do not have to be minimized or eliminated. Rather, the will must be reoriented to God through faith so that it is open to theological questioning and truth. Because the search for a more objective theological orientation is motivated by the Enlightenment's prejudice against prejudice, the choice of a dogmatic method cannot change the orientation of the will because the choice is subject to the very influences of the will the method seeks to overcome.

59. Wittgenstein, *Culture and Value*, 85.

Part Two

A Hermeneutical Model of Rationality

3

Rationality, Relativism, and Skepticism

How can we form our beliefs on matters of maximal concern such as ethics and religion when we cannot appeal to a shared and unified tradition? According to Nicholas Wolterstorff, this is the cultural crisis that John Locke addressed with his vision of the responsible believer. If tradition is fractured, we cannot appeal to the rational norms embodied in a tradition of rational inquiry in order to settle disagreements. Reason must be our guide rather than tradition. This conviction motivates the foundationalist project. But, as Wolterstorff argues, it is not clear how we can let reason be our guide by setting aside all unverified tradition. For the examination of tradition can take place only in the context of unexamined tradition.[1] The fracturing of tradition has become more pressing since Locke. The emergence of cultural diversity in the West has been exacerbated by a general mood of skepticism and the pernicious social effects of relativism. Both have eroded our confidence in reason to produce rational consensus.

It has been argued that skepticism and relativism are different reactions to diversity that should not be confused. Unlike skepticism, which doubts our capacity to know truth at all, relativism does not doubt whether there is truth relative to a conceptual scheme.[2] Relativism does doubt, however, whether common rational norms or criteria of meaning and intelligibility are available to us by casting suspicion on existing rational norms as a way to proceed in the face of disagreement. Thus, relativism involves skepticism about rationality rather than truth. Because relativism pressures us to find common rational norms or criteria of meaning and intelligibility in advance of a mutual interaction between differing points of view, it

1. Wolterstorff, *John Locke*, 246.

2. Meiland and Krausz, "Introduction," vii.

presents an immediate obstacle to the practice of rational inquiry. To avoid this problem, I will develop a hermeneutical model of rational inquiry that is substantively shared by the analytic and continental traditions in philosophy. Since relativism is connected to the idea of a conceptual scheme, we may avoid the skeptical doubt that prevents us from proceeding in the face of strong disagreement by shifting the debate about rationality from the internalist Cartesian framework of conceptual schemes to the externalist framework of traditions of rational inquiry. This externalist framework enables us to appeal to what we hold in common rather than private and parochial foundations in order to adjudicate strong disagreement about truth in religion and theology.

The Problem of Rationality

Alasdair MacIntyre has argued that a degree of circularity is ineliminable in the problem of rationality: "disagreement arises concerning the fundamental nature of rationality and extends into disagreement over how it is rationally appropriate to proceed in the face of these disagreements."[3] However we proceed, we cannot address skeptical challenges to rational inquiry by finding a model of rationality that prevents skeptical challenges from arising. After the demise of classical foundationalism, we do not need to find new standards of rationality as a basis for meaningful disagreement. Rather, we need to formulate a new doxastic practice that makes meaningful disagreement possible by correcting extreme skeptical reactions to diversity on the basis of existing rational norms. Such a doxastic practice addresses skeptical challenges as they arise rather than once and for all. Although it takes the skeptic's challenge seriously in allowing doubts to arise, it prevents doubt from degenerating into a general mood of skepticism by critically appraising the reasonableness of our doubts as well as beliefs. The question of rationality is not posed with regard to whether a belief or doubt is rational, but whether a person in a given context is rational in the manner he has come to acquire or hold the belief or doubt. Thus, as Wolterstorff argues, the question of whether a person is rational in holding certain beliefs or doubts cannot be settled in advance of an evaluation of the actual epistemic situation in which the belief or doubt arises. For the question of rationality depends on how a person has used his epistemic mechanisms

3. MacIntyre, *Whose Justice? Which Rationality?*, 4.

in a given situation.[4] This approach to the problem of rationality relies on context as a way to proceed in the face of disagreement about rationality. It depends on the rational norms or criteria of meaning and intelligibility already objectively instantiated in the practice of rational inquiry, in contrast to norms that we must invent and then agree on in advance of the practice of rational inquiry.

Because the ideal of an unsituated rationality is untenable, we must make sense of the alternative hypothesis that rationality is situated in a tradition of rational inquiry. As Hans-Georg Gadamer suggests, rationality is situated in a tradition whose horizon is always in motion and thus rational norms are subject to change.[5] Similarly, Hilary Putnam argues that norms and standards of warrant evolve with time and that they can be reformed in the face of challenges.[6] Although everyone is aware of the historicity of rational norms and standards, Putnam argues that we still need some picture of how they change. Such a picture of rational inquiry must take into account two things. First, when norms, standards, and judgments about particular cases conflict, we are pushed to a special kind of reflection that Nelson Goodman called reconstructive reflection. Just because we must abandon the ideal of a total and unique reconstruction of our belief system as in classical foundationalism does not mean that we cannot learn a great deal from partial reconstructions, or from reconstructing our beliefs in alternative ways. Thus, Putnam argues that a delicate mutual adjustment of beliefs, norms, and standards to each other is a fertile source of change in all three. Second, there is a kind of feedback loop. By trusting existing norms and standards of warrant, we sometimes unexpectedly discover facts that lead to a change in the picture of knowledge that informs those norms and standards. At the same time, such a change in the picture may indirectly lead to a change in the norms and standards of warrant themselves.[7]

In light of Putnam's suggestion, one possible candidate to replace classical foundationalism is a hermeneutical model of rationality. Like the classical picture of knowledge, the hermeneutical model provides common rational norms or criteria of meaning and intelligibility that permit the adjudication of differing points of view. Unlike the classical picture, however, the hermeneutical model is not based on a special class of beliefs

4. Wolterstorff, "Belief in God," 176.

5. Gadamer, *Truth and Method*, 293.

6. Putnam, *Realism with a Human Face*, 25–26.

7. Ibid.

that are self-evident and critique-immune. Both the picture of knowledge that informs the rational norms and the rational norms that underlie the picture can change through mutual interaction within a feedback cycle of legitimation. According to MacIntyre, there is an interdependent relation between the experience deposited in tradition and the concepts formed by interpreting that tradition. Tradition and interpretation mutually determine each other. They interact within a feedback cycle of legitimation. Thus, rationality is at once tradition-constituted and tradition-constitutive. MacIntyre distinguishes three stages in this process. First, every form of rational inquiry originates in some condition of historical contingency. There are givens that constitute the beliefs, practices, and institutions of a particular community. These givens are initially exempt from skepticism. Thus, in theology, MacIntyre argues, "it is indeed one of the marks of what is taken to be sacred that it is so exempted."[8] Second, incoherence in this system of belief may become evident with time. This creates an epistemological crisis that pressures us to examine the givens underlying the practice of rational inquiry. Wolterstorff describes these givens as control beliefs because they control our acceptance and non-acceptance of other beliefs.[9] Third, such an examination produces more truth-preserving beliefs, judgments, or interpretations.

Nicholas Rescher presents a similar picture of how our beliefs change.[10] Like MacIntyre, Rescher argues that the formation of our belief system takes place through the mutual interaction of experience and concepts within a feedback cycle of legitimation. Both MacIntyre and Rescher propose a retrojustification of the givens of rational inquiry. Legitimation is undertaken retrospectively within the practice of rational inquiry, not in advance of it. Thus, we are never rationally justified in doubting our inherited belief system as a whole. Such skeptical doubt is unintelligible. Rather, we doubt the reliability or truth of a given belief in light of counterevidence within the practice of rational inquiry. Unlike MacIntyre, however, Rescher argues for a strong empiricist interpretation of the givens of rational inquiry. This leads him to postulate a sharp logical distinction between the nondiscursive and discursive modules of human information processing. I will return to this issue after developing the groundwork for my criticism.

8. MacIntyre, *Whose Justice? Which Rationality?*, 355.

9. Wolterstorff, *Bounds of Religion*, 94.

10. Rescher, *Pragmatic Idealism*, chapters 2, 4, 10.

Conceptual Schemes vs. Traditions of Rational Inquiry

Donald Davidson has argued that two different metaphors lead to the idea of a conceptual scheme. The first metaphor is expressed by Peter Strawson, and the second metaphor is expressed by Thomas S. Kuhn. Whereas Strawson's many imagined worlds are described from the same point of view, Kuhn's one world is seen from different points of view.[11] Although both metaphors require a distinction between concepts and contents, they are problematic for different reasons. According to Strawson's metaphor, a system of concepts is comprised of words with fixed meanings that describe alternative universes. According to Kuhn's metaphor, the dualism is between total conceptual scheme and uninterpreted content. A conceptual scheme, the organizing system, is radically juxtaposed to empirical content, the something waiting to be organized. The empirical content is alleged to be fixed, neutral, and supplied by nature. Davidson focuses on Kuhn's metaphor because it has become the dominant metaphor of conceptual relativism. In fact, playing on the words of W. V. Quine's famous essay "Two Dogmas of Empiricism," Davidson tells us that Kuhn's metaphor has become the third dogma of empiricism.

Davidson draws a distinction between two cases of Kuhnian incommensurability, partial and dramatic, both of which he rejects. In both cases, two conceptual schemes are subsets of the same empirical content. In the case of partial incommensurability, both conceptual schemes intersect, sharing some region of beliefs in common. In the case of dramatic incommensurability, however, the region of shared beliefs is negligible. The relativist thesis in the form of partial incommensurability is evident through our experience with diversity, and is intelligible because of shared beliefs between conceptual schemes. Thus, Davidson suggests that the relativist thesis in the form of partial incommensurability can be viewed as a productive skepticism because it can make us aware of problems in the received tradition of the past that must be addressed. But the relativist thesis in the form of dramatic incommensurability claims that there are no substantial shared beliefs, including beliefs about what is reasonable and unreasonable. Thus, it can be viewed as an unproductive skepticism because it casts suspicion on all existing rational norms as a way to proceed in the face of strong disagreement. In contrast to Strawson's words with fixed meanings, Kuhn

11. Davidson, "Conceptual Scheme," 187.

invokes the notion of a common ontology as the foundation for his picture of knowledge. But, as Kuhn later recognized, such an ontology begs the question of how people living in dramatically different conceptual schemes can communicate if there is no "basic vocabulary consisting entirely of words which are attached to nature in ways that are unproblematic and, to the extent necessary, independent of theory."[12] Unless we have access to a neutral translation language, which Kuhn rejects, Davidson argues that we cannot compare dramatically differing points of view or conceptual schemes on the basis of a common ontology.

Neither Strawson's fixed stock of meanings nor Kuhn's theory-neutral reality can provide a stable foundation for the practice of rational inquiry. Either a single conceptual scheme comprised of words with fixed meanings provides a stable foundation for alternative worlds, or a fixed empirical content provides a stable foundation for alternative interpretations of the world in differing points of view or conceptual schemes. Both metaphors misrepresent the mutual interaction between contents and concepts. If Davidson is right, we need to abandon the metaphor of conceptual schemes as distortive of the practice of rational inquiry. In its place, we ought to adopt the picture of a hermeneutical relation between contents and concepts within a language game or system of belief. If we define contents as meanings or interpretations deposited in a tradition of rational inquiry and concepts as the further interpretation or refinement of those meanings, then understanding rationality is narrating the story of how tradition and interpretation, or contents and concepts, have changed through mutual interaction. Thus, as Kuhn recognizes, there can be no stock of fixed meanings embodied in a tradition of rational inquiry as in Strawson's metaphor because meanings change as differing interpretations compete for our rational allegiance. But, as Kuhn also recognizes, there can be no fixed empirical content without a neutral observation language that gives us unproblematic access to this content in order to adjudicate differing conceptual schemes competing for our rational allegiance.

Within the tradition of meanings or contents we inherit, our interpretations or concepts are refinements of a more primitive language game called trust. Ludwig Wittgenstein argues that the human being should be regarded in the first instance as an animal, as a primitive being to which one grants *instinct* but not reason.[13] Like all creatures, we have a natural instinct

12. Quoted in Davidson, "Conceptual Scheme," 190.

13. Wittgenstein, *On Certainty*, ¶ 475.

to trust our surroundings. Doubt is a refinement of the more primitive language game of trust that is necessary to preserve the integrity of our belief system for survival.[14] If we do not acquire the habit of scrutinizing the reasonableness of our doubts as well as beliefs, however, doubt may degenerate into a general mood of skepticism. Whereas trust is a natural reaction, doubt is a learned reaction.[15] Thus, like tautologies and contradictions in the case of language, fideism and skepticism are extreme and degenerative reactions to diversity in the case of knowledge. Whereas fideism involves trusting everything we are told without rational justification, skepticism involves trusting nothing we are told without strong evidence.

Wittgenstein argues that we are engaged in a struggle with language. It is not language itself that is important, but the foundationalist picture of rational inquiry and associated doxastic practice that is instantiated in language. The foundationalist picture of rational inquiry assumes that trust must be suspended in order to properly ground our allegiances on what is rationally acceptable. According to Wittgenstein, this picture presents an immediate obstacle to the practice of rational inquiry. The obstacle cannot be overcome because the practice of rational inquiry, in which it could be overcome, cannot begin unless we first trust many things. Wittgenstein argues that trusting the received tradition of the past is a natural reaction: "For how can a child immediately doubt what it is taught? That could mean only that he was incapable of learning certain language games."[16] For example, Wittgenstein asks, "what if the pupil refused to believe that this mountain had been there beyond human memory? We should say that he had no *grounds* for this suspicion."[17] Continuing, Wittgenstein says "if he calls *that* in doubt—whatever 'doubt' means here—he will never learn this game . . . Only in such-and-such circumstances does a reasonable person doubt *that*."[18]

Although tradition provides a reliable and nonarbitrary foundation for rational inquiry, Wittgenstein argues that our knowledge of this foundation is wrongly expressed by the words "I know."[19] There is nothing intrinsically basic about the system of belief that we have been taught as

14. Ibid., ¶¶ 115, 354.

15. Ibid., ¶¶ 143, 160.

16. Ibid., ¶ 283. See Reid, *Inquiry*, 281–82.

17. Ibid., ¶ 322.

18. Ibid., ¶¶ 329, 334.

19. Ibid., ¶ 414.

children. As Putnam argues, basicality is conferred on these beliefs in the sense that we take them as basic in the practice of rational inquiry.[20] Similarly, Wolterstorff argues that they function as control beliefs that govern our acceptance and non-acceptance of other beliefs. Instead of claiming to know that *p* at this first-order level of basic doxastic ascent, Wittgenstein suggests that we should say that it stands fast for me that *p*. Further, that it stands fast for me and many others.[21] At this primitive level of basic doxastic ascent, belief has not yet been transmuted into knowledge. It is simply trust, a natural reaction to believe what we are told. Thus, contrary to classical foundationalism, Wittgenstein argues that a foundation is not an infallible and incorrigible basis for rational inquiry. Rather, it is an ungrounded natural reaction to believe what we apprehend other people as telling us as true.

Wittgenstein tells us that the statement "I know that *p*" expresses the readiness to believe certain things.[22] Similarly, the Scottish Common Sense philosopher Thomas Reid describes the readiness to believe as a credulity disposition. But at the first-order level of basic doxastic ascent, Wittgenstein suggests that credulity may misrepresent the epistemic status of the beliefs all normal human beings must take for granted in the living of their lives in the everyday. For, as Wittgenstein argues, "that something stands fast for me is not grounded in my stupidity or credulity."[23] A credulity disposition implies that a person might have come do believe something out of haste, carelessness, or gullibility. Thus, the person has not been epistemically responsible in the way he has acquired or come to hold his beliefs. Credulity, however, corresponds to a first-order level of basic doxastic ascent that is spontaneous, involuntary, and innocent with regard to the manner in which beliefs are acquired. For Wittgenstein, like Reid, it is not within our power to choose which beliefs we will accept and which beliefs we will reject at this primitive level of belief-formation.[24]

How do we know that such beliefs are reliable, that they are truth conducive and not prone to error? Wolterstorff argues that "our situation is not that to be rationally justified in accepting the deliverances of the credulity disposition we need evidence in favor of its reliability. Rather, we

20. Putnam, *Reason, Truth, and History*, 38.

21. Wittgenstein, *On Certainty*, ¶ 116.

22. Ibid., ¶ 330.

23. Ibid., ¶ 235.

24. Wittgenstein, *Investigations*, 1, ¶ 219. See Reid, *Inquiry*, 9.

are rationally justified in accepting its deliverances until such time as we have evidence of its *unreliability* for certain types of cases."[25] The problem with reliabilism as a theory of knowledge is that we must first establish the reliability of a cognitive process before we are justified in trusting its deliverances. Here Wolterstorff illuminates a neglected aspect of the ethics of belief tradition. We must also seek to be reasonable in the doubts we hold. The question of reliability is appropriately raised at a second-order level of doxastic ascent. The rational justification of our convictions, as well as the question of whether they are true or false, is a higher level cognitive process that takes place at a second-order level of doxastic ascent that must be carefully distinguished from the first-order level of basic doxastic ascent. Although the word "knowledge" is commonly used to characterize doxastic ascent at both cognitive levels, the type of ascent involved is quite different.[26]

It is at this second-order level of doxastic ascent that we distinguish between what Putnam calls real doubt and philosophic doubt.[27] Philosophic doubt, or what the Reformed theologian Karl Barth calls skeptical doubt, consists of unreasonable doubts or unproductive skepticisms that present obstacles to belief-formation and revision by circumventing the pressure to know. In contrast, real doubt, or what Barth calls Socratic doubt, consists of reasonable doubts or productive skepticisms that pressure us to revise our beliefs in view of incoherence in order to increase the reliability of the connection between rationality and truth. This, as Wolterstorff argues, is how we get down to what Locke called "the things themselves." Therefore, although we do not explicitly learn the beliefs that stand fast for us, Wittgenstein argues that we "can discover them subsequently like the axis around which a body rotates. This axis is not fixed in the sense that anything holds it fast, but the movement around it determines its immobility."[28] Such a discovery does not occur in advance of the practice of rational inquiry, but involves a retrojustification of the givens of rational inquiry within the practice of rational inquiry. These givens consist of the beliefs all normal human beings must take for granted that control our acceptance and nonacceptance of other beliefs.

25. Wolterstorff, "Belief in God," 163.

26. This distinction is based on the argument of Lehrer and Cohen, "Justification, Truth, and Coherence," 192.

27. Putnam, *Realism with a Human Face*, 221.

28. Wittgenstein, *On Certainty*, ¶ 152. See Reid, *Inquiry*, 281–82.

If the more ordinary metaphor of a foundation is correct, the empiricist foundation of Rescher's interactionist model of rational inquiry must be scrutinized. Rescher, as I have said, draws a sharp logical distinction between nondiscursive and discursive cognitive functions. Experience gives rise to raw data such as immediate experience, raw feels, sensa, or perhaps even direct religious experiences. Operating on these raw data, the discursive information processing module of cognition produces data *in advance* of the feedback cycle of legitimation. This empiricist aspect of Rescher's model is a throwback to logical positivism, made plausible by a precommitment to what Davidson calls Kuhn's third dogma of empiricism: the dualism of scheme and content, of an organizing system and something waiting to be organized. Rescher's information processing metaphor of the mind assumes that the practice of rational inquiry is based on a person's internal and private encounter with experience. It also assumes that the deliverances of these encounters can be compared intersubjectively with the deliverances of other people's internal experience. Like Roderick Chisholm's notion of the directly evident in empirical experience, these self-presenting mental states form the basis for agreement in opinions.[29]

But if the externalist metaphor I have urged is correct, we cannot arrive at the objective if we begin with the subjective within an internalist Cartesian framework. Agreement in opinions or consensus is different from agreement in judgments or natural reactions. Whereas agreement in opinions involves a conscious and epistemically responsible process, agreement in judgments involves a spontaneous, involuntary, and epistemically innocent process. The grammar of knowing is different from the grammar of believing. Knowing and believing correspond to higher and lower levels of doxastic ascent respectively. Wittgenstein argues that the basis for agreement in opinions is agreement in judgements or natural reactions, not agreement in self-presenting mental states.[30] The conditions of belief acceptance and non-acceptance are external and contextual, not internal and psychological. If experience is to function as a common exchange rate in our language, it must be accessible in ways that the third dogma of empiricism rejects. The accessibility must be extra-mental and objective, which is incompatible with the internalist Cartesian framework of classical foundationalism.

29. See Chisholm, *Theory of Knowledge*, chapter 2; and *First Person*, chapter 8. See Wolterstorff, *John Locke*, 16.

30. Wittgenstein, *Investigations*, 1, ¶ 241.

As Alvin Plantinga argues, the concept of rational justification seems to require internalism.[31] Like Plantinga, we must challenge the dogma that our connection with reality is primarily mediated through the inner realm of the mind, but for different reasons than he proposes. Wittgenstein claims that something must be taught us as a foundation.[32] We acquire a system of belief, or a shared world picture, as a foundation for rational inquiry. For instance, "the child learns to believe a host of things . . . it learns to act according to these beliefs. Bit by bit there forms a system of what is believed, and in that system some things stand unshakably fast and some are more or less liable to shift. What stands fast does so, not because it is intrinsically obvious or convincing; it is rather held fast by what lies around it."[33] Experience, in the ordinary sense of a foundation, consists of a system of belief inherited from a tradition of rational inquiry. The meanings we acquire as part of our shared world picture are given to us already in the form of interpretations by a host of significant others. Reid argues that we rely on this tradition as a trustworthy point of departure for further rational inquiry, not as a more or less arbitrary and doubtful starting point.[34] Similarly, Wittgenstein argues that "all testing, all confirmation and disconfirmation of a hypothesis takes place already within a system. And this system is not a more or less arbitrary and doubtful point of departure for all our arguments: no, it belongs to the essence of what we call an argument. The system is not so much the point of departure, as the element in which arguments have their life."[35]

The Parallel between Wittgenstein and Reid

Wolterstorff argues that there is a striking similarity between Reid's doctrine of the principles of Common Sense and Wittgenstein's account of our shared world picture in *On Certainty*. Both philosophers are interested in identifying the same phenomenon—the beliefs all normal human beings take for granted in the living of their lives in the everyday. These beliefs comprise a substratum, common background, or inescapable framework

31. Plantinga, "Justification," 354.
32. Wittgenstein, *On Certainty*, ¶ 449.
33. Ibid., ¶ 144.
34. Reid, *Inquiry*, 281–82.
35. Wittgenstein, *On Certainty*, ¶ 105.

for human activity. Whereas Reid identifies this substratum as the principles of Common Sense, Wittgenstein identifies it as our shared world picture. Although both philosophers ascribe the same features to this substratum, Wolterstorff argues that the account they offer of the features is quite different. Whereas Reid thinks the reason we take for granted the beliefs we do is that the constitution of our nature leads us to believe them, Wittgenstein thinks that we take them for granted because in performing the activities of life in the everyday *we just do* take them for granted.[36]

Wolterstorff denotes the beliefs we take for granted as deeply ingressed beliefs. Because these beliefs are deeply ingressed, they are exempt from doubt. Thus, Wolterstorff argues that "doubt cannot get at them there. Too many other beliefs stand guard."[37] Certain passages in *On Certainty* give one this impression. Wittgenstein, for example, tells us that "the expression 'it is my unshakable conviction' means that I have not consciously arrived at the conviction by following a particular line of thought, but that it is anchored in all my *questions and answers*, so anchored that I cannot touch it."[38] Contrary to Wolterstorff, however, it does not follow that the beliefs that stand unshakably fast for us are exempt from doubt (1) because they are deeply ingressed or (2) because we wish to avoid toppling the totality of our system of belief should we discover some of our beliefs to be unreliable or false. Both of these claims concern the question of what makes a belief exempt from doubt. In the case of Wolterstorff's second claim, reflective knowledge is presupposed at a first-order level of basic doxastic ascent that Wittgenstein argues is purely instinctive. The reason we take for granted the beliefs we do has to do with a natural reaction to trust what we apprehend other people as telling us as true. The purely instinctive character of basic doxastic ascent involves no thought about the coherence or reliability of our belief system. As we will see, such a thought occurs only at a higher level of doxastic ascent in which we become conscious of the beliefs whose reliability we have taken for granted in light of counterevidence.

In the case of Wolterstorff's first claim, although we take many beliefs for granted, it does not follow that we *always* take them for granted, or equivalently, that we *never* doubt them.[39] Given appropriate circumstances, the maximally ingressed beliefs that comprise our shared world picture

36. Wolterstorff, *Thomas Reid*, 242.

37. Ibid., 237, 241.

38. Wittgenstein, *On Certainty*, ¶ 103.

39. Wolterstorff, *Thomas Reid*, 233.

may become doubtful. As Wittgenstein points out, beliefs whose veracity we now take for granted may become doubtful at another time.[40] Other beliefs that are more truth-preserving may take their place in the substratum of our shared world picture. Here Wittgenstein stresses the contingent nature of the relation between beliefs that stand unshakably fast and beliefs that are more or less subject to alteration.[41] This corresponds to his criticism of the classic philosophical distinction between necessary and contingent propositions. Wolterstorff's omission of this theme in Wittgenstein's account of our shared world picture leads to a contradiction in his reading of *On Certainty*: maximally ingressed beliefs are indubitable (they cannot be doubted), but they are not infallible (they can be false).[42] But if maximally ingressed beliefs are always exempt from doubt, never questioned, it is not clear how we can subsequently discover that some of these beliefs are unreliable or false as Wittgenstein argues.[43] The question of whether a belief is true or false is incompatible with an epistemic disposition whereby the veracity of the belief is always taken for granted. As Wittgenstein argues, beliefs that are initially exempt from doubt may become doubtful at another time.

Wolterstorff makes two additional claims, this time concerning the question of what makes a belief certain. Wolterstorff claims that a belief is certain (3) because it is deeply ingressed or entrenched in our shared world picture and (4) because it is surrounded or guarded by the totality of beliefs in our shared world picture. In the case of the third claim, however, a belief is not certain because of the *position* it occupies in our shared world picture as in classical foundationalism. In the case of the fourth claim, a belief is not certain because other beliefs *surround* it and support it like a scaffolding as in coherentism. Indeed, Wittgenstein identifies these features of the beliefs we take for granted in his account of our shared world picture. But these features do not explain why we are led to take them for granted. Contrary to Wolterstorff's interpretation of Wittgenstein's account, certainty is not a characteristic of a belief, that is, something that a belief enjoys[44] Rather, as Wittgenstein argues, certainty is a characteristic of an ungrounded natural

40. Wittgenstein, *On Certainty*, ¶ 211.

41. Ibid., ¶¶ 96–97.

42. Wolterstorff, *Thomas Reid*, 238–39.

43. Wittgenstein, *On Certainty*, ¶ 152. See Reid, *Inquiry*, 281–82.

44. Wolterstorff, *Thomas Reid*, 238.

reaction or way of acting that may or may not be expressed by a belief.[45] Language and beliefs are refinements and expressions of ungrounded natural reactions.[46] But behavior may also simply take the place of beliefs as an expression of our natural reactions.[47] It is not a belief that is certain therefore, but the natural reaction expressed by the belief.[48] Consequently, we do not take for granted the beliefs we do because in performing the activities of life *we just do* take them for granted as Wolterstorff claims. Rather, the natural reactions expressed in our everyday activities or behavior lead us to take them for granted.

Although Wolterstorff acknowledges that the beliefs we take for granted are not grounded in rational intuition or experience, he is reluctant to accept Wittgenstein's account of the primitive nature of our agreement in such beliefs: "the origin and the primitive form of the language game is a reaction; only from this can more complicated forms develop. Language—I want to say—is a refinement, 'in the beginning was the deed.'"[49] But, as Wittgenstein himself acknowledges, "it is so difficult to find the *beginning*. Or, better: it is difficult to begin at the beginning. And not try to go further back."[50] Contrary to the presupposition of modern philosophy beginning with Descartes, Wittgenstein argues that our shared world picture is based on agreement in judgments or natural reactions, not on agreement in opinions.[51] Unlike agreement in opinions, agreement in judgments or natural reactions does not refer to a conscious and critical process. Rather, it refers to the groundless substratum of belief that is inherited from a tradition of rational inquiry. These basic beliefs are produced spontaneously in an involuntary and epistemically innocent manner at a first-order level of basic doxastic ascent by trusting the beliefs handed down to us in a tradition of rational inquiry. This first-order level of doxastic ascent is so basic that it is given a special name. Wittgenstein describes the certainty characteristic of this agreement in judgments or natural reactions as a form of life: "now I would like to regard this certainty, not as something akin to hastiness or superficiality [credulity], but as a form of life. (That is very badly expressed

45. Wittgenstein, *On Certainty*, ¶¶ 358–59, 427.

46. Wittgenstein, *Culture and Value*, 46; and *Investigations*, 1, ¶ 546.

47. Wittgenstein, *On Certainty*, ¶¶ 7, 254.

48. Ibid., ¶ 360.

49. Wittgenstein, *Culture and Value*, 31.

50. Wittgenstein, *On Certainty*, ¶ 471.

51. Ibid., ¶ 131.

and probably badly thought as well.) But that means I want to conceive it as something that lies beyond being justified or unjustified; as it were, as something animal."[52] Thus, for Wittgenstein, certainty is a characteristic of our agreement in natural reactions. It is not a characteristic or property of a belief, or the position of a belief relative to other beliefs in our shared world picture.[53] It follows that Wolterstorff's suggestion of a continuum of beliefs in a person's belief system, in which a belief is more firmly held in proportion to its depth of ingression, is incompatible with Wittgenstein's account.[54]

Wolterstorff also claims that Wittgenstein fails to draw an important distinction between personal and human frameworks. Whereas a personal framework is comprised of beliefs that are peculiar to a single person, a human framework is comprised of the beliefs that are common to all of us in our shared world picture.[55] But, as Wittgenstein argues, personal reactions such as "I have two hands" are not peculiar to a single person. They are shared by other normal human beings.[56] It is not just that we take most of the same beliefs for granted, but more fundamentally, that we share most of the same reactions to life that are expressed by these beliefs.[57] Wittgenstein, as I have said, describes this natural fact as a form of life.[58] Under more or less identical circumstances, a normal adult person reacts or responds to a situation in the same way as other normal adult human beings.

As an example of a deeply ingressed belief that is peculiar to a single person, Wolterstorff cites one of Wittgenstein's own examples out of context, namely, the belief that "I am called Ludwig Wittgenstein." But, as the context of this example shows, Wittgenstein argues that "it is part of the language game with people's names that everyone knows his name with the greatest certainty."[59] This reaction is not idiosyncratic because it is shared by other normal people. Of course, as Wittgenstein points out, we can imagine people who may have different reactions, but they would involve a form of life different from our own. In normal circumstances, for example, we would not say that a person who constantly checked to see whether he had

52. Ibid., ¶¶ 358–59.

53. Ibid., ¶ 174.

54. Wolterstorff, *Thomas Reid*, 235.

55. Ibid., 237.

56. Wittgenstein, *On Certainty*, ¶ 281; and *Zettel*, ¶ 567.

57. Wittgenstein, *Zettel*, ¶ 540.

58. Wittgenstein, *Investigations*, 1, ¶ 241; 2, ¶ 226.

59. Wittgenstein, *On Certainty*, ¶ 579.

two hands or was uncertain of his own name was reasonable.[60] As Norman Malcolm argues, "the framework propositions that we accept, grow into, are not idiosyncrasies but common ways of speaking and thinking that are pressed on us by our human community."[61] The distinction between personal and human frameworks is plausible only if we accept the internalist Cartesian framework of classical foundationalism. Differences in belief do not correspond to differences in personal or conceptual frameworks as in internalism, but to differences in forms of life or natural reactions as in externalism. It follows that religious beliefs do not hover somewhere between the two frameworks as Wolterstorff suggests.[62] Rather, religious beliefs belong to the shared world picture of a religious community.

For Wittgenstein, what we find reasonable and unreasonable is not determined by consensus, convention, rules, or the infallible and incorrigible foundations of self-evident principles, but by our agreement in judgments or natural reactions.[63] Our shared reactions determine the beliefs we take for granted. What we call reasonable is a reaction in conformity with the majority of other normal adult people's reactions in similar circumstances. What we call unreasonable is a reaction that deviates from this natural norm. Thus, Wittgenstein argues that the expression "'we are quite sure of it' does not mean just that every single person is certain of it, but that we belong to a *community* which is bound together by science and education . . . Thus, we should not call anybody reasonable who believed something in despite of scientific evidence."[64] As Malcolm explains, "it is an immensely important fact of nature that as people carry on an activity in which they have received a common training, they do largely agree with one another, accepting the same examples and analogies, taking the same steps. We agree in what to say, in how to apply language. We agree in our responses [reactions] to particular cases."[65]

This fact of human nature cannot be explained by consensus or convention, which Wittgenstein describes as agreement in opinions, for that presupposes language and reflective knowledge at a level that Wittgenstein argues is purely instinctive. Nor can it be reduced to behavior because we

60. Ibid., ¶ 255.

61. Malcolm, *Thought and Knowledge*, 203.

62. Wolterstorff, *Thomas Reid*, 237.

63. Wittgenstein, *On Certainty*, ¶ 140.

64. Ibid., ¶¶ 298, 324.

65. Malcolm, *Thought and Knowledge*, 208.

can also express our certainty in language and beliefs that may simply take the place of performing the activities of life in the everyday as in the case of J. L. Austin's performative utterances. If we cannot explain why we are lead to take for granted the beliefs we do in terms of consensus, convention or behavior, this natural fact must correspond to something deep in human nature itself. Although our shared reactions manifest our common human nature, Wittgenstein argues that we cannot explain the reactions themselves in terms of efficient causes. Although we can describe how we are led to take the same beliefs for granted on the basis of shared reactions, we cannot explain *why* we react in the same ways in terms of an underlying causal mechanism. Similarly, Reid argues that we cannot know the true causes of things.

Thus, what lies at the bottom of our shared world picture is not a special class of deeply ingressed beliefs as Wolterstorff claims, but our shared instinct to respond to situations in the same way in the same circumstances. Wittgenstein argues that this instinct is something more basic and primitive than agreement in opinions. For example, "the squirrel does not infer by induction that it is going to need stores next winter as well. And no more do we need a law of induction to justify our actions or our predictions."[66] Whether we characterize our agreement in natural reactions as a credulity disposition or as an animal instinct is less important than the fact that we share a common constitution that leads us to believe the same things, that we are "hard wired" in the same way, and that this commonality determines what we find reasonable and unreasonable, whatever its causal nature.[67] Thus, contrary to Wolterstorff, Wittgenstein and Reid both argue that our common constitution consists in our agreement in judgments, forms of life, or the principles of Common Sense. This constitution is simply there like our life. It is neither reasonable nor unreasonable.[68]

Like Wolterstorff, however, most epistemologists find Wittgenstein's account of our shared world picture unsatisfactory as a response to skepticism. Ernest Sosa, for example, draws a distinction between animal knowledge and reflective knowledge that is analogous in many respects to the grammatical distinction I have drawn between lower and higher levels of doxastic ascent.[69] Sosa is the first analytic philosopher to shift the

66. Wittgenstein, *On Certainty*, ¶ 287.

67. Ibid., ¶¶ 254, 325.

68. Ibid., ¶ 559.

69. See Sosa, *Virtue Epistemology*, chapter 2.

discussion in epistemology from its internalist Cartesian framework to an externalist framework in the ethics of belief tradition. According to Sosa, to have animal knowledge that *p* is to believe that *p*, and for this belief to be apt, that is, accurate or conducive to truth because it has been skillfully formed due to the intellectual virtue of the agent. In contrast, to have reflective knowledge that *p* is to aptly believe that you aptly believe that *p*. These two levels of knowledge are related in Sosa's virtue epistemology through the central notion of an epistemic perspective, which is comprised of a set of second-order beliefs about one's first-order beliefs and the reliability of their sources. My main disagreement with Sosa concerns the condition of apt belief or competence in the case of animal knowledge. For this condition presupposes reflective knowledge at a doxastic level that Wittgenstein argues is purely instinctive, and suffers from the same problem as reliabilism.

In contrast, Wittgenstein argues that our agreement in judgments or natural reactions is mystical. When we try to express the nature of our common constitution in terms of self-evident principles, we bump up against the limits of language and thought. In struggling to express his anti-skeptical convictions without falling into the conundrums of G. E. Moore, Wittgenstein tells us that the difficulty is to realize the groundlessness of our believing at the first-order level of basic doxastic ascent.[70] Similarly, in attempting to express the principles of Common Sense, Reid argues that "when men attempt to deduce such self-evident principles from others more evident, they always fall into inconclusive reasoning."[71] For both Wittgenstein and Reid, we cannot satisfy our avidity to know the true causes of things.

This leads to another theme in *On Certainty* overlooked by Wolterstorff. The pressure to find a transcendental explanation for why we take for granted the beliefs we do is connected to the rational aspect of our nature. At the same time, when we attempt to explain our common constitution either in terms of self-justifying reasons or the *a priori*, we obscure the primitive nature of the agreement underlying the beliefs we take for granted. The fact that our agreement in opinions is grounded in ungrounded natural reactions collides with the rational aspect of our nature, which requires a rational explanation of something that is neither rational nor irrational. Although our agreement in natural reactions is the foundation for the rational aspect of our nature, it eludes our rational grasp. Although shared beliefs and behavior are characteristics and manifestations of this

70. Wittgenstein, *On Certainty*, ¶ 166.

71. Quoted in Wolterstorff, *Thomas Reid*, 242.

natural fact, the fact cannot be reduced to them. Instead, it corresponds to something deep in human nature itself beyond the limits of language and justification, to something mystical that shows itself in behavior, language and beliefs, but cannot be expressed in words. This is the "phenomenon" that both Wittgenstein and Reid identify in their accounts and describe in similar ways.

Contrary to Wittgenstein and Reid's externalist account of experience as a substratum of commonly held beliefs or principles of Common Sense, the third dogma of empiricism depends on an internalist account of experience based on the unintelligible notion of the directly evident. The dualism of uninterpreted content and total conceptual scheme requires a sharp logical distinction between a fixed foundation for rational inquiry and the practice of rational inquiry, such as the distinction Rescher draws between the nondiscursive and discursive modules of human information processing. In place of this logical distinction, Wittgenstein and Reid suggest a grammatical distinction between first-order and second-order levels of doxastic ascent. The first-order level of basic doxastic ascent involves trusting the beliefs given to us in our common experience of a received tradition. We inherit a tradition of rational inquiry or system of belief that is initially exempt from skepticism as a foundation for further rational inquiry. Trust is a natural reaction to believe what we apprehend other people as telling us as true.[72] At the level of basic doxastic ascent, beliefs are produced spontaneously. Thus, the manner in which we acquire them or come to hold them is involuntary and epistemically innocent. As Wittgenstein argues, the child learns to react in a certain way and in so reacting it does not so far know anything. Knowing only begins at a later stage.[73]

In contrast, the second-order level of doxastic ascent involves reflective knowledge about the beliefs whose veracity we have trusted at the first-order level of basic doxastic ascent. Reflective knowledge arises from the awareness of incoherence in our established system of belief that may become evident with time. This incoherence pressures us to examine the beliefs underlying the practice of rational inquiry that have become doubtful in light of counterevidence. Thus, reasoning is a refinement of the more primitive language game of trusting that depends critically on the human will. At the level of critical belief, the control beliefs that comprise the foundation of rational inquiry are open to questioning and revision, thereby

72. Wittgenstein, *On Certainty*, ¶ 344.

73. Ibid., ¶ 538.

averting the problem of fideism. We become intellectually responsible for continuing to hold doubtful beliefs in light of accumulating counterevidence. In this way, the interpretations or meanings inherited from tradition can change as we reinterpret them to remove anomalies in our belief system. We consciously choose to accept one interpretation from among many different interpretations competing for our rational allegiance.

At this second-order level of doxastic ascent, immediate belief is transmuted into knowledge through critical belief. Reasoning about the beliefs whose veracity we have trusted or taken for granted produces beliefs that are more truth-preserving, thereby enhancing the reliability of the connection between rationality and truth. Thus, a reasoned trust, which Wittgenstein calls judging, involves a mutual hermeneutical interaction between the epistemic processes of trusting and reasoning. The justification of our control beliefs is undertaken, not in advance of the practice of rational inquiry, but retrospectively within the practice of rational inquiry as the evidence demands. As Wolterstorff argues, we are never rationally justified in doubting our inherited system of belief as a whole. Such global skepticism is unintelligible. Rather, we doubt the reliability or veracity of some beliefs on grounds of evidence that may come to light through the practice of rational inquiry.

Such a hermeneutical model of rational inquiry does not need to make sense of the dualism of uninterpreted content and total conceptual scheme. Consequently, it does not need to make sense of the metaphor of a single space within which each scheme has a position and provides a point of view. Further, unlike the foundationalist project, it does not pressure us to find common rational norms or criteria of meaning and intelligibility in advance of a mutual interaction between differing points of view. The doxastic practice associated with the hermeneutical model makes meaningful disagreement possible by trusting existing rational norms as they stand. For, as Wittgenstein argues, judging involves reasoning about the beliefs whose veracity we have trusted. Trust is part of judging, and we use judgments as principles of judgment.[74] Thus, in the case of religion and theology, a rational faith or reasoned trust implies a more subtle relation between faith and reason in contrast to their classic opposition. Trusting and reasoning are complementary epistemic mechanisms that produce more truth-preserving beliefs or judgments, not mutually exclusive paths to knowledge of God that we must choose between.

74. Ibid., ¶¶ 124, 150.

Although these judgments or principles of Common Sense do not provide infallible and incorrigible foundations for rational inquiry, they do provide a reliable and nonarbitrary point of departure for conducting further rational inquiry. As Wolterstorff argues, trust requires appropriate forms of doubt in order to produce more truth-preserving beliefs that get down to "the things themselves." The movement from trust to doubt and back again as the evidence demands is what makes reasoning or reflective knowledge dialectical and distinguishes it from animal knowledge, that is, the natural reaction to believe what we apprehend other people as telling us as true. Whereas responsible doubt pressures us to believe in a deeper way which leads to knowledge, irresponsible doubt can circumvent the pressure to know which leads to skepticism. Extreme skeptical reactions to disagreement cast suspicion on existing rational norms as a way to proceed in the face of strong disagreement and lead to a breakdown in rational inquiry. In order to correct this extreme and degenerate reaction to diversity, we must question whether we are rationally justified in holding our doubts as well as beliefs. This does not mean preventing doubts from arising with a philosophical refutation of skepticism, only correcting habitual doubt with a doxastic practice that prevents the habit from spilling over into every area of human life.

4

Tradition, Worldviews, and Conflict

Two developments are frequently cited as factors in the fracturing of tradition in the modern West. First, the once unified ethical and religious tradition in Europe has fractured because of the sovereignty of modern scientific thought. The knowledge of nature is no longer easily related to our sense for conduct and beauty as it was for the medieval mind. Consequently, Western culture has become fragmented into warring scientific and humanistic factions, subcultures or worldviews, each struggling to dominate the other by subjugating it to its authority. Second, the emergence of cultural pluralism in the West has resulted in extreme skeptical reactions to diversity and the relativity of differing points of view which challenge the validity of a single worldview as never before. Both factors have become more prominant since the time of John Locke in light of the increasing secularization of Western culture.

I will argue that Wilhelm Dilthey's theory of worldviews gives us insight into the problem of disagreement and, in particular, the conflict between science and theology. Dilthey's conception of tradition as an acquired mental structure suggests a parallel, both with Ludwig Wittgenstein's account of our shared world picture and with Thomas Reid's doctrine of the principles of Common Sense. Like Wittgenstein and Reid, Dilthey is interested in identifying the beliefs all normal human beings take for granted in the living of their lives in the everyday. Tradition is at once the source and product of an acquired mental structure. When the critical activity of mental life is suppressed, different interpretations of the experience of mental life harden into conflicting worldviews or ideologies. This fractures the shared and unified mental structure that we call tradition. Unlike Reid, however, Dilthey and Wittgenstein suggest that the conflict of worldviews is rooted in different reactions to life and their attitudes of alienation rather than in incommensurable systems of belief or conceptual schemes. This implies that the problem of disagreement has to do with our being closed to differing points of view through the decay of critical belief. If science and theology express different activities of mental life or ways of living based on different attitudes toward life, they may be viewed as complementary traditions of rational inquiry that give us a more comprehensive view of the common experience of the world given to us in tradition.

The Sovereignty of Scientific Thought

Early modern scientists such as Isaac Newton argued that the creator has partially revealed himself in the Book of Nature, and that natural philosophy provides a method for interpreting this Book. Science and theology were regarded as complementary parts of a conceptual and rational whole that reveal our central place in the scheme of things. But as the philosophy of nature separated from metaphysics and theology, the connection between the physical and spiritual realms strained. At one extreme, we find the Roman Church banishing the scientific works of Galileo because they contradicted the official position of Aristotelian physics. At the other extreme, we find Holbach's *System of Nature* banishing religion and metaphysics from the philosophy of nature. As E. A. Burtt argues, this polarization led to the despiritualization of nature.[1] The scientific attitude toward life hardened and become more skeptical and enclosed in relation to the religious or spiritual attitude toward life. Modernity came to view the relation between science and theology as one of irreconcilable conflict. Thus, Holbach argues that theology is the born enemy of experience and an insuperable obstacle to the progress of natural science. In describing Holbach's extreme skeptical reaction to theology, Ernst Cassirer writes that "only a resolute and radical break with all spiritualism can cure this situation. The notions of God, freedom and immortality are to be uprooted once and for all, so that the rational order of nature shall not be threatened and overthrown by constant intervention from the supernatural world which these notions seem to construct."[2] Cassirer argues that the scientific worldview overreacts to the challenges of the humanistic worldview in seeking to "eliminate from

1. Burtt, *Metaphysical Foundations*, 262.
2. Cassirer, *Philosophy of the Enlightenment*, 70.

the philosophy of nature not only all religious, but all aesthetic elements as well, and to neutralize all the forces of feeling and phantasy."[3]

Given the hostile conflict between science and theology in the past, we should not be surprised to learn that the scientific and religious worldviews should have a curious distorted image of each other, or that their attitudes toward life should be so different. Contrary to C. P. Snow's analysis of the conflict, the divide involves more than illiteracy on both sides.[4] The conflict involves a breach with the other side's point of view as something alien and irreconcilable in principle. There is an *attitude of alienation* on both sides of the debate. Galileo's persecution by the Roman Church and Holbach's extreme skeptical reaction to theology illustrate the impulse to separate the study of nature from the human studies once and for all. The differences between these worldviews are exaggerated to the point of mutual incomprehension and suspicion. The tendency to draw the boundary between these worldviews once and for all is an extreme skeptical reaction to disagreement. According to the scientific worldview, the scientific method of experiment must be freed from its bondage to the systematizing spirit of metaphysics and theology. For, whereas science is concerned with the living world of physical change, metaphysics and theology are concerned with the petrified world of tradition. Today, this conflict has led to a choice between two apparently mutually exclusive worldviews. Either we adopt a scientific worldview intent on overcoming the constraints of tradition and nature, or we adopt a humanistic worldview that views the attempt to overcome these constraints as potentially harmful to our humanity.

When abstracted from the historical and social context in which science has developed side by side with theology, one thinks of each worldview developing according to its own internal dynamical principle. But, in truth, their development has been one of mutual interdependence. If science were free of metaphysical assumptions, it is difficult to imagine how Dalton's atomic theory could have become the accepted paradigm in modern chemistry. Without metaphysical assumptions of space and time, it is difficult to imagine how Newton's mechanics could have developed, despite his belief that it was free of such assumptions. Conversely, if the human studies developed autonomously in relation to experimental science, it is difficult to imagine how the combination of cognitive psychology and philosophical epistemology could have led to the new fertile

3. Ibid., 72–73.

4. See Snow, *Two Cultures*.

point of view of cognitive science. Such developments are the product of a cross-fertilization of ideas from different areas of knowledge. The obstacle to mutual comprehension between worldviews is not epistemological or methodological. Although the conflict between worldviews involves different systems of belief, these systems are rooted in different reactions to life and their attitudes of alienation, which must be addressed by taking into account more than epistemology.

Dilthey's Theory of Worldviews

Dilthey argues that the problems of epistemology and methodology that plague modernity arise from a disregard of the historical forces that shape the conflict between worldviews. Hans-Georg Gadamer describes this disregard as the Enlightenment's prejudice against prejudice.[5] Dilthey argues that the legacy of the Enlightenment, given its emphasis on universally valid knowledge based on a concept of pure reason abstracted from contingency, must be corrected by the historical consciousness that human rationality is always situated in a cultural context. Our understanding of the physical and human worlds is determined by historical forces ignored by pure reason. In his theory of worldviews, Dilthey attempts to unite the need in human psychology for universally valid knowledge with the fact that understanding is radically conditioned by history. This manifests itself in a palpable tension between the critical activity of mental life and metaphysical conceptions of it. Whereas mental life flows in a restless stream of events like the movement of waters on a riverbed, the objectification of mental life in metaphysical systems tends to remain at rest like the riverbed itself. Whereas mental life is involved in activity and becoming, metaphysics tends to congeal this activity into a doctrine of being. Dilthey argues that the problem is a pinning down in thought of what is itself an occurrence or trend.[6] This problem concerns how to restore the vital connection between the objectifications of mental life and the critical mental activity that produced them. Similarly, Thomas S. Kuhn argues that the textbook paradigm in science is an objectification of scientific thought that disguises the scientific revolutions that produced the objectification.[7]

5. Gadamer, *Truth and Method*, 270.
6. Dilthey, "Historical World," 200.
7. Kuhn, *Scientific Revolutions*, 136–43.

According to Dilthey, the relation of the objectifications of mental life to the critical activity of mental life that produced them is complex. Thus, the subject-matter of the human studies, which concerns the connectedness of mental life, requires several methods. Dilthey formulates a methodology that expresses the critical activity of mental life in dynamic language analogous to the way power expresses the rate work is done on a body by a force in nature. According to Newtonian mechanics, when a body is displaced by a force in nature, there is a transfer of energy to the body in the form of positive work. Power denotes the rate of change in this transfer of energy. In the human studies, power is the expression of something that can be directly experienced, namely, mental life. The activity of mental life is the force that drives the individual in self-development as it transfers energy to him in the consolidation of personality. The power of an individual life is proportional to the intuition of life: the more immediate the experience of the connectedness of mental life, the greater the transfer of energy to the individual and goad to self-development. Thus, the greatest minds of a culture, its geniuses, are moved farther than others in their self-development and understanding of mental life. The products of their critical mental activity—science, art, literature, poetry, philosophy, ethics, and religion—are expressions of our fullest humanity. As Dilthey explains, "in so far as history strives to understand and express change, it must operate with concepts which express energy, trends and regroupings of historical forces. The more historical concepts assume this character the better will they express the nature of their subject-matter."[8]

Contrary to both empiricism and rationalism, Dilthey argues that mental life cannot be grasped through "The Way of Ideas" or through rational intuition. Like Wittgenstein and Reid, Dilthey stands apart from the philosophical mainstream of his day. Mental life cannot be expressed in language, but discloses (shows) itself in the hermeneutical interaction of experience and understanding. It is gradually elucidated through the mutual interaction of these two classes of truth. The narrow and erroneous interpretations of mental life, initially determined by the world of objective mind, are replaced by more truth-preserving interpretations in the mind-constructed world as the individual becomes conscious of mental life through his interaction with things and people.[9] The individual's knowledge

8. Dilthey, "Historical World," 217.

9. Ibid., 189–90.

of mental life springs from these historical and social interactions.[10] Bit by bit the individual is oriented in the world of objective mind, which is the established worldview in which the critical activity of mental life has become objectified in language, custom, economics, politics, law, religion, art, and science. Although a person's mental life is inaccessible to direct scientific observation, it is mediated to the first-person and others in the same way through the externalism of an inherited system of belief. Thus, Dilthey argues that the objective mind consists of "the manifold forms in which what individuals hold in common have objectified themselves in the world of the senses. In this objective mind the past is a permanently enduring present for us . . . From this world of objective mind the self receives sustenance from earliest childhood. It is the medium in which the understanding of other people and their expressions takes place. For everything in which the mind has objectified itself contains something held in common by the I and the Thou . . . Before [the child] learns to talk it is already wholly immersed in that common medium."[11] Like Wittgenstein's account of our shared world picture and Reid's doctrine of the principles of Common Sense, Dilthey's account of mental life describes a structure that has priority in determining human subjectivity. The world of objective mind is the common realm of experience in which humans orient themselves through tradition.

Although the world of objective mind is initially exempt from skepticism, the elementary forms of understanding make a transition to a higher form of understanding when the individual becomes conscious of incoherence in the world of objective mind. When the individual encounters "an inner difficulty or a contradiction of what he already knows, he is forced to re-examine the matter . . . So, for different reasons, we must consider other expressions [of mental life] or go back to the whole context of life in order to still our doubts."[12] Doubt pressures the higher forms of understanding to reexamine the interpretations of the experience of mental life given in the world of objective mind. Thus, the world of objective mind in which the past has become a permanently enduring present for us does not provide a fixed and permanent precondition for rational inquiry. Like Hans-Georg Gadamer's conception of tradition, the world of objective mind is always in motion. When an alternative interpretation of the experience of mental life becomes stable, it provides a new foundation for our common experience.

10. Ibid., 179.

11. Ibid., 221.

12. Ibid., 223.

The mind-constructed world alters the world of objective mind in order to eliminate incoherence between different interpretations of mental life. Like Alasdair MacIntyre's conception of tradition, the mind-constructed world of the understanding (rationality) is at once constituted by the world of objective mind (tradition) and constitutive of the world of objective mind.[13] Whereas tradition consists of the beliefs and rational norms objectified in the world of objective mind, rationality or interpretation consists of the critical mental activity that produced them in the mind-constructed world.

The Parallel between Dilthey and Wittgenstein

Victor Preller has argued that there is a deep affinity between Dilthey and Wittgenstein.[14] Preller considers Dilthey's influence on the young Wittgenstein essential for understanding the motivations that led to Wittgenstein's later philosophy. Whereas Preller identifies this affinity primarily in Wittgenstein's philosophical psychology such as *Zettel*, I locate the affinity primarily in *On Certainty*. There Wittgenstein describes the relation between the interpretations of the experience of mental life, objectified in tradition, and the critical activity of mental life that produces them. Toward the end of his life, Wittgenstein wrote that "it might be imagined that some propositions, of the form of empirical propositions, were hardened and functioned as channels for such empirical propositions as were not hardened but fluid; and that this relation altered with time, in that fluid propositions hardened, and hard ones became fluid. The mythology may change back into a state of flux, the river-bed of thoughts may shift. But I distinguish between the movement of the waters on the river-bed and the shift of the bed itself; though there is not a sharp division of the one from the other."[15]

The riverbed of thoughts corresponds to Dilthey's world of objective mind or tradition. According to Dilthey, tradition consists of the interpretations of the experience of mental life deposited in the world of objective mind, which are acquired unconsciously and involuntarily by the elementary forms of understanding. This corresponds to the first-order level of basic doxastic ascent discussed in the previous chapter, based on Reid's conception of a credulity disposition. In contrast, the movement of

13. See MacIntyre, *Whose Justice? Which Rationality?*

14. The parallel was developed in a 1993 doctoral seminar in hermeneutics at Princeton University.

15. Wittgenstein, *On Certainty*, ¶¶ 96–97.

waters on the riverbed corresponds to the conscious and critical mental activity of the mind-constructed world, which consists of different interpretations of the experience of mental life as yet not hardened but fluid. This corresponds to the second-order level of doxastic ascent discussed in the previous chapter. As new interpretations of the experience of mental life acquire stability, they petrify and settle to the bottom of the riverbed of thoughts. These interpretations subsequently function as a new foundation or channel for rational inquiry. Given the emergence of different historical conditions, the relation between the riverbed of thoughts and the thoughts moving on the riverbed may change. What we now take as a foundation, the stabile interpretations of the experience of mental life deposited in the riverbed, may shift as other interpretations in the mind-constructed world take their place in the substratum of our belief system.

Thus, for both Dilthey and Wittgenstein, there can be no sharp division between the world of objective mind and the mind-constructed world, between the riverbed of thoughts (tradition) and the movement of the thoughts on the riverbed (interpretation). Although we may distinguish between empirical propositions that belong to one class or the other, there can be no fixed or permanent division between the two. The division is not logical and *a priori*, but empirical and contingent, dependent on historical forces that may change with time. Because the structure of mental life is perpetually changing, it cannot be captured in any single worldview that attempts to pin down this activity and becoming in a doctrine of being. Although the objectifications of mental life in different worldviews may give us partial reconstructions of this structure, the structure as a whole cannot be expressed in any single worldview. When we attempt to express the structure of mental life as a whole, we bump up against the limits of language and thought. Like Wittgenstein's analogy between the logical structure of language and scaffolding in the *Tractatus*, the logical structure or scaffolding of mental life cannot be fully articulated. It is something mystical, which manifests itself in the critical activity of mental life, yet remains incapable of full articulation in any single point of view. As Wittgenstein argues, what cannot be expressed in language shows itself instead.

In the hermeneutical interaction of experience and understanding, or tradition and interpretation, the goal of the highest form of understanding is to relive the present objectified in the past by means of hermeneutics.[16] As Dilthey argues, the approach of higher understanding to its object is

16. Dilthey, "Historical World," 210.

determined by its task of discovering a vital connection in what is given in the world of objective mind.[17] We cannot grasp an interpretation of the experience of mental life without grasping the system of interactions in which it originated. Thus, Dilthey claims that "even when we analyze objectifications of mental life as something complete and, as it were, at rest, we still need to grasp the system of interactions from which these objectifications originated."[18]

Similarly, Wittgenstein argues that "each morning you have to break through the dead rubble afresh [the objectifications of mental life] so as to reach the living warm seed [the critical activity of mental life that produced them]."[19] The objectifications of mental life correspond to what Wittgenstein calls wisdom, which "is like cold grey ash, covering up the glowing embers."[20] Whereas wisdom conceals the critical activity of mental life, empathy reveals it by reliving and re-experiencing it. In poetry, for example, the poet expresses an experience of mental life. Dilthey argues that empathy is the process of understanding in which every line of a poem is retransformed into life through the inner context of experience and the critical activity of mental life.[21] Thus, contrary to logical positivism, Dilthey argues that poetry is not merely an expression of emotion, but is "made up of assertions about life which it expresses vigorously . . . through his empathy the poet restores the relationship to life which receded in the course of intellectual development and practical interests."[22]

According to Dilthey, empathy does not subjectivize and fragment mental life into autonomous frameworks. On the contrary, it enables us to transcend our own direct experience of mental life, which is otherwise limited by our historical and social situatedness. As Dilthey explains, "limited by circumstances one can yet glimpse alien beauty in the world and areas of life beyond his reach."[23] Empathy widens the horizon of our own direct experience of mental life by re-establishing vital connections between different interpretations of the experience of mental life deposited in the world of objective mind. Understanding these interpretations, however,

17. Ibid., 226.

18. Ibid., 200.

19. Wittgenstein, *Culture and Value*, 2.

20. Ibid., 56.

21. Dilthey, "Historical World," 226.

22. Ibid., 241.

23. Ibid., 228.

requires more than scientific observation and analysis because "[mental] life discloses itself at a depth inaccessible to observation, reflection and theory."[24] Empathy involves more than understanding the surface grammar of the interpretation objectified in tradition. It involves understanding the depth grammar of the interpretation found in the critical mental activity that produced the objectification. For, as Wittgenstein argues, "the problems of life [with which ethics and religion deal] are insoluble on the surface and can only be solved in depth. They are insoluble in surface dimensions."[25] This means that the past experience of mental life, which has become objectified in the world of objective mind and expressed vigorously in an interpretation, must be reproduced in the present. No person can accomplish this appropriation for another. The interpretation cannot be understood merely by acquiring objective knowledge about a metaphysical worldview. The interpretation can be fully understood only by activating capacities in the self, which enable a person to re-experience the activity of mental life that originally produced it.

Dilthey argues that the enigma of mental life is an acquired mental structure that cannot be fully expressed in words, but manifests itself in mental activity through a nexus of historical and social connections. This nexus consists of what individuals hold in common, or the beliefs all normal human beings take for granted in the living of their lives in the everyday. This mental structure is the same "phenomenon" identified by Wittgenstein as our shared world picture, and by Reid as the principles of Common Sense. Dilthey argues that this acquired mental structure is given to us directly in experience, not in the philosophical sense of a rational intuition or sense datum, but in the ordinary sense of being mediated by the common realm of objective mind in which all humans orient themselves. But this mental structure cannot enter consciousness as a whole. When we try to understand it or express it as a whole, we bump up against the limits of language and thought. As Dilthey argues, "it is clear in detail but enigmatic as a whole."[26] This mental structure can only be reproduced bit by bit.[27] Similarly, Wittgenstein argues that light dawns gradually over our acquired system of belief, not all at once.[28]

24. Ibid., 220.

25. Wittgenstein, *Culture and Value*, 74.

26. Dilthey, "Types of World-view," 136.

27. Dilthey, "Descriptive Psychology," 93.

28. Wittgenstein, *On Certainty*, ¶ 141.

Dilthey tells us that the unmethodical knowledge of mental life, which is acquired unconsciously and involuntarily by the elementary forms of understanding, must be developed into a conscious general evaluation of mental life by the higher forms of understanding. This development corresponds to a deeper kind of believing called knowing, in which we learn to reason about the beliefs whose veracity we have trusted as a foundation for rational inquiry. The gradual elucidation of our acquired mental structure requires empathy.[29] For the higher forms of understanding require us to analyze the intuition in which the whole context of mental life, with its unvarying characteristics, manifests itself to us in spatially and temporally differentiated instances.[30] In the hermeneutical interaction of experience and understanding, or tradition and interpretation, the individual encounters conflicting worldviews, each of which seeks to establish its own interpretation of the experience of mental life as universally valid. Like J. G. Fichte, Dilthey argues that these worldviews are not based on reason, but on different attitudes toward life that are connected to our conduct or action.[31] Thus, contrary to the presupposition of modern philosophy, reason is not the ground of a worldview. Rather, a worldview is grounded in an ungrounded reaction to mental life, which is expressed vigorously in an interpretation of the experience of mental life that is alleged to be universally valid. Similarly, Wittgenstein argues that what lies at the bottom of a worldview is not an ungrounded presupposition, but an ungrounded way of acting that is expressed in our most fundamental convictions and beliefs.[32]

The Conflict of Worldviews

Dilthey's theory of worldviews suggests that the mutual interaction between different worldviews through the hermeneutical interaction of experience and understanding breaks down when one worldview exaggerates its truth-claims relative to another. When differences between worldviews or belief systems are emphasized to the point of dramatic incommensurability, we overlook the beliefs that we hold in common. As I argued in chapter 1 about

29. Dilthey, "Types of World-view," 143.
30. Dilthey, "Historical World," 232.
31. Ibid., 240.
32. Wittgenstein, *On Certainty*, ¶ 110.

the autonomy of religious language, such an overemphasis on differences between beliefs across various areas of knowledge and regions of language leads to relativism. As Wittgenstein argues, "in an age without culture [or a shared and unified tradition], forces become fragmented, and the power of an individual is used up in overcoming opposing forces and frictional resistances. It does not show in the distance one travels, but perhaps only in the heat one generates in overcoming friction."[33] Dilthey argues that the drive toward universally valid knowledge inherent in human psychology pressures us to make excessive claims about the scope of a worldview, interpretation, or abstraction. In the face of strong disagreement, in which we ignore what we hold in common, the inability to adjudicate conflicting interpretations leads to alienating attitudes of skepticism based on the contradiction of human opinions. Consequently, vital connections between different areas of knowledge and regions of language are severed as one worldview becomes alienated from another. This leads to isolated, autonomous interpretations of the experience of mental life, which fragment the unity and integrity of mental life as it is originally given to us in our common experience of the world of objective mind.

Conceptual relativism is a skeptical backlash to the inability to satisfy the inherent drive in human psychology to establish a single worldview or interpretation as universally valid. This inherent drive corresponds to the avidity to know the true causes of things in Reid's epistemology and, more generally, to the ideal of universal reason in the Enlightenment. Although we may encounter conceptual differences in the task of mutual comprehension, conceptual relativism overemphasizes these differences to the point of dramatic incommensurability by casting suspicion on what we hold in common. This includes existing rational norms or criteria of meaning and intelligibility as a way to rationally proceed in the face of strong disagreement. As Dilthey and Wittgenstein suggest, relativism is rooted in attitudes of alienation from the world and from the community. As Hilary Putnam argues, "it never dies because the attitude of alienation from the world and from the community is not just a theory, and cannot be overcome by purely intellectual argument."[34] This illuminates an important limitation in the scope of Reid's naturalist response to skepticism. A wider view that takes more into account than epistemology is needed to address the different reactions to life underlying conflicting systems of belief.

33. Wittgenstein, *Culture and Value*, 6.

34. Putnam, *Renewing Philosophy*, 178.

Although no single worldview can provide a total and unique reconstruction of our belief system that reveals the structure of mental life as a whole, Dilthey argues that the various experiences of mental life expressed in different worldviews can bring us nearer to such a view by widening our own direct experience of mental life.[35] For the fullness of mental life expresses itself in innumerable nuances.[36] The reality of the world is not relative to a worldview, perspective, or conceptual scheme. Rather, each worldview discloses how the reality of the world is given to us through the different activities of the mind. In epistemology, this corresponds to a shift from internalism to externalism. Thus, science and theology are not incommensurable systems of belief or conceptual schemes, but complementary ways of intending the world. These basic attitudes toward life, Dilthey tells us, disclose different aspects of the world.[37] Whereas the natural sciences disclose the structure of nature comprised of a system of causal interactions, the human studies disclose the structure of mental life comprised of a system of historical and social interactions. Together, these interactions form a nexus that enables us to make sense of human existence in a physical universe through a shared and unified mental structure. The dominant subject-object scheme of modern philosophy, however, has alienated the self from these interactions. The self has become alienated, both from the physical world and from the human world. In contrast, Dilthey argues that mental life cannot understand its strivings and goals apart from the nexus of historical, social, and causal interactions that determine it.

For Dilthey, the conflict of worldviews is a conflict of metaphysical systems "ultimately *rooted in life itself*, in the knowledge of life and one's attitudes to its problems."[38] Consequently, the question of whether there can be harmonious agreement between science and theology, or whether we must accept sharp disagreement between these different systems of belief, misconstrues the relation between the two. Rather, the question is how two basic, irreducible, conflicting attitudes toward life can interact to achieve a deeper understanding of mental life, its strivings, and goals. Dilthey suggests that the conflict between science and theology is not rooted

35. Dilthey, "Nature of Philosophy," 123.

36. Dilthey, "Historical World," 192. Similarly, John E. Smith argues that experience has several "dimensions based on [different] purposes and each has its own part to play in the disclosure of reality." See Smith, *Experience and God*, 40.

37. Dilthey, "Types of World-view," 146.

38. Ibid., 145.

in incommensurable systems of belief or dramatically different conceptual schemes, but in different reactions to life and their attitudes of alienation. If these worldviews were completely commensurable, or if the incommensurability were dramatic, science and theology could not interact to widen the horizon of our own direct experience of mental life. Although both worldviews seek to establish their interpretations as universally valid, neither worldview has sufficiently grasped its role in disclosing the connectedness of mental life, not from a parochial perspective motivated by political, ideological, or other practical interests, but from the whole context of mental life as experienced and expressed in an interpretation. Science and theology are not two different conceptual schemes that provide a point of view within a common neutral framework that must still be discovered. Rather, they are two different traditions of rational inquiry, both of which are products of our common rational nature. Thus, the question of whether a scientific interpretation of our common experience of the world is more objective and rational than a theological interpretation overlooks the fact that both types of interpretations are required to relate the manifold dimensions of our common experience.

Matthew Arnold once said that a culture without science evokes in us a sense of dissatisfaction because the instinct for knowledge is suppressed. But a scientific culture that suppresses reflexivity also dissatisfies us because the desire to relate the new conceptions of the universe to our sense for conduct and beauty is baulked.[39] Despite the appearance of sharp conflict, most scientists and theologians desire to relate their different reactions and attitudes toward life in a shared and unified conception of the universe that gives meaning and significance to our various mental activities. Dilthey suggests that the fracturing of the Western tradition is not due to the sovereignty of modern scientific thought, but to the excessive claim made by modern science to explain everything, including the mystical in ethics and religion. When the critical belief characteristic of the activity of mental life is suppressed, different interpretations of the experience of mental life harden into conflicting metaphysical worldviews, thereby fracturing what we hold in common. Similarly, John E. Smith argues that difference and diversity may be seen as sources of strife that lead to conflicting relativities. Or they may be seen as the dynamic force of life in a culture that leads to opportunities for creative interchange through mediation and human experience that overcomes insularity and parochialism. According to Smith,

39. Arnold, "Literature and Science," 83.

mediation attempts to transform the dyadic relation of claim and counter-claim which, in the impasse, is not acknowledged by either party, into the establishment of what Josiah Royce called a "community of interpretation" in which each party can be made to hear and understand the claim of the other. This transformation depends on human experience that transcends its expression in natural languages and points of view. The main obstacle to the *will to interpret* across disciplinary or cultural boundaries is the belief that experience is completely bound and limited to its expression in a particular natural language or point of view. That we constantly strive to find the most adequate expression of what we experience, however, and that we discover in this process that we can recognize some forms of expression as inadequate cuts against this belief. Experience, Smith tells us, has its own transcendence.[40]

At a time when the once unified ethical and religious tradition in Europe seemed hopelessly fractured, John Stuart Mill wrote: "In the case of any person whose judgment is really deserving of confidence, how has it become so? Because he has kept his mind open to criticism of his opinions and conduct. Because it has been his practice to listen to all that could be said against him; to profit by as much of it as was just, and to expound to himself, and upon occasion to others, the fallacy of what was fallacious . . . No wise man ever acquired his wisdom in any mode but this . . . The steady habit of correcting and completing his own opinion by collating it with those of others, so far from causing doubt and hesitation in carrying it into practice, is the only stable foundation for a just reliance on it."[41] This is the "community of interpretation" Royce had in mind. It is perhaps well to remember, as Mill observed, that a unified tradition is marked by an inevitable and gradual narrowing of the bounds of diversity of opinion and the disappearance of controversy. W. W. Bartley has described this phenomenon as the morbidity of critical belief.[42] This may happen over a period of time to a person, a worldview, or the entire culture. The reappearance of difference and diversity signals an opportunity to establish new connections between long established and defended boundaries, including the boundary delimiting the much disputed sphere of modern science.

If Dilthey and Smith are right, we do not need to find a more objective perspective or common coordinate system on which to plot the scientific

40. Smith, "Mediation, Conflict, and Creative Diversity," 44.

41. Mill, *On Liberty*, 25.

42. Bartley, *Retreat to Commitment*, xix.

and religious points of view. We do not need to find a translation language with neutral rational norms or criteria of meaning and intelligibility to advance the science-religion dialogue. Rather, we need to restore our trust in the ability of reason to produce rational consensus in the face of strong disagreement by acknowledging the rational norms or criteria of meaning and intelligibility that we already hold in common through our experience of tradition. So long as the dialogue is posed in terms of incommensurable conceptual schemes, we will never find a sufficiently objective point of view according to which we can adjudicate different interpretations of our common experience of the world. If, instead, the dialogue is posed in terms of the mutual task of relating the various activities of mental life in a way that gives us a more comprehensive view of the experience of mental life given to us in tradition, we may make progress by realizing that any interpretation is limited in scope, however valid within its own intent and under the control of its own purpose. This will be the subject of the next chapter.

5

Science, Rationality, and Theology

THE RAPID SUCCESS OF modern science is largely due to the ability of scientists to create idealizations or abstractions for the purpose of understanding some aspect of nature. But there is a tendency to identify the aspect with the whole. As John E. Smith argues, "an abstraction is seen as partial, *not from within* the purpose which controls it since it was made precisely to fulfill that purpose, but only in relation to some wider purpose which takes more into account. But the fact that an abstraction does not fulfill some other purpose does not preclude its being well founded within its own intent and under the control of its own purpose."[1] Similarly, Albert Einstein and Leopold Infeld argue that creating a new scientific theory is not like destroying an old barn and erecting a skyscraper in its place. Rather, it is like climbing a mountain that gives us new views that reveal unexpected connections between our starting point and its surroundings. Although the starting point still exists and can be seen, it now appears as an aspect of a wider view rather than the whole.[2]

This metaphor suggests a broader conception of rational inquiry that takes more into account than science. The evidentialist model of rational inquiry extrapolated from the success of the physical sciences claims that scientific belief is well founded compared to religious belief. In response to the evidentialist challenge, theologians and philosophers may try to find a criterion for the directly evident in religious knowledge or experience. Or, as I will urge, they may question whether the evidentialist model that pressures the project of rational justification in theology is valid. Based on the seminal work of Thomas S. Kuhn, I will argue that the structure of

1. Smith, "Critique of Abstractions," 24–25.
2. Einstein and Infeld, *Evolution of Physics*, 152.

rational inquiry in science is hermeneutical like theology, and that not even the most conscientious scientist can live up to the ideal of the evidentialist model. In order to avert the conceptual relativism of Kuhn's position, however, I will refine the hermeneutical model of rational inquiry developed in previous chapters based on Niels Bohr's principle of complementarity and correspondence principle. This model permits us to view science and theology as complementary interpretations of our experience of the world rather than as incommensurable systems of belief or conceptual schemes. Although these interpretations serve different purposes and goals, they must correspond in the limit where the scientific or causal interpretation reduces to the theological or teleological interpretation in illuminating our central place in the scheme of things.

The Nature of Scientific Inquiry

The conventional interpretation of the blackbody radiation problem credits Max Planck with the discovery of the concept of a restricted or discrete energy spectrum.[3] Contrary to the conventional interpretation, Kuhn argues that Albert Einstein and Paul Ehrenfest originated the concept.[4] Based on a historiographical analysis of Planck's papers on the blackbody radiation problem, Kuhn argues that Planck did not actually hold this concept until 1908, two years after it was first proposed by Einstein and Ehrenfest. The concept appears regularly in Planck's discussions after 1909. Although Kuhn's historiographical analysis is quite technical, it raises epistemological issues that illuminate the hermeneutical nature of rational inquiry in science.

In the years preceding Planck's acceptance of the concept of energy quantization, Kuhn meticulously documents how Planck was still struggling to derive his radiation law from the principles of classical physics. Repeated attempts to reconcile the law with classical theory eventually led to an epistemological crisis that precipitated a conceptual change or gestalt switch. Kuhn argues that this conceptual change was accompanied by two alterations in Planck's technical vocabulary. First, Planck replaced the phrase "energy element" with the phrase "energy quantum." Whereas the first phrase refers to a mathematical subdivision of the classical energy

3. See, e.g., Thornton and Rex, *Modern Physics*, 91–95.

4. See Kuhn, *Black-Body Theory*.

continuum, the second phrase refers to a physically separable and indivisible atom or unit of energy. Second, Planck replaced the term "resonator" with the term "oscillator." Whereas the first term refers to hypothetical entities that absorb and emit energy to the electromagnetic medium in a continuous manner, the second term refers to hypothetical entities that absorb and emit energy in a discontinuous manner. Kuhn argues that this alteration in technical vocabulary is the central symptom of incommensurability. It signals a change in the meaning of the fundamental quantity of energy $h\nu$ from a mental subdivision of the energy continuum to a physically separable atom of energy. Consequently, there are two incommensurable ways of understanding the expression $E = h\nu$, where h is Planck's constant and ν is the frequency of oscillation.

Kuhn argues that Planck's conceptual change is an example of a paradigm shift or scientific revolution. The most significant feature of such revolutions is that they remain invisible to both the discoverer and his or her colleagues during the period of discovery. As Kuhn explains, "creative scientists can be, and typically are, responsible for the emergence of beliefs that they did not hold themselves, at least not during the period when their discoveries were made."[5] In reconstructing past discoveries, however, Kuhn argues that there is a tendency to disguise this fact by creating the impression that the discoverer had always held the belief, albeit unconsciously, or that he somehow knew the outcome of his scientific activity in advance of the discovery. We see this in the case of the blackbody radiation problem. It is curious, both historiographically and epistemologically, that the standard interpretation of this problem relies on the term "oscillator," which Kuhn argues was only used by Planck after his gestalt switch in 1909. Planck's references to the term before this time occur only in relation to the use of the term by other physicists. Here Kuhn notes a resistance on the part of discoverers and the scientific community in accepting the mode of thought of a past generation of scientists after a discovery has revealed its failure to solve all its problems. After the concept of quantization had been discovered and the tradition of normal science was revised in light of this new concept, physicists found it very difficult to return to the classical mode of understanding the problem of blackbody radiation.

The resistance to an older mode of understanding a problem after a scientific revolution has occurred is in part epistemological. Scientists claim to hold their beliefs about nature on strong evidence. The evidentialist

5. Ibid., 362.

model of rational inquiry in science has become the gold standard against which every tradition of rational inquiry is measured. This evidentialist model is succinctly stated by W. K. Clifford when he writes that "it is wrong always, everywhere, and for anyone, to believe anything upon insufficient evidence. If a man, holding a belief which he was taught in childhood or persuaded of afterwards, keeps down and pushes away any doubts which arise about it in his mind . . . the life of that man is one long sin against mankind."[6] Thus, the evidentialist model of rational inquiry implies that a rational person is *always* critical. This implication explains in part why the scientist is so resistant in accepting an older mode of thought. For in the transition to a new research paradigm, as Kuhn argues, new possibilities are opened at the expense of old ones, thereby "exposing the foundations of a previous life form as contingent and threatening the integrity of the life one had lived before. Ultimately the experience [of a scientific revolution] can be liberating, but it is always threatening."[7]

What is threatening, as Clifford suggests, is not whether an older mode of thought or belief turns out to be true or false, but whether the scientist had a right to believe on such evidence as was before him.[8] That an older mode of thought or belief turns out to be false in light of a discovery suggests that the scientist was not performing his duty in holding his scientific beliefs on strong evidence. It is not so much that a scientific belief turns out to be false as that the scientist who holds the belief turns out to be irresponsible in adhering to the belief in light of accumulating evidence against it. Thus, Kuhn is right when he characterizes the crisis that precipitates a scientific revolution as an epistemological crisis. A detailed historiographical analysis of scientific discoveries reveals that the epistemological foundations of scientific belief do not measure up to the gold standard of rationality articulated by Clifford. In the practice of science, the scientist is not always critical, nor can she always be critical. Kuhn argues that the reaction to such a revelation is a retreat to commitment in which the scientific community attempts to cover up the epistemological problem through the distortion of personal and communal memories.

Michael Polanyi compares the way one learns science to the way one learns an art. Like an art, science "can be transmitted only by examples of the practice which embodies it. He who would learn from a master by

6. Clifford, *Ethics of Belief*, 77.

7. Kuhn, *Black-Body Theory*, 368.

8. Clifford, *Ethics of Belief*, 71.

watching him must trust his example. He must recognize as authoritative the art which he wishes to learn and those of whom he would learn it. Unless he presumes that the substance and method of science are fundamentally sound, he will never develop a sense of scientific value and acquire the skill of scientific enquiry. This is the way of acquiring knowledge, which the Christian Church Fathers described as *fides quaerens intellectum*, 'to believe in order to know.'"[9] Similarly, Kuhn suggests that one acquires a system of scientific belief in the same manner as one acquires a system of religious belief. In both cases, one must trust the authority of a tradition of rational inquiry. Just as one cannot become a Christian without trusting the authority of the Christian tradition, one cannot become a scientist without trusting the authority of the scientific tradition. Like the Christian tradition, the scientific tradition is initially exempt from skepticism. Kuhn argues that this is precisely what characterizes a tradition as *normal*. In science and in theology, a normal tradition provides rational norms or criteria of meaning and intelligibility for rational inquiry. Like the believer, the scientist must trust the rational norms embodied in the exemplars of the scientific tradition as a reliable foundation for further scientific inquiry, not as a more or less arbitrary and doubtful point of departure.

It would be a mistake, however, to suppose that the acquisition of a system of scientific belief or religious belief occurred in a critical manner. Like theology, science involves training in a normal paradigm. By trusting the paradigm of normal science, Kuhn argues that one learns to see the same things as his predecessors when confronted by the same stimuli. The child or novice is shown examples of situations that his predecessors have already learned to see as like each other and as different from other sorts of situations.[10] In this way, the young scientist learns to see a network of connections or patterns. Similarly, N. R. Hanson argues that the scientist is taught to see the world in a different way from the nonscientist. When a child or novice sees an X-ray tube, he does not see the same thing as the physicist. As Hanson argues, "the infant and the layman can see: they are not blind. But they cannot see what the physicist sees; they are blind to what he sees . . . The elements of the [layman's] visual field, though identical with those of the physicist, are not organized for him as for the physicist;

9. Polanyi, *Science, Faith, and Society*, 15.

10. Kuhn, *Scientific Revolutions*, 193–94.

the same lines, colours, shapes are apprehended by both, but not in the same way."[11]

According to the evidentialist model of rational inquiry, what the scientist sees or observes is the result of learning how to interpret a common visual experience or sense datum shared by other scientists. As a research physicist trained in the techniques of scientific observation, Hanson argues to the contrary that what the physicist sees is the result of learning how to *react* to examples rather than interpret them in the same way as other physicists. Whereas interpretation involves thinking or reasoning, seeing involves a spontaneous, involuntary reaction.[12] Thus, whereas interpretation refers to a critical process, seeing refers to a groundless reaction. In learning how to react to problem situations in the same way, Hanson argues that one acquires a way of seeing or organizing objects. But we do not see the organization of an object, say, a drawing, in the way we see the lines, shapes, and colors that comprise the drawing. For the organization itself is not a line, shape, or color. Unlike the elements of organization, the organization of the elements is not an element in the visual field. Thus, Hanson argues that "the plot is not another detail in the story. Nor is the tune just one more note. Yet without plots and tunes details and notes would not hang together."[13] Like the plot in relation to the details of a story, the tune in relation to the notes of a musical piece, or the meaning of a proposition in relation to its elements, the organization of elements in the visual field cannot be expressed by another detail, note, or symbol. Rather, the organization shows itself.

Therefore, contrary to the sense datum or empiricist account of observation, Hanson argues that the physicist must be taught how to see elements in the visual field in a certain organization, pattern, or arrangement. What she sees or observes, however, is not determined by the underlying psychological processes of interpretation, but by an objective context supplied by a normal paradigm. This organization is acquired by learning how to react to the paradigm, not by learning how to interpret it. The ability to interpret the organization embodied in the paradigm, to see alternative ways of organizing its elements, occurs only after the physicist has acquired a way of seeing the world through the paradigm. As Hanson argues, theories and

11. Hanson, *Patterns of Discovery*, 17.

12. Ibid., 10–11.

13. Ibid., 13.

interpretations are there in the seeing from the outset.[14] But the scientist learns how to see an arrangement of objects or phenomena according to a scientific interpretation before he is conscious that it is an interpretation.

In drawing a similar distinction, Kuhn opposes "the attempt, traditional since Descartes but not before, to analyze perception as an interpretive process, as an unconscious version of what we do after we have perceived."[15] But when we confuse the fundamental act of learning how to see nature in a certain pattern or organization with an interpretive process, we obscure the primitive nature of trusting the authority of the scientific tradition. According to the evidentialist model of rational inquiry, the scientist acquires rules and the ability to apply them from exemplars in a critical manner. On the contrary, Kuhn argues:

> That description is tempting because our seeing a situation as like ones we have encountered before must be the result of neural processing . . . once we have learned to do it, recognition of similarity must be as fully systematic as the beating of our hearts. But that very parallel suggests that recognition may also be involuntary [spontaneous], a process over which we have no control. If it is, then we may not properly conceive it as something we manage by applying rules and criteria. To speak of it in those terms implies that we have access to alternatives, that we might, for example, have disobeyed a rule, or misapplied a criterion, or experimented with some other way of seeing. Those, I take it, are just the sort of things we cannot do.[16]

Thus, contrary to the evidentialist model of rational inquiry, Kuhn argues that a normal paradigm organizes our perception and experience of the world before we are critical. It not only provides the condition for seeing; it determines what we can see. Alternative ways of organizing our perception and experience of the world are precluded by the very nature of a normal paradigm as a shared worldview, inescapable framework, or form of life.

Like the certainty characteristic of a religious form of life, the certainty characteristic of a normal paradigm in science is not a property of scientific belief, but a function of learning how to react to examples in the same way as other scientists who share the paradigm. Thus, Kuhn argues that a second source of resistance to alternative paradigms or modes of thought

14. Ibid., 10.

15. Kuhn, *Scientific Revolutions*, 195.

16. Ibid., 194.

"is the assurance that the older [normal] paradigm will ultimately solve all its problems, that nature can be shoved into the box the paradigm provides . . . That same assurance is what makes normal or puzzle-solving science possible."[17] Hence, despite mounting counterevidence, Planck struggles to reconcile his radiation law with the normal paradigm of classical physics with certainty. His effort is rewarded by solving the puzzle of the ultraviolet catastrophe with an empirical formula of unprecedented accuracy.

At some point, however, the normal paradigm is unable to solve all its problems and we are led to a critical examination of the paradigm. At the same time, Kuhn argues that there is a tendency to adhere to the normal paradigm despite accumulating doubts, anomalies, and counterevidence. Thus, a third source of resistance to alternative modes of thought is ideology.[18] In contrast to the spontaneous and involuntary manner in which a normal paradigm is acquired, ideology arises from a conscious and deliberate resistance to change the normal paradigm regardless of facts. W. W. Bartley has characterized this resistance to alternative modes of thought as the morbidity or decay of critical belief. As Bartley explains, the morbidity of critical belief "investigates what can happen to an objective system of belief to lead it, after being held for a time quite critically, to be gradually or abruptly, as the case may be, transformed into a dogmatically held ideology."[19] If the morbidity of critical belief is deliberate as Bartley argues, then we bear responsibility for the decay of critical belief. As Clifford argues, the sacred tradition of humanity does not consist "in propositions or statements which are to be accepted and believed on the authority of the tradition, but in questions rightly asked, in conceptions which enable us to ask further questions, and in methods of answering questions. The value of all these things depends on their being tested day by day. The very sacredness of the precious deposit imposes upon us the duty and the responsibility of testing it, of purifying and enlarging it to the utmost of our powers."[20]

Ideology, then, is to reason what the natural process of decay is to the body. Further, ideology is to scientific belief what fideism is to religious belief. In order to prevent the decay of critical belief in both cases, we must test and scrutinize the normal paradigm. But, as Kuhn argues, we cannot always be critical according to the evidentialist model of rational

17. Ibid., 151–52.

18. Ibid., 138.

19. Bartley, *Retreat to Commitment*, xix.

20. Clifford, *Ethics of Belief*, 91.

inquiry described by Clifford. Rather, critical belief occurs at special moments when the normal paradigm is threatened by the accumulation of counterevidence. Contrary to Karl Popper, who argues that the scientist must always be critical, Kuhn argues that such moments are in fact rare. Scientific activity is largely occupied with working out the details and consequences of a normal paradigm. We see this near the end of the nineteenth century during the discovery of X-rays, radioactivity, the electron, and the Zeeman effect. In large part, scientists were busy measuring physical parameters such as specific heats, densities, compressibility, resistivity, indices of refraction, and permeabilities. Only a small group of scientists were concerned with the anomalies presented by the new and often unexpected discoveries.[21]

More fundamentally, Kuhn argues that we cannot just break out of a normal paradigm or framework at any time.[22] Scientific revolutions, which consist of fundamental changes in the organization of our perception and experience of the world, occur through crisis. So long as the normal paradigm is able to solve all its problems, the possibility of extraordinary science cannot occur. Thus, the epistemological crisis that emerged from Planck's inability to reconcile his radiation law with the normal paradigm of classical physics prepared the way for a scientific revolution. Before Planck could see the alternative paradigm of a discrete energy spectrum, he had to fully acknowledge his inability to explain blackbody radiation in terms of the normal paradigm of a continuous energy spectrum. Just as the religious believer must fully acknowledge his inability to overcome error before he can see the point of grace, the scientist must acknowledge his inability to overcome the problems of a normal paradigm before he can see the point of an alternative paradigm.

Although the process leading to a scientific revolution is gradual, Kuhn argues that the revolution itself is sudden like a religious conversion experience. Like Kuhn, Hanson argues that such a revolution is not the result of deliberation and interpretation, but the result of an abrupt change in the conceptual organization of what one sees.[23] Just as there is a marked discontinuity between natural consciousness and Christian consciousness, there is a marked discontinuity between an older scientific paradigm and a new one. Like the religious believer, the scientist must change his mode

21. Thornton and Rex, *Modern Physics*, 16.

22. Kuhn, "Reflections on My Critics," 232.

23. Hanson, *Patterns of Discovery*, 12.

of thought or reflection. As new evidence comes to light, the context of a problem situation changes. Kuhn suggests that it is this context, not a mysterious intuition, that is responsible for the sudden reorganization of the familiar elements of the old paradigm into a new pattern. At some unexpected moment, the new pattern just emerges like a hidden figure in a picture puzzle. Following Hanson, Kuhn describes this abrupt psychological experience as a gestalt switch.

The Hermeneutical Dimension of Science

Kuhn's historiographical account of the blackbody radiation problem is illustrative of a paradigm shift in the image of science just as revolutionary as the paradigm shift he describes in science. Based on historiographical analysis of this and other scientific discoveries, Kuhn develops an anti-evidentialist model of rational inquiry that has largely replaced the conventional image of science as a steady, accumulative, and linear march toward truth. This new image of science is similar in many respects to rational inquiry in theology. We inherit a system of scientific belief that functions as a normal paradigm in providing a reliable and nonarbitrary point of departure for further scientific inquiry. This system of belief is initially exempt from skepticism, which is what characterizes it as normal. Contrary to the evidentialist model of rational inquiry, which claims that the scientist must always be critical in relation to the scientific tradition, Kuhn argues that the scientist reacts in accordance with the normal paradigm so long as it is able to solve all its problems. Crises emerge, however, when accumulating doubts, anomalies, and counterevidence arise in relation to a problem that the normal paradigm cannot solve. An epistemological crisis elicits critical belief or extraordinary science that pressures us to examine the normal paradigm, propose alternative versions of the solution of a problem within the paradigm, and ultimately modify or change the normal paradigm by adopting an alternative paradigm. The new paradigm subsequently functions in a normal role in determining further scientific inquiry.

Thus, the structure of scientific revolutions exhibits an interdependent relation between normal science and extraordinary science, in which the scientific interpretations of the present are at once constituted by the interpretations of earlier generations and constitutive of the interpretations for future generations. For this reason, Richard J. Bernstein argues that Kuhn's structure of scientific revolutions intimates the hermeneutical circle of tradition and interpretation.[24] As the normal paradigm of traditional science is examined and interpreted as a result of crisis, it is purified and enlarged through the critical activity of extraordinary science in the manner described by Clifford. Just as extraordinary science is impossible without normal science, extraordinary science or critical belief is necessary to keep the normal paradigm from decaying into a dogmatically held ideology. Thus, the relation between normal science and extraordinary science involves an essential tension necessary for the growth of scientific knowledge. In the words of Alasdair MacIntyre, the normal paradigm of science is at once tradition-constituted and tradition-constitutive.[25]

Although Bernstein may be right in arguing that the structure of scientific revolutions intimates the hermeneutical circle of tradition and interpretation, Kuhn never develops this structure into a hermeneutical model of rationality because of his metaphor of conceptual schemes. Despite Kuhn's rejection of a neutral translation language that could provide a way of comparing incommensurable paradigms, he argues that we must still translate one paradigm into the language of another paradigm in its entirety. Here, as Donald Davidson argues, Kuhn's metaphor of different observers of the same world who come to it with incommensurable systems of concepts leads to the idea of conceptual schemes and ultimately to conceptual relativism.[26] Although Bernstein is right in suggesting that Kuhn never intended his criticism of objectivism to lead to relativism, Davidson's conclusion is valid. Given the sharp contrast Kuhn draws between subject and object, between the organizing system of a conceptual scheme and the neutral empirical content supplied by nature waiting to be organized, it is difficult to see how scientists living in dramatically different worlds can understand one another without a common coordinate system such as a neutral translation language. Thus, contrary to Bernstein, the very idea of a conceptual scheme is incompatible with the hermeneutical circle of tradition and interpretation.

Davidson urges that we must abandon the idea of conceptual schemes as distortive of the practice of rational inquiry. In place of the metaphor of

24. Bernstein, *Objectivism and Relativism*, 131–33.

25. See MacIntyre, *Whose Justice? Which Rationality?*

26. Davidson, "Conceptual Scheme," 187.

conceptual schemes, we ought to adopt the metaphor of a system of belief in which the scientific interpretations of the past and present determine each other. This suggests that we ought to replace the phrase "conceptual translation" between paradigms with the phrase "hermeneutical interaction" between paradigms. But this alteration in vocabulary signals a conceptual change analogous to the one Kuhn discusses in relation to the blackbody radiation problem. Therefore, just as it is a mistake to suppose that Planck held the concept of a discrete energy spectrum during the period of his discovery, it is a mistake to suppose that Kuhn held the concept of the hermeneutical circle of tradition and interpretation during the period of his discovery.

The problem of conceptual relativism raised by Kuhn's metaphor of conceptual schemes may be illuminated by the morbidity of critical belief. In the absence of critical belief, Bartley argues that a system of belief tends to decay into a dogmatically held ideology. Recall the distinction drawn in the previous chapter between the riverbed of thoughts and thoughts moving on the riverbed, based on Ludwig Wittgenstein's metaphor of the relation between tradition and interpretation. The morbidity of critical belief explains how beliefs that were once fluid became hardened. Beliefs that are critically held for a period of time are eventually taken for granted. Their role or logical status within our belief system changes. In the absence of critical belief, Wilhelm Dilthey argues that the unity and integrity of our experience of the world given to us in tradition becomes fractured into conflicting metaphysical systems or worldviews. Contrary to Kuhn, Dilthey argues that the conflict is not rooted in dramatically incomparable systems of belief, but in the different reactions to life and their attitudes of alienation that underlie these worldviews.[27] This implies that the problem of incommensurability lies in our being closed to different interpretations through the decay of critical belief. According to Bartley, there is a retreat to commitment in the face of extramural challenges from other worldviews. Thus, the problem of conceptual relativism may be averted by locating the source of incommensurability in the morbidity of critical belief rather than in dramatically different conceptual schemes.

Dilthey's claim that worldviews are based on different reactions to life rather than differing points of view is compatible with Kuhn's account of the way in which scientific knowledge is acquired, not by consciously choosing a paradigm, but by reacting to the normal paradigm in a spontaneous

27. Dilthey, "Types of World-view," 133–54.

manner. Dilthey's claim is also consistent with Kuhn's parallel between a scientific revolution and a religious conversion experience. For this parallel implies that there can be no direct and gradual transition from the normal paradigm of a continuous energy spectrum to the extraordinary paradigm of a discrete energy spectrum, any more than there can be a direct and gradual transition from the normal paradigm of knowing about Christ to the extraordinary paradigm of accepting the things of Christ crucified through faith. In both cases, there is no neutral language in which we can translate the whole of one paradigm into another paradigm. For, unlike Popper, Kuhn argues that a neutral observation language is impossible because words change their meaning from one paradigm to another paradigm. In the transition from one paradigm to another, words attach themselves to nature in different ways.

Kuhn's parallel also implies that the problem of reorganizing one's perception and experience of the world has as much to do with the morbidity of critical belief as it has to do with a new way of seeing the world. The scientist acquires an organized way of seeing the world through a normal paradigm in an uncritical manner that is independent of the human will. But the resistance to alternative ways of seeing the world due to the decay of critical belief is a difficulty having to do with the will. Before one's perception and experience of the world can be reorganized, the will must be reoriented as a result of crisis. The epistemological crisis that emerges from the inability of the normal paradigm to solve all its problems makes the will more open and receptive to alternative paradigms. Similarly, according to the Christian tradition, the will must be converted through crisis or suffering before one can see the world differently through faith.

Contrary to Kuhn, the hermeneutical circle of tradition and interpretation tells us that we do not have to break out of a normal paradigm before we can understand another paradigm. The prejudices that are inherited from a normal paradigm are not only obstacles to understanding other paradigms, but are the conditions for understanding them. As Bernstein argues, "it is true, of course, that understanding requires effort and care, imagination and perceptiveness, but this is directed to the *pathos* of opening ourselves to what we seek to understand—of allowing it to 'speak to us.' And such receptiveness is possible only by virtue of those 'justified prejudices' that open us to experience."[28] But pathos involves an act of the human will. The will, although enclosed in itself through the decay of criti-

28. Bernstein, *Objectivism and Relativism*, 137.

cal belief, may become open and receptive to other interpretations through an epistemological crisis. As Kuhn argues, the crisis that emerges from the inability of the normal paradigm to solve all its problems leads to a breakdown of the normal paradigm. Because neither problems nor puzzles often yield to the first attack, the proliferation of versions of a theory within the normal paradigm is a very usual symptom of crisis.[29] Although scientists may begin to lose faith and then consider alternatives, they do not renounce the normal paradigm that has led them into crisis.[30]

This suggests that scientific interpretations are justified by appealing to the other interpretations or parts of a normal scientific tradition that have arisen in the fracturing of the normal paradigm. Like interpretations in theology, interpretations in science are validated in the practice of working out alternative interpretations of a problem within the hermeneutical circle of tradition and interpretation. Like the rule of faith in which one part of scripture may be illuminated by its other parts, a scientific problem may be illuminated by different interpretations of the problem within the normal paradigm. Thus, Kuhn argues that crisis loosens the rules of normal puzzle solving in ways that ultimately permit a new paradigm to emerge by proliferating versions or alternative interpretations of the normal paradigm.[31]

In this way, an epistemological crisis loosens the grip of the normal paradigm on the human will by opening it to new possibilities. As Bernstein suggests, through crisis the emergence of critical belief opens us "to the 'newness' of what is handed down to us, through the play of our forestructures [normal paradigm] and the 'things themselves' [problems] we can become aware of those prejudices that blind us to the meaning and truth of what we are trying to understand and those prejudices that enable us to understand."[32] Critical belief permits us to distinguish between prejudices that enable our understanding of a problem, and prejudices that present obstacles to understanding. In light of the various interpretations of a problem that have been made available within the normal paradigm, we must decide which parts of the paradigm to preserve and which parts of the paradigm to change. Thus, Kuhn argues that a fundamental source of

29. Kuhn, *Scientific Revolutions*, 71, 75.

30. Ibid., 77.

31. Ibid., 80.

32. Bernstein, *Objectivism and Relativism*, 138.

scientific change is "the divergent nature of the numerous partial solutions that concentrated attention to the problem has made available."[33]

The Blurring of the Subject-Object Scheme

The adoption of a hermeneutical model of rational inquiry in science in place of an evidentialist model is supported not only by historiographical analysis, but by the development of quantum physics. Both have significantly changed the image of science. As Stephen Toulmin writes, "on the minutest level of scientific analysis, Laplace's ideal of the scientist, as 'an unobserved, uninfluencing observer' studying the world of nature through a one-way mirror, is unattainable in principle for reasons of basic physical theory. There can be no simple, one-way coupling between a physicist and (say) the electrons that he selects as his objects of study. However delicate and miniscule our acts of observation on any subatomic particle may be, they will alter the particle's existing position or momentum, and so limit the precision with which its current condition can be known."[34] When we observe objects on the microscopic scale, we find that the observer and the object of study are interdependent parts of the same physical system. Like Kuhn's historiographical analysis, the development of quantum theory raises epistemological issues that illuminate the hermeneutical nature of rational inquiry in science. These issues lead us to question the sharp contrast between subject and object drawn by modern philosophy. This problem, known as the observational problem, is still of great concern to physicists. Einstein and Bohr discussed the problem at great length. In recounting these discussions, Bohr argues that "they implied the impossibility of any sharp separation between the behavior of atomic objects and the interaction with the measuring instruments which serve to define the conditions under which the phenomena appear."[35]

The observational problem can be illuminated by the uncertainty principle first enunciated in 1927 by the German physicist Werner Heisenberg. The first form of the principle, $\Delta p \Delta x \geq \hbar/2$, tells us that no matter how good an experimental measurement is made there is uncertainty in knowing the particle's momentum and position at the same time. In fact, the more

33. Kuhn, *Scientific Revolutions*, 83.

34. Toulmin, *Return to Cosmology*, 249–50.

35. Bohr, *Physics and Knowledge*, 39–40.

precisely we measure the particle's momentum, the larger the uncertainty we must accept in knowing the particle's position, and vice versa. The second form of the principle, $\Delta E \Delta t \geq \hbar/2$, tells us that if the change in the energy of a particle is small then the rate of change must be very gradual. Conversely, if the energy of a particle changes rapidly then the uncertainty in the energy must be large. This uncertainty is intrinsic and is not due to our inability to measure more precisely.[36] The generalized uncertainty principle allows us to formulate uncertainty principle relations for every pair of observables whose operators do not commute, such as angular momentum L and angle θ or rotational inertia I and angular velocity ω.[37] Because the value $\hbar = h/2\pi$ is very small, however, the uncertainty principle is evident only on the atomic level.[38]

A measuring instrument such as an electron microscope emits high-frequency radiation when it measures some property of a particle, say, the position of an electron. This radiation is emitted in quantized packets of energy called photons. Because particles of matter interact with photons, when we try to locate or localize the position of an electron precisely in a limited space-time (xt) domain, Bohr argues that the uncertainty principle implies that there is an exchange of momentum and energy between the measuring instrument and the electron. As can be seen from an examination of Heisenberg's uncertainty principle in either of its forms, the smaller the domain chosen, the greater the exchange of momentum and energy.[39] When a photon collides with an electron, the photon transfers momentum and energy to the electron. According to the conservation of momentum and energy, the total momentum and energy of the photon-electron system before the collision must be identical with the total momentum and energy of the system after the collision. But this transfer of momentum and energy to the electron influences the very properties we wish to measure. Thus, when we shine a source of light or radiation on an atomic object in order to measure its position, the measuring instrument introduces uncertainty into the measurement of the particle's momentum as a result of the beam of photons emitted by the instrument.

Since electronic measuring instruments are extensions of our unaided observational abilities, it follows that the very act of observation or

36. Griffiths, *Quantum Mechanics*, 114–16.

37. Ibid., 111.

38. Thornton and Rex, *Modern Physics*, 177–79.

39. Bohr, *Physics and Knowledge*, 89.

perception influences what is observed, although the influence is evident only on the atomic level. Thus, Bohr argues that the uncertainty principle illuminates a limitation in the scope of the normal paradigm of classical physics:

> While, within the frame of classical physics, there is no difference in principle between the description of the measuring instruments and the objects under investigation, the situation is essentially different when we study quantum phenomena, since the quantum of action imposes restrictions on the description of the state of the systems by means of space-time coordinates and momentum-energy quantities. Since the deterministic description of classical physics rests on the assumption of an unrestricted compatibility of space-time coordination and the dynamical conservation laws, we are obviously confronted here with the problem of whether, as regards atomic objects, such a description can be fully retained.[40]

Although we may draw a sharp distinction between the observer and the object of study within the normal paradigm of classical physics, the uncertainty principle implies the impossibility of a sharp separation between the behavior of atomic objects and the act of observing these objects with measuring instruments. On the atomic level, there is no sharp distinction between subject and object. Consequently, Toulmin argues that "we can no longer regard the world simply as a view, because we are agents or participants in all that we observe."[41] The observer and the object of study are interdependent parts of the same quantum system. The quantum mechanical approach to nature reveals different aspects of an atomic object that cannot be measured or described together. Similarly, the normal paradigm of classical physics and the extraordinary paradigm of quantum physics reveal different aspects of nature that cannot be described together, such as the wave and particle nature of both matter and radiation. Bohr relates these different aspects of a phenomena with his principle of complementarity. Because the uncertainty principle forbids the precise measurement of both aspects of an atomic object at the same time, we must view them as complementary parts of the whole we are trying to understand.

In the limit, however, where classical physics and quantum physics should agree—when the orbit of the electron is large, or equivalently, when the principal quantum number is large—the results of quantum physics

40. Ibid., 89.

41. Toulmin, *Return to Cosmology*, 238.

must reduce to the results of classical physics. Bohr calls this requirement the correspondence principle. For example, the frequencies of radiated energy predicted by quantum physics should agree with the frequencies predicted by classical physics for large values of an electron's orbit where quantization effects are minimized. In order to maintain this equivalence, Planck's constant h must decrease as the electron's orbit increases. Thus, in the limit when the principal quantum number is large, where quantization effects are minimized, the finite size of Planck's constant is unimportant.[42] Similarly, when the velocity of an object is a significant fraction of the speed of light ($v \leq 0.14c$), or equivalently, when the kinetic energy of the object is significantly smaller than its rest energy ($K << E_0 = mc^2$), where relativistic effects are minimized, the results of special relativity should reduce to the results of classical physics.

We see, therefore, that Planck's constant plays a role in quantum theory analogous to the speed of light in Einstein's theory of special relativity. In both cases, h and c define the correspondence of modern physics with classical physics, that is, the limiting conditions under which the results of quantum theory and special relativity must reduce to the results of classical physics respectively. Thus, we can translate the results of quantum physics into classical physics, or the results of special relativity into classical physics, in the limits where they must reduce to the same physical description of nature. Contrary to Kuhn, however, Bohr argues that we cannot translate the *whole* paradigm into the language of another paradigm beyond the scope determined by these theoretical limits. Rather, as Einstein and Infeld's metaphor of scientific discovery suggests, a scientific paradigm provides a partial view and fragmentary reconstruction of nature that complements the partial views and fragmentary reconstructions of other paradigms in giving us a wider conception of nature as a whole.

Like the rationalists of the Enlightenment, Bohr was convinced that the symmetry he observed in nature must also be mirrored in our common experience of the world. Consequently, Bohr did not hesitate to extend his principle of complementarity to observational problems outside the domain of physics:

> When studying human cultures different from our own, we have to deal with a particular problem of observation which on closer consideration shows many features in common with atomic or psychological problems, where the interaction between objects

42. Thornton and Rex, *Modern Physics*, 132–38.

> and measuring tools, or the inseparability of objective content and observing subject, prevents an immediate application of the conventions suited to accounting for experiences of daily life. Especially in the study of cultures of primitive peoples, ethnologists not only are, indeed, aware of the risk of corrupting such cultures by the necessary contact, but are even confronted with the problem of the reaction of such studies on their own human attitude. What I here allude to is the experience, well known to explorers, of the shaking of their hitherto unrealized prejudices through the experience of the unsuspected inner harmony human life can present even under conventions and traditions most radically different from their own.[43]

Like Bohr, Ludwig Wittgenstein argues that the reactions of primitives and the reactions of modern people are much the same. In both cases, culture is an expression and refinement of those ungrounded reactions. The experience of the unsuspected inner harmony of human life reveals that all human beings share a common constitution. This experience is the basis for Wittgenstein's account of our shared world picture, Thomas Reid's account of the principles of Common Sense, and Dilthey's account of our acquired mental structure. Although forms of life may be expressed in cultures whose conventions and traditions are most radically different from our own, there is still an inner harmony and commonality that binds us together at the deepest level of human nature.

Like Dilthey, Bohr acknowledges that the methodologies of the physical sciences and human studies must be appropriate to their disparate subject matters. Nevertheless, Bohr argues that we can extract a general epistemological attitude or strategy from the lessons learned in the development of quantum theory. Just as the appearance of different physical phenomena reveal partial but complementary aspects of nature, different manifestations of mental life in the world's great cultures and civilizations reveal partial but complementary aspects of our common experience of the world as human beings. Further, just as different paradigms in physics are necessary to achieve a wider view of the physical world, different human cultures or forms of life are necessary to achieve a wider view of our common human nature. Here our prejudices and differences are not only obstacles to understanding alien cultures, but conditions for understanding them. It is a matter of distinguishing between prejudices that enable understanding and prejudices that impede understanding. But we cannot

43. Bohr, *Physics and Knowledge*, 30.

draw this distinction apart from a mutual interaction between different interpretations of a problem competing for our rational allegiance within a shared paradigm.

Although Bohr understands that the analogy between physical problems and human problems is limited in scope, he describes a constructive metaphor for approaching the problem of strong disagreement within these limits that averts the problem of conceptual relativism connected with Kuhn's metaphor of conceptual schemes. The prejudices or interpretations that the observer brings to a problem are at once conditions of and obstacles to understanding the problem. Because the observer is an active agent or participant in what she is trying to understand, it is impossible to work out which prejudices enable understanding and which prejudices impede understanding apart from an open and lively interaction between different interpretations of a problem within a shared paradigm. Like Kuhn, Bohr suggests that alternative interpretations and partial solutions of a problem within the normal paradigm are necessary to discover the scope and limitations of the established paradigm. They reveal complementary aspects of a problem that may lead to a more comprehensive view that takes more into account. As Smith, Einstein, and Infeld suggest, the older way of looking at the problem is still valid. Only now, after we have achieved a more comprehensive view of the problem by overcoming those prejudices that impede understanding, we see how the starting point for our understanding of a problem is connected to a much richer environment. Further, as Bohr's correspondence principle suggests, regardless of how different our interpretations may be, they must reduce to a set of common beliefs in the limit where one interpretation stands in an exclusive relationship of complementarity to another interpretation. We saw this in the case of Gordon Kaufman's criticism of Karl Barth's Christocentric method in chapter 2. The arguments of both theologians can be reduced to a common belief in the exclusive disjunction of objectivism or relativism influenced by the Cartesian persuasion.

This approach to the problem of disagreement implies that there is a hermeneutical dimension of science analogous to the hermeneutical dimension of theology argued for in chapter 2. Like theological inquiry, scientific inquiry depends on the interdependent relation or hermeneutical interaction between the scientific interpretations of the past and present.

If this is true, we cannot expect theological inquiry to do what scientific inquiry cannot, namely, to resolve disputes and justify truth-claims from a perspective that stands outside a tradition of rational inquiry. The scientific ideal of the unobserved, uninfluencing observer is unattainable on both philosophical and scientific grounds. Although there can be no perception of the whole without its parts, the meaning of the parts cannot be fully comprehended without relating them to the whole in a complementary manner. Whereas the former activity corresponds to the analytic function of reason, the latter activity corresponds to the synthetic function of reason. If, as Smith argues, the limitations of a particular interpretation or abstraction can be seen only in relation to some wider purpose that takes more into account, science cannot preclude theology as a complementary interpretation of our common experience of the world that may illuminate the limits of the much disputed sphere of natural science.

Bohr's approach to the problem of disagreement suggests that it is a mistake to think of science and theology as incommensurable systems of belief or conceptual schemes that must be plotted on a common coordinate system. Instead, we may regard them as complementary interpretations of our experience of the world that are well founded within their own intent and under the control of their own purpose, but are nevertheless limited in scope. Although science and theology are shaped by two different normal paradigms or traditions of rational inquiry, there is no reason to suppose that the causal interpretation of the universe in science and the teleological interpretation of the universe in theology are incompatible. In fact, classical mechanics seeks to explain the causal mechanism of events in a universe that very much has a goal and directedness. This may be seen in the transition from Newtonian mechanics, in which the net force on a body is calculated by adding up all the individual forces acting on it, to Lagrangian and Hamiltonian dynamics which arrive at the same result using energy methods. Hamilton's Principle states that the actual path along which a dynamical system moves is the one that minimizes the time integral of the difference between the kinetic and potential energies. This principle is influenced by Maupertuis's principle of least action based on the theological concept that action is minimized through the wisdom of God.[44] As Stephen Thornton and Jerry Marion explain, "in the Newtonian formulation, a certain force on a body produces a definite motion—that is, we always associate a definite *effect* with a certain *cause*. According to Hamilton's Principle,

44. Thornton and Marion, *Classical Dynamics*, 230.

however, the motion of a body results from the attempt of nature to achieve a certain *purpose*, namely, to minimize the time integral of the difference between the kinetic and potential energies."[45] On the macroscopic scale, then, nature tends toward the goal of minimized action.

But the teleological character of the universe and the principle of least action are also evident on the microscopic scale. In quantum theory, for example, the electrons in the Bohr model of the atom *tend* to occupy the lowest energy levels available to them and, according to the Pauli exclusion principle, only one electron can be in a state with a given set of quantum numbers.[46] Thus, in the case of X-rays, physicists say that the electrons of heavy atoms that occupy the higher shells are *likely* to change their state in filling the inner-shell vacancies at lower energy levels, thereby emitting electromagnetic radiation. The characteristic X-ray energies are simply the energy differences between the shells.[47] In thermodynamics, the experimental fact that energy moves from a hot object to a cooler object is not explained by a causal mechanism. Rather, the random motions of particles in a system *tend* to distribute the energy of the system more uniformly among all its parts. As Daniel V. Schroeder explains, "the spontaneous flow of energy [heat] *stops* when a system is at, or very near, its *most likely macrostate*, that is, the macrostate with the greatest multiplicity. This 'law of increase of multiplicity' is one version of the famous second law of thermodynamics."[48]

Thus, nature may be interpreted not only as a causal system of interactions, but as a teleological system with goals and directedness. Further, the causal and teleological views in science are not mutually exclusive descriptions of nature, but complementary interpretations that give the scientist a more comprehensive understanding of how nature works. This suggests that the conflict between science and theology is not so much a conflict between a causal worldview and a teleological worldview, as it has been portrayed in the past. Rather, it is a conflict between a scientific worldview that takes both causal and teleological interpretations into account and a scientific worldview that seeks to reduce all interpretations to a single causal account. Similarly, Alvin Plantinga has recently argued that the conflict between science and religion is not so much a conflict between science and theism as it is a conflict between science and naturalism. According to Plantinga,

45. Ibid., 258.

46. Thornton and Rex, *Modern Physics*, 250.

47. Ibid., 142.

48. Schroeder, *Thermal Physics*, 59.

the scientific worldview does not necessarily include naturalism, which has become a worldview in its own right which many scientists reject. Nor does the scientific worldview commit the scientist or anyone else to naturalism. Thus, "if the most satisfactory Christian (or theistic) theology endorses the idea that the universe did indeed have a beginning, the believer [whether she is a scientist or not] has a perfect right to accept that thought."[49]

Plantinga's argument is further supported by the Planck time in the early universe which places a limit on our knowledge of the creation event. A rough formula for the Planck time can be derived from the consideration of a primordial black hole of mass M, which is the most compact region within which a mass can be contained. Because we are dealing with a very small mass at extremely high temperatures, quantum mechanics and relativity are involved in addition to gravitation. Thus, we should expect that the fundamental constants of nature will be involved, including Planck's constant h, Newton's gravitational constant G, and the speed of light c. If we let the Schwarzschild radius of the black hole R_S approximate the change in position in Heisenberg's uncertainty principle, we can determine the change in momentum of the singularity. The change in momentum can be used to estimate the kinetic energy of the singularity in the relativistic limit K. Since gravitation is also involved, we can find a Newtonian expression for the gravitational potential energy of the black hole U. Depending on which term dominates, the gravitational potential energy or the kinetic energy, the black hole will either be bound or the singularity could emerge from behind the event horizon in violation of the "Law of Cosmic Censorship." Thus, there will be a conflict between the application of quantum and classical physics to gravitation when the kinetic energy of the singularity is comparable to the magnitude of the gravitational potential energy of the black hole. This condition can be used to determine the Planck mass m_p, which gives us an estimate of the least massive primordial black hole. The Planck length ℓ_p, which describes the horizon distance or size of the observable universe at the Planck time, is given by the Schwarzschild radius of the black hole, where M is the Planck mass. Then, the Planck time t_p is just the time required for light to travel the Planck length.[50]

49. Plantinga, *Where the Conflict Really Lies*, 121. See also chapter 9.

50. The derivation of the Planck time is as follows. (1a) $\Delta x \Delta p \approx \hbar$, with $\Delta x \approx R_S$. Thus, $K \approx \Delta E = (\Delta p)c = \hbar c/R_S$. (1b) $U \approx -GM^2/R_S$. (1c) When $K + U = 0$, $M = \sqrt{\hbar c/G} \equiv m_p$. Thus, (2) $\ell_p \equiv R_S = 2GM/c^2 = Gm_p/c^2 = \sqrt{\hbar G/c^3}$, neglecting the factor of two in the order-of-magnitude estimate. Finally, (3) $t_p \equiv \ell_p/c = \sqrt{\hbar G/c^5}$. Recall that $\hbar = h/2\pi$. See Carroll and Ostlie, *Modern Astrophysics*, 1233–34.

Although this derivation is little better than a dimensional analysis, it is sufficient to show that the Planck time, $t_p \equiv \sqrt{\hbar G/c^5}$, involves a melding of quantum mechanics, gravitation, and relativity that has yet to be achieved in a unified theory. For this reason, the Planck time delimits the earliest time in the universe that can be addressed with current physical theory. Before the Planck time, cosmologists argue that "it is an article of faith for physicists that . . . the four fundamental forces of nature (the gravitational force, the electromagnetic force, and the strong and weak nuclear forces) were merged into one all-encompassing Theory of Everything."[51] Likewise, the Planck time places a limit on our ability to answer the question of whether the universe had a beginning. Science cannot definitively tell us what happened before the Planck time when the universe was smaller than the Planck length. Thus, naturalism cannot tell us with certitude that the universe did not have a beginning. Further, naturalism cannot rule out the possibility that the theological interpretation of the beginning of the universe, found in the Christian doctrine of creation, could be true. Finally, naturalism cannot reject the theological claim about the transcendent or mystical character of the universe in which human beings have a central role on the basis that it is less authoritative than its own claim to have reduced this transcendent character to a naturalistic interpretation; both claims are articles of faith. If naturalism is to avoid the fate of an ideology devoid of critical belief, it must remain open to these possibilities. Although science cannot definitively answer the question of whether the universe had a beginning, the idea that it did have a beginning has led to an impressive intellectual achievement for a theory that could turn out to be wrong. Unlike theories in modern cosmology which presuppose that there was no creation event, the Big Bang theory has allowed scientists to explain how the universe has rapidly evolved from an infinite singularity into a large-scale, causally connected region of space-time suitable for human life relative to a cosmological time-scale. With the additional hypothesis of the Theory of Everything, this idea has allowed scientists to explain how a single, all-encompassing force spontaneously separated into the four fundamental forces of nature we observe today through a process called symmetry breaking as the universe expanded and cooled.

How does this argument against naturalism contribute to the science-religion dialogue? In considering difference and diversity, Smith suggests that the achievement of mutual understanding in science and theology

51. Ibid., 1235.

depends on the possibility of a higher synthesis, in which their points of convergence may serve as a basis for a scheme that embraces their divergences as indispensable elements in a more comprehensive interpretation.[52] The possibility of this synthesis in turn depends on the recognition that our experience of the world cannot be reduced to but one of its dimensions. As Bohr, Dilthey, and Smith suggest, science and theology disclose different dimensions of our experience of the world. These dimensions of experience need to be related in a more comprehensive interpretation on the basis of beliefs that are substantively shared by scientists and theologians. These beliefs cannot be restricted to rationality, as in the current science-religion dialogue, because rational norms and standards of warrant are subject to change. Progress in the science-religion dialogue requires a more stable foundation in experience that transcends its expression in any one point of view.

Unlike naturalism, which ridicules the instinct to transcend our experience of the world, science and theology share the substantive belief that the universe has a transcendent character that cannot be reduced to a single dimension of experience. When we study science or theology, we bump up against something that possesses its own independence. Science and theology, each in their own way, seek to transcend the boundaries of our experience of the world. Our experience of the world as a single significant whole is limited not only by the fundamental structure of human consciousness as a synthesis of the ideal and the real, but by the Planck time in the early universe. As Plantinga suggests, the belief in the transcendent character of the universe in which human beings have a central role may be rooted in our constitution as rational creatures made in the image of God (Psalm 8:3–5). Regardless of the source or cause of this belief, this point of deep convergence may serve as a basis for a higher synthesis in which the scientific and theological communities are bound together in a single community of interpreters interpreting the world.

52. Smith, "Mediation, Conflict, and Creative Diversity," 42.

Part Three

A Kierkegaardian Perspective on Religious Knowledge

6

Faith, Knowledge, and Belief

ALTHOUGH ONE MAY HAVE the impression that skepticism is a modern problem, it was also prevalent in the ancient world. In one of Plato's dialogues, Socrates and Theaetetus discuss the nature of knowledge and how it is acquired through perception and sensation. The dialogue addresses the skeptic's challenge to our comfortable conclusions about the world issued by the Protagoreans: "Socrates: 'And if you have an idea must it not be an idea of *something*?'—Theaetetus: 'Necessarily.'—Socrates: 'And if you have an idea of something, mustn't it be of something real?'—Theaetetus: 'It seems so.'"[1] Notice Theaetetus's uncertain response to Socrates' question. Apparently, the commonsense empirical belief in things existing in space outside the mind is not self-evident. Today, it is argued that such a commonsense belief must be inferred from another empirical belief that is self-evident to perception and the senses. Thus, it is claimed that the former is indirectly evident based on the latter which is directly evident or immediate.

This thesis concerning the structure of empirical knowledge is at the heart of classical foundationalism. According to the strong version of justified true belief defended by Roderick Chisholm, the phenomenological fact that Theaetetus is immediately aware that his idea is of something is directly evident. The question is whether his idea puts him in touch with reality.[2] Suppose that Theaetetus discovers that one of his commonsense empirical beliefs is mistaken, that one of his ideas fails to put him in touch with reality, so that he does not know what he believes to be true about the world in one particular case. The question occurs whether he might be mistaken about other commonsense beliefs whose knowledge he has taken for

1. Quoted in Wittgenstein, *Philosophical Grammar*, 164. See *Investigations*, 1, ¶ 518.

2. See Chisholm, *Theory of Knowledge*.

granted. One case of doubt casts suspicion on all the beliefs whose veracity he has trusted. In this way, doubt may degenerate into a general mood of skepticism that can take hold of us. The question is whether there can be a response to such a skeptical mood that does not dismiss the skeptic's challenge to our comfortable conclusions about the world, or result in an explanation with no more genuine satisfaction than the skeptical conclusion it was meant to avoid. I will describe the features of what I take to be an anti-skeptical response of the right general form. Then I will discuss some problems with applying such a response to the problem of skepticism about the rationality of religious belief.

Skepticism and the Ordinary Deliverances of Experience

The skeptical challenge to our comfortable conclusions about the world is at odds with the ordinary deliverances of empirical experience. If asked whether one of our empirical beliefs about the world is of something real, we do not typically respond by saying "it seems so." Instead, as the Scottish Common Sense philosopher Thomas Reid argues, we are naturally disposed to believe the ordinary deliverances of our empirical experience with certainty. The commonsense image of the world precludes the possibility that we might be mistaken or deceived in our empirical beliefs. Ordinary empirical beliefs about the world do not misrepresent the external world to us. They provide genuine knowledge of the world as we actually experience it. They do not create internal mental representations that might disagree with the way the world really is independent of empirical experience.

Religious belief is analogous to empirical belief in this respect. Religious believers hold a commonsense image of God analogous to the commonsense image of the world. If asked whether one's belief in God is of something real, the believer does not typically respond by saying "it seems so." Instead, as the Reformer John Calvin argues, we are naturally disposed to believe in God with certainty.[3] Like the commonsense image of the world, the commonsense image of God precludes the possibility that one might be mistaken or deceived in one's religious beliefs. Ordinary religious beliefs about God do not misrepresent God's nature to the believer. They provide genuine knowledge of God as religious believers actually experience him in

3. Calvin, *Institutes*, 44.

the practice of their faith. They do not create internal mental representations that might disagree with the way God really is independent of religious experience.

After learning that perception and sensation are fallible, however, we are not so readily disposed to trust the commonsense images of the world or God given by the ordinary deliverances of experience. We learn that we are epistemically fallible and thus prone to make mistakes in our believings. Thus, the foundationalist is right in claiming that we are responsible for the beliefs that we hold. But he is wrong in claiming that our commonsense beliefs about the world and God are irrational if they are not supported by strong evidence. The foundationalist argues that we are not entitled to hold our most fundamental convictions with warrant until we base them on a special class of beliefs that are directly evident, incorrigible, and self-justifying. Without proper noetic foundations, a person cannot claim that her personal convictions are rational or true. For if they are rational, they must be supported by strong evidence. If they are true, they must agree with the way things are independent of any epistemic practice of justification.

According to this strong view of justified true belief, the commonsense images of the world and God are epistemically below par. If we lack evidence for such beliefs, we are intellectually irresponsible if we continue to hold them. For in so doing we dodge the skeptic's challenge to our comfortable conclusions about the world and God, either by retreating to ideology in the case of empirical belief or fideism in the case of religious belief. We have an epistemic duty to hold at least our most important beliefs on strong evidence. Only beliefs that are directly evident or immediate to the senses can provide the fixed and stable foundation for deriving all our other beliefs with some measure of assurance. If at least some of our most fundamental beliefs are not grounded in immediate experience or the directly evident, the truth-preserving nature of all our other beliefs becomes suspect. Thus, today, as in the ancient world, if asked whether our commonsense empirical and religious beliefs about the world and God are of something real, the uncertain response "it seems so" reveals a deep skepticism about their rationality and truth-condition. Here, as Ludwig Wittgenstein argues, doubt comes after belief.[4]

The difficulty of justifying our most basic beliefs in response to the evidentialist challenge has precipitated a backlash of skepticism about traditional religious, moral, and even scientific beliefs. As doubt about the

4. Wittgenstein, *On Certainty*, ¶ 160.

agreement of our commonsense beliefs with reality has become widespread, we have grown suspicious of our capacity to know. We no longer trust the ordinary deliverances of experience. In order to reclaim initial certitudes, we feel compelled to explain why we are entitled to hold our most formative beliefs without strong evidence. As Clifford Geertz writes, "the thing we seem least able to tolerate is a threat to our powers of conception, a suggestion that our ability to create, grasp, and use symbols may fail us."[5] Because relativism involves skepticism about rationality rather than truth, or our ability to produce rational consensus in the face of strong disagreement, it expresses a threat to our powers of conception. After the demise of classical foundationalism, we have become alienated from the commonsense images of the world and God that we acquired naturally and innocently as children. There is a growing dissatisfaction with the intellectual underpinnings of our commonsense beliefs in every area of knowledge. Geertz argues that we cannot just look at such anomalies without trying to develop some notions about how they might be reconciled with the ordinary deliverances of experience. In religion and theology, the failure of classical foundationalism has led to skepticism about the rationality of religious belief. As anomalies have accumulated and traditional norms have failed to address them, reflection about the reasonableness of religious belief has become intensely reconstructive. In the search for the new foundations of theism, the question of whether religious belief is rational looms large.

As Nicholas Wolterstorff has pointed out, responses to this question remained polarized for years by classic rivals in the theory of knowledge—coherentism versus foundationalism.[6] Today, this impasse has come unstuck as the structure of these epistemological alternatives has been reexamined in light of developments in the theory of knowledge. Prior to these developments, realism and pragmatism were regarded as mutually exclusive alternatives we had to choose between. It is now widely argued that one can be pragmatist with respect to knowledge and realist with respect to truth. If part of the classical picture of knowledge must be rejected, Wolterstorff argues that we do not have to reject the whole picture. We can reject the evidentialist challenge embedded in classical foundationalism without flouting our obligations to rationality or sacrificing claims to objective truth. Just because knowledge is fallible does not mean that it is

5. Geertz, *Interpretation of Cultures*, 99.

6. See Sosa, "The Raft and the Pyramid," for a discussion of coherence versus foundations in the theory of knowledge.

not rational or objective. Just because an unsituated rationality is an untenable ideal does not mean that anything goes in our believings. There are still better and worse ways of believing.[7]

The emergence of Reformed epistemology has had a dominating influence on current discussions of faith and reason. Wolterstorff and Alvin Plantinga have applied these developments in the theory of knowledge to religious belief in arguing that belief in God is rational as it stands. The approach of both philosophers to the question of whether belief in God is rational is shaped by the anti-evidentialist impulses of the Reformed theological tradition. Although there may be no self-evident beliefs that justify belief in God as in the case of strong foundationalism, there may still be justification-conferring conditions that justify the rationality of its acceptance. Although both philosophers argue that we are justified in holding our commonsense religious beliefs until such time as there is evidence not to believe in particular cases, they appeal to quite different doctrines. Whereas Wolterstorff appeals to Reid's doctrine of the principles of Common Sense, Plantinga appeals to an exotic epistemological doctrine known as weak foundationalism. According to this doctrine, belief in God is properly basic or self-justifying rather than self-evident, and thus lies at the foundation of our noetic structure like other properly basic beliefs such as the belief in other minds. In this way, Plantinga develops Calvin's theological claim that belief in God is implanted in everyone into an epistemological doctrine.

Contrary to Plantinga's weak foundationalism, Wolterstorff appeals to the ordinary deliverances of experience and the rational norms or criteria of meaning and intelligibility available to us in a tradition of rational inquiry. These rational norms are not based on exotic foundations, but on our shared sense of agreement about what is and is not reasonable. Like John Locke's vision of the responsible believer, Wolterstorff urges us to take the skeptic's challenge to our comfortable conclusions about the world and God seriously. For in matters of maximal concern such as ethics and religion, it is not permissible to hold beliefs without considering their reasonableness and truthfulness. Unlike Locke, however, Wolterstorff proposes a doxastic practice in place of classical foundationalism, based on a distinction between reasonable and unreasonable cases of belief and doubt. Reasonable

7. Developments in the theory of knowledge over the last several decades provide a good example of progress in philosophy, as well as a counterexample to the claim that genuine progress is possible only in science.

doubt, or what Karl Barth calls Socratic doubt, arises in specific noetic situations and is necessary to fulfill our epistemic duty to produce more rational and truth-preserving beliefs. In contrast, unreasonable doubt, or what Barth calls skeptical doubt, arises apart from any specific noetic situation and thus presents an obstacle to the epistemic goal of increasing our stock of true beliefs. Thus, the question of whether a particular religious belief is rational is meaningful. For it can be answered by examining how the belief was acquired in a specific noetic situation. But the question of whether religious belief in general is rational is nonsense. Wolterstorff therefore urges the believer to form the habit of interrogating the reasonableness of his doubts as well as beliefs in order to prevent the belief-forming mechanism of doubt from degenerating into a general mood of skepticism.

In contrast to Locke's evidentialism and Plantinga's weak foundationalism, Wolterstorff argues that the rationality of religious belief is based on common rational norms, not private and parochial foundations. Wolterstorff appeals to Reid's doctrine of the principles of Common Sense in describing what we hold in common. This includes our shared sense of agreement about what is and is not reasonable. As such, Wolterstorff appeals to the natural rather than transcendental in human nature, to how we are constituted as rational creatures and to what we actually do in the arena of believing. Most importantly, Wolterstorff argues that we must once again learn to trust our capacity to know by trusting these ordinary deliverances of experience. At the same time, we must learn to question the general mood of skepticism that has robbed us of initial certitudes and barred the way to productive belief. Here, as John Paul II argues, "in reaffirming the truth of faith, we can both restore to our contemporaries a genuine trust in their capacity to know and challenge philosophy to recover and develop its own full dignity."[8] Wolterstorff has done much to advance both objectives through his Reidian approach to skepticism.

Misgivings about a Religious Epistemology

The application of a naturalist response to empirical skepticism, however, to the problem of skepticism about the rationality of religious belief is problematic for several reasons. Perhaps most importantly, the Reformed

8. John Paul II, *Fides et ratio*, § 1.

definition of faith as knowledge becomes a source of confusion when knowledge is defined in the philosophical sense of justified true belief. Plantinga claims that belief in God means trusting God.[9] At the same time, he claims that belief in God is properly basic in the sense that it is grounded in justification-conferring conditions that make it a case of knowledge just in case the belief is true. Like other properly basic beliefs that are produced immediately such as the belief in other minds, Plantinga argues that belief in God is included in the foundations of our noetic structure. Of course these claims are not incompatible on Plantinga's view because faith is construed as a matter of belief alone. This follows from the Reformed definition of faith as knowledge combined with the philosophical definition of knowledge as justified true belief. Thus, Plantinga argues that faith itself is a matter of believing something rather than doing something.[10] To complicate matters, Plantinga is not clear about which religious beliefs are properly basic. At times he speaks of belief in God as including only the minimal belief in God's existence. At other times he implies that belief in God may include knowledge of God's nature and attributes, which are considered to be objects of faith rather than natural reason by the Christian tradition. Thus, there is a lack of precision in the definition of the scope of properly basic belief.

Unlike Plantinga, Wolterstorff argues that faith is an act of the whole person that cannot be reduced to a matter of believing something. Faith as a whole is not identical with belief because the organizing center of faith is trust rather than belief.[11] Like Plantinga, however, Wolterstorff suggests that believing or accepting something as coming from God may well be a case of knowledge.[12] In quoting Rudolf Bultmann, Wolterstorff argues that knowledge must also be an element of faith since knowledge begins with faith and all faith is to become knowledge. In a much stronger claim, Wolterstorff argues that to have faith in God is to know him, and conversely, to know God is to have faith in him.[13] This claim may be expressed more formally by saying that a person has faith in God if and only if he has knowledge of God. Apparently, knowledge is not merely an element of faith, but is somehow identical with faith itself. Analogous to Plantinga in the case

9. Plantinga, "Belief in God," 18.

10. Plantinga, *Warranted Christian Belief*, 249.

11. Wolterstorff, "Introduction," 13.

12. Ibid., 14.

13. Ibid., 15.

of properly basic belief, there is a lack of precision in the definition of the scope of knowledge in relation to faith. It is not clear whether knowledge is logically equivalent to faith or whether it is a component of faith and, if so, in what sense and to what extent. In contrast to Plantinga and Wolterstorff, I will argue that faith involves knowledge in the more ordinary sense of having acquired a system of religious belief by trusting the authority of the Christian tradition. Faith is a relationship with what is believed rather than belief itself. This relationship involves a conscious, deliberate, and continuing action of the human will. Thus, contrary to Plantinga, I will argue that faith is a matter of doing something, not merely believing something.

Wolterstorff invokes the use of the word "know" by the New Testament writers in support of his claim that faith may be a case of knowledge. It is doubtful, however, whether these writers actually use the word "know" in the philosophical sense proposed by Wolterstorff and Plantinga. As I argued in chapter 3, Wittgenstein tells us that the statement "I know that *p*" expresses the readiness to believe certain things. As Wittgenstein and Reid suggest, a system of religious belief is acquired in a spontaneous, involuntary, and epistemically innocent manner by believing or trusting the authority of the Christian tradition. Belief acquisition occurs through a credulity disposition implanted by nature. This process is immediate and corresponds to a first-order level of basic doxastic ascent that is independent of the will. Thus, as we saw in the previous chapter, the scientist, like the theologian, acquires a system of belief by reacting to a normal paradigm, trusting and following its exemplars, prior to the critical process of interpretation. Here, as the Danish philosopher Søren Kierkegaard argues, the question of truth does not arise. In the words of the philosophical pseudonym Johannes Climacus, "immediacy is indefiniteness. In immediacy relationships are absent; for as soon as relationships exist, immediacy is annulled. In immediacy therefore everything is true; but this truth is straightway untrue; for in immediacy everything is untrue . . . If consciousness can remain in immediacy then the whole question of truth is done away."[14] Thus, one sense of "knowledge" or believing something as coming from God refers to the *acquisition* of a system of religious belief in an uncritical or immediate manner. It is in this ordinary sense of knowledge that the apostle Paul speaks of knowing and proclaiming the things of Christ crucified.

But there is another sense of "knowledge" or believing something as coming from God that refers to the *acceptance* of a system of religious belief

14. Kierkegaard, *De Omnibus Dubitandum Est*, 147.

in a critical or reflective manner. These two senses of knowledge are based on the grammatical distinction drawn in chapter 3 between two different levels of doxastic ascent. Whereas belief acquisition occurs at a first-order level of basic doxastic ascent that is independent of the will, belief acceptance occurs at a second-order level of doxastic ascent that is critically dependent on the will. In contrast to a credulity disposition, which is a natural reaction implanted by nature that enables us to trust what we apprehend other people as telling us as true, faith is an emotional disposition implanted by grace that enables us to react or respond to God in obedience. These dispositions correspond to lower and higher levels of doxastic ascent respectively. Whereas the credulity disposition is an unmediated immediacy, faith is a mediated immediacy. Thus, Kierkegaard argues that faith is a critical mode of acceptance that opens the will to the knowledge of God rather than implanting this knowledge in us in an immediate manner. As Climacus explains, "when I accept a proposition in faith, I am unable straightway to understand it or carry it out, but yet I receive it because I believe [trust] the person who asserts it."[15] Through the critical disposition of faith the believer comes into *relationship* with the proposition. Because relationships are absent in the case of an unmediated immediacy, faith cannot be conceived as an immediate belief-forming process. Rather, the knowledge of God involves the transmutation of what is believed or accepted through faith into knowledge through the natural belief-forming processes of critical belief. Since faith and knowledge both depend critically on the will, they belong to a second-order level of doxastic ascent that must be carefully distinguished from the first-order level of basic doxastic ascent.

Like faith, doubt may also disturb the natural immediacy of our acquired system of belief or shared world picture. Climacus tells us that "in immediacy the falsest and the truest things are equally true. In immediacy the most possible and the most impossible things are equally actual. So long as the alternating [between these opposites] takes place without any collision, consciousness is not really present."[16] Thus, as one matures in the Christian faith, doubts may arise as the religious beliefs acquired through trusting the Christian tradition come into conflict or collision with beliefs acquired through trusting other formative traditions of rational inquiry such as science. Here, as Climacus argues, doubt disturbs the natural im-

15. Ibid., 137.

16. Ibid., 149.

mediacy of our acquired worldview as consciousness brings two opposing beliefs into *relationship*. The emergence of responsible doubt pressures us to hold our religious beliefs in a deeper way which we call knowledge. Thus, consistent with Augustine and Anselm, the question of whether our religious beliefs have epistemic warrant and the question of whether they are true or false are appropriately raised at a second-order level of doxastic ascent, only after one has accepted the Christian teachings through faith.

Although faith is implanted by the activity of the Holy Spirit, as Wolterstorff contends, it cannot be properly conceived as a new cognitive disposition or belief-forming process that produces religious beliefs immediately in a way that makes them knowledge. This epistemic conception of faith is at the heart of Ralph McInerny's charge of fideism against Reformed epistemology.[17] On the contrary, faith is a passion that creates a new relationship between the self and God, and through this relationship, establishes a new connection between rationality and truth such that genuine knowledge of God is possible. Faith is a new emotional disposition implanted by grace that reorients the will to the knowledge of God, opening our heart to accept something as coming from God, and thereby allowing our natural belief-forming processes to properly function as God created them. Thus, contrary to Wolterstorff and Plantinga, faith is not a new cognitive device that repairs our natural cognitive equipment from the noetic effects of sin. Faith creates a new will or heart in us, not new knowledge. The problem, therefore, is not that our natural belief-forming processes are defective or incapable of properly functioning due to the noetic effects of sin. Rather, the problem is that our will is fallen. According to Augustine and the Reformer Martin Luther, the will is closed to the knowledge of God in its natural state.[18] If reason is wounded, as John Paul II tells us, it is because of disobedience. Because the will is closed to the knowledge of God, it has blinded our natural powers of conception with prejudices that impede our understanding of truth. Only if the will is reoriented to the knowledge of God through faith can reason perceive truth in its fullness.[19]

Kierkegaard argues that there is a leap between faith and knowledge, not a leap of blind faith that somehow puts us in a state of knowledge, but a grammatical distinction between the fundamental act of trusting God with the endurance of a deep passion and the epistemic process of knowing God

17. McInerny, "Christian Philosophy," 257–75.

18. Augustine, *Confessions*, 48. See Luther, *Bondage of the Will*, 67.

19. John Paul II, *Fides et ratio*, § 2.

in the sense of holding beliefs about him with warrant. The grammar of faith is different from the grammar of knowledge. The Christian tradition produces religious beliefs in us in the same way as other traditions of rational inquiry. They are produced spontaneously or immediately through the ordinary deliverances of a credulity disposition. Although a system of religious belief is acquired naturally through a credulity disposition by trusting the authority of the Christian tradition, the activity of the Holy Spirit creates a new relationship to these beliefs through the supernatural disposition of faith, such that the beliefs become formative of a religious way of living in addition to informing a religious point of view. This distinction between faith and knowledge implies that the knowledge of God, in the ordinary sense of having acquired a system of religious belief by trusting what the Christian tradition tells us about Christ, does not necessarily lead to the acceptance of the Christian teachings through faith. As I argued in chapter 3, although we have no choice or control over which beliefs are acquired at the level of basic doxastic ascent, we do have a choice in whether to accept this system of belief in whole or in part at the level of critical belief.

The epistemic conception of faith involves an inversion of the two levels of doxastic ascent described above. Faith is defined, not in the critical sense of accepting a system of religious belief in a way that depends on the will at the second-order level of doxastic ascent, but in the uncritical or immediate sense of acquiring a system of religious belief through a credulity disposition that is independent of the will at the first-order level of basic doxastic ascent. This inversion creates two problems. First, the justification-conferring conditions offered in support of our most basic religious beliefs obscure the primitive nature of trusting the authority of the Christian tradition at the first-order level of basic doxastic ascent. Belief acquisition is spontaneous, involuntary, and epistemically innocent with regard to the manner in which we come to hold these beliefs. For Wittgenstein, like Reid, it is not within our power to choose which beliefs we will accept or reject at this basic level.[20] Thus, the conception of a belief-forming process that produces religious beliefs with just the right sort of justification-conferring conditions is at odds with both Wittgenstein and Reid's accounts. Second, these same justification-conferring conditions effectively transmute religious belief into knowledge in advance of the acceptance of the Christian teachings through faith, thereby dodging the difficulty of accepting these teachings by circumventing the critical role of the will at the second-order

20. Wittgenstein, *Investigations*, 1, ¶ 219. See Reid, *Inquiry*, 9.

level of doxastic ascent with an immediate belief-forming process at the first-order level of basic doxastic ascent.

The epistemic conception of faith as justified true belief is problematic for another reason. In arguing that faith can be transmuted into knowledge through justification-conferring conditions rather than what is believed or accepted through faith, Wolterstorff and Plantinga presume that faith can change its essential nature. In the transmutation of what is believed through faith into knowledge, however, the essential nature of faith remains unchanged. Faith is an emotional disposition implanted by grace that creates a new relationship between the self and the truth of the Christian teachings by reorienting the will to the knowledge of God. The Christian tradition claims that salvation depends on a saving obedience to God through an act of faith or trust in Jesus Christ, not the degree or quality of one's religious knowledge. The apostle Paul urges the believer to transmute the *deposit* of faith into knowledge, not faith itself. The deposit of faith consists of a system of religious belief acquired in a spontaneous, involuntary, and epistemically innocent manner by trusting the authority of the Christian tradition. Although a rational faith or reasoned trust seeks to transmute what is believed through faith into knowledge, it cannot transmute faith itself into knowledge without changing the means by which God has chosen to save us.

We are redeemed through a saving act of obedience made possible by the inward work of grace, not through an epistemic state or process. But, as Gerhard O. Forde argues, when we speak of the Pauline teaching about justification by faith alone, "we are usually driven to define, qualify, and hedge about the faith of which we speak so that no one will get the 'wrong idea' . . . Protestants eager to attest their orthodoxy and 'safeness' are drawn into the same game, put on the defensive, and the battle is lost."[21] Forde argues that "it is precisely that *alone*, that *sola*, especially when combined with *faith*, that makes us think there surely must be something missing and leads us, both Protestant and Catholic, to rush in with all our interpretative additions."[22] In the case of Reformed epistemology, the interpretative addition is faith conceived as an immediate belief-forming process with justification-conferring conditions that make it a case of knowledge just in case the belief is true. But if we are to take the Reformers seriously, faith *alone* is incompatible with this or any other interpretative addition.

21. Forde, *Justification by Faith*, 10.

22. Ibid., 9.

The account of the relation between faith and religious belief in Reformed epistemology also raises the question of whether faith is compatible with a *prima facie* theory of justified true belief. According to the weak version of justified true belief proposed by Wolterstorff and Plantinga, the justification-conferring conditions for our beliefs must be understood as conferring *prima facie* rather than *ultima facie* justification.[23] Consistent with the anti-evidentialist impulses of the Reformed tradition, both philosophers wish to avoid the strong version of justified true belief in classical foundationalism in which degrees of certainty are proportional to the strength of the evidence. According to the *prima facie* account, we are justified in holding our religious beliefs until such time as there is evidence to believe that some of these beliefs are unreliable or false. Since apparently all religious beliefs are defeasible in principle, the *prima facie* justification of these beliefs can be overridden. This is compatible with Plantinga's view that some religious beliefs are properly basic. Although basic religious beliefs are produced immediately in a way that confers *prima facie* justification on them, the justification can be overridden by potential defeaters. In this way, Plantinga hopes to avert the charge of fideism.

As Wolterstorff has pointed out, however, this account of the relation between faith and religious belief is incompatible with the absolute faith stance of Christianity. For the Christian tradition speaks of faith as an act of holding fast to our most basic religious convictions, in times of adversity as well as in times of prosperity, not until such time as we have evidence not to believe. Holding our most basic religious beliefs until such time as we have evidence not to believe is incompatible with the certainty that is characteristic of faith. Such a tentative posture is not even possible for the scientist. For, as we saw in the previous chapter, the scientist continues to hold his most basic scientific convictions with the assurance that the normal paradigm will solve all its problems, despite evidence that some of his beliefs about nature may be unreliable or false.

According to the rational norms or criteria of meaning and intelligibility established in the Christian tradition through its creeds, confessions and doctrines, several beliefs are basic to orthodox Christianity: the belief in the Trinity, the incarnation, the full divinity and full humanity of Jesus of Nazareth, the physical death and bodily resurrection of Jesus, his power to forgive sin and give eternal life through faith, and the belief that there is no other name in heaven or on earth by which we are saved, a stumbling block

23. Plantinga, "Belief in God," 83.

for Jews and Gentiles alike. If these basic beliefs are defeasible in principle, upon what rock shall we stand? This suggests that not all religious beliefs are compatible with a *prima facie* theory of justified true belief. For the Christian tradition has established a set of basic beliefs that are exempt from skepticism. One cannot be a Christian and seriously doubt them because they connect the believer to God in an intimate relationship through faith. Here, as Wittgenstein argues, trusting God "means submitting to an authority. Having once submitted, you can't then, without rebelling against it, first call it in question and then once again find it acceptable."[24]

Gary Gutting argues, therefore, that we must draw a distinction between beliefs that are basic to the absolute faith stance of Christianity and beliefs that are not. Gutting attempts to elucidate Plantinga's distinction between basic and non-basic religious beliefs in terms of Imre Lakatos's distinction between core and outer beliefs in science. Whereas the core beliefs within the Christian tradition are based on direct religious experience, Gutting argues that outer beliefs are *prima facie* accounts of God about which it is possible to be mistaken. We are *prima facie* justified in holding outer beliefs until such time as we have adequate reason in specific cases to believe that they are unreliable or false.[25] But how can we define a criterion for the directly evident in religious experience when we cannot do so in the case of empirical experience? The notion of the directly evident in religious experience is plagued by the same vagueness as the notion of the directly evident in empirical experience. This raises the question of whether any epistemic theory, regardless of whether it is based on a strong or weak version of foundationalism, can distinguish a set of basic beliefs without appealing to tradition. If a theory of religious knowledge cannot define a criterion for proper basicality without appealing to tradition, we must rely on tradition as our only source for adjudicating religious disagreement. Unless an epistemic theory can supply a more trustworthy norm, we must rely on the norm already established in the practice of the Christian tradition. But the appeal to tradition is the very problem we hoped to avoid with a foundationalist theory of religious knowledge. Although Gutting is right when he argues that the core beliefs of the Christian tradition are exempt from doubt, he attempts to prove too much when he argues that they are exempt because they are based on direct religious experience.

24. Wittgenstein, *Culture and Value*, 45.

25. Gutting, *Religious Belief*, 175.

Although the core or basic beliefs of Christianity may be exempt from doubt within the Christian tradition, they are not necessarily exempt from doubt within other traditions of rational inquiry. Just because these beliefs are taken for granted in living life in the everyday within the Christian community does not mean that this is the case for other communities. In his recent work, Plantinga appears to dodge the skeptic's challenge to our comfortable conclusions about God by dismissing skepticism and relativism as potential defeaters of warranted Christian belief, thereby inviting the charge of fideism he hopes to avert.[26] Apparently, for Plantinga, some religious beliefs are so deeply ingressed in the foundations of our noetic structure that doubt cannot get at them.[27] Unlike Plantinga, Wolterstorff takes the skeptic's challenge seriously. In his recent work, Wolterstorff attempts to address the challenges of skepticism and relativism to the problem of disagreement with Reid's doctrine of the principles of Common Sense. Wolterstorff argues that the cultural crisis that confronted Locke is still with us, perhaps more so than ever. If tradition is fractured, we cannot appeal to tradition to settle disputes about matters of maximal concern such as ethics and religion. This is the predicament that motivates the foundationalist project. But, as Wolterstorff argues, the solution is not to set aside all unverified tradition and let reason be our guide as Locke claims. Rather, we must establish a new doxastic practice in order to prevent habitual doubt from spilling over into every area of human life.

In this way, Wolterstorff argues that the problem defined by Locke may be better solved by Reid. Whereas skepticism doubts whether we can know truth, relativism doubts whether we can find a sufficiently objective perspective to adjudicate strong disagreement about truth. Although doubt is necessary to produce more truth-preserving beliefs that put us in touch with reality, Wolterstorff argues that we must learn to scrutinize our doubts as well as beliefs in order to prevent the belief-forming mechanism of doubt from degenerating into a general mood of skepticism about rationality and truth. If Wolterstorff is right, we do not need to find a more objective perspective to achieve rational consensus in the face of strong disagreement. Rather, we need to restore trust in the rational norms or criteria of meaning and intelligibility already available to us in a tradition of rational inquiry

26. Plantinga, *Warranted Christian Belief*, 422–99.

27. The phraseology of this sentence is based on Wolterstorff's criticism of Wittgenstein's account of our shared world picture, which may be more appropriately applied to Plantinga's religious epistemology. See Wolterstorff, *Thomas Reid*, 240; and chapter 3 of this book for my critique of Wolterstorff's reading of *On Certainty*.

as they stand. Thus, in contrast to the parochial concerns of Plantinga's religious epistemology, Wolterstorff, like Locke, attempts to engage his philosophy with the wider culture in developing a general theory about how we may understand our differences in terms of what we hold in common.

A naturalist response to empirical skepticism, however, cannot be automatically applied to skepticism about the rationality of religious belief without considering how religious belief is different from empirical belief, and how Christian faith is different from both. Kierkegaard's philosophical pseudonym Climacus argues that doubt is never necessary. For if it were, it could never be overcome.[28] Rather, as Wittgenstein argues, doubt rests on what is exempt from doubt. Wolterstorff's naturalist response to skepticism is compatible with this claim. For Wolterstorff argues that the examination of tradition can take place only in the context of unexamined tradition. Further, in arguing that we must restore trust in our capacity to know and in the rational norms already available to us in a tradition of rational inquiry, Wolterstorff enables us to draw a distinction between basic and non-basic beliefs within the Christian tradition. Through the rational norms established in the practice of the Christian tradition, we may distinguish between theological interpretations of God and humanity that are fixed and interpretations that are not fixed but subject to alteration.[29] But, as Wolterstorff concedes, we cannot reconcile the fixed theological interpretations of the Christian tradition that comprise the absolute faith stance of Christianity with a *prima facie* theory of justified true belief. Here a naturalist response to skepticism that views all beliefs or interpretations as defeasible in principle is incompatible with the certainty that is characteristic of faith.

28. Kierkegaard, *Fragments*, 102.

29. Wittgenstein, *On Certainty*, ¶¶ 48, 392, 458, 519.

7

Faith, Knowledge, and Truth

LUDWIG WITTGENSTEIN ONCE REMARKED that the question, What is its verification?, is a good translation of the question, How can one know it?[1] But the translation does not hold in the case of the truth in Christianity. Here the question, How can one know it?, is different from the question, What is its verification? The problem of knowing or understanding the truth in Christianity is not a problem of verification based on reason or evidence. Rather, it is a problem of making a transition or shift in one's way of thinking about the truth. There is a deep affinity between Wittgenstein and the Danish philosopher Søren Kierkegaard about this problem. Both philosophers argue that the objective problem of the truth arises from a misunderstanding of the logic or grammar of truth in Christianity and how we may know it. The relationship between a person and the truth in Christianity is different from their relationship to truth in other areas of knowledge.

I will develop this affinity into a Kierkegaardian perspective on religious knowledge informed by Wittgenstein's philosophy. I will use this perspective to refine the criticism of Reformed epistemology in the previous chapter, and to present an alternative response to skepticism and relativism in the case of religious knowledge. The perspective is based on the hermeneutical model of rationality developed in previous chapters which depends on a distinction between two different levels of doxastic ascent. Like a system of empirical belief, the beliefs of the Christian tradition are acquired spontaneously through a credulity disposition or natural reaction. This credulity disposition corresponds to a first-order level of basic doxastic ascent that is independent of the will. Also like a system of empirical

1. Wittgenstein, *Wittgenstein's Lectures*, 19–20.

belief, this system of religious belief is accepted in whole or in part through critical belief at a second-order level of doxastic ascent that depends critically on the will. In the case of Christianity, the mode of acceptance is faith. This supernatural disposition is a critical mode of acceptance that creates a new relationship between the self and the truth by opening the will to the knowledge of God. Consequently, I will argue that the attempt in Reformed epistemology to transmute religious belief into knowledge at the level of basic doxastic ascent obscures the primitive nature of trusting the authority of the Christian tradition. Further, because this transmutation takes place in advance of the acceptance of the truth through faith, it dodges the difficulty of establishing a new relationship with the truth by circumventing the critical role of the will with an immediate belief-forming process.

Knowledge as an Obstacle to Faith

Kierkegaard thought that the educated class of his day was in the grip of an illusion fostered by the rapid success of modern science. The illusion of scientific objectivity, in relation to theology, involves two claims. First, that the truth in Christianity can be objectively verified either through speculative philosophy or through the historical-critical method. Second, that a person can make a direct or immediate transition from this objective verification to the acceptance of the truth through faith. Kierkegaard argues that both claims reduce the problem of understanding the truth to a problem of knowing the truth only. Thus, the problem is posed in the form of the objective question, What is its verification? If the truth of the Christian teachings can be verified from the objective standpoint of a disinterested relationship to the problem, a person will prove ready and willing to accept it.[2] Johannes Climacus, Kierkegaard's philosophical pseudonym, calls this the objective problem of the truth in Christianity.

In the case of speculative philosophy, a person seeks to know the truth as an ordinary object of abstract thought on the basis of reason. Kierkegaard is especially concerned about this approach in light of the dominating influence of G. W. F. Hegel's philosophy on Christianity in Europe. Although Kierkegaard has the highest admiration for Hegel as a philosopher, he argues that Hegel's speculative philosophy sustains the illusion of scientific objectivity. Hegel's philosophical translation of faith into knowledge,

2. Kierkegaard, *Postscript*, 45.

or subjectivity into objectivity, creates an intellectual obstacle to faith by misrepresenting the relationship between a person and the truth in Christianity. Although the truth is indeed objective, Kierkegaard argues that it cannot be known objectively. For the speculative philosopher must overcome his actual present situation in existence. Reflection must turn away from the subject and his existence toward the truth as an ordinary object of abstract thought. But then the subject cannot have a personal relationship with the truth. The relationship becomes purely abstract and disinterested. Instead of grasping the truth therefore, speculative philosophy chases a chimera. As Climacus argues, Hegel's "notion of truth as identity of thought and being is a chimera of abstraction . . . not because the truth is not such an identity, but because the knower is an existing individual for whom the truth cannot be such an identity as long as he lives in time."[3]

The nature of truth in Christianity is different from the nature of truth in other areas of knowledge because God does not exist in the sense of an ordinary object of abstract thought. Wittgenstein argues that we do not learn the meaning of the word "God" by pointing to its object: "if the question arises as to the existence of a god or God, it plays an entirely different role to that of the existence of any person or object I ever heard of. One said, had to say, that one *believed* in the existence, and if one did not believe, this was regarded as something bad. Normally if I did not believe in the existence of something no one would think there was anything wrong in this."[4] Like Augustine, Kierkegaard argues that God is a spirit rather than a metaphysical object. God does not exist in the sense humans exist because he is eternal.[5] Some have misread these remarks about the grammar of God as anti-realist. Hence the truth in Christianity is reduced to a linguistic or epistemic practice enshrined in fideism. For both Kierkegaard and Wittgenstein, however, God exists apart from our conceptualizations and interpretations. The question is not whether God objectively exists in a sense that is independent of human thought therefore, but whether we can know God objectively outside a contingent tradition of rational inquiry through abstract thought.

The Bible claims that the truth is not revealed in abstract thought, but in the concrete person of Jesus of Nazareth, a subject who existed like

3. Ibid., 176.

4. Wittgenstein, *Lectures & Conversations*, 59.

5. Kierkegaard, *Postscript*, 178, 296; and "Strengthening in the Inner Being," 88. See Augustine, *Confessions*, 64.

us within a contingent tradition of rational inquiry. This particular truth does not exist as an ordinary object of abstract thought because it seeks its locus in another subject or person. Therefore Kierkegaard argues that truth is subjectivity rather than objectivity in the case of Christianity. Because the Bible claims that Jesus of Nazareth is God, the remarks about the grammar of God may also be applied to the relationship between an existing individual and Jesus of Nazareth. Thus, they are remarks about the kind of relationship one person may have with another person, not the kind of relationship a person may have to an object of abstract thought. When Kierkegaard argues that the truth has no "objective" existence therefore, he means that it has no existence for a person whose reflection is bound to a tradition of rational inquiry. Although the eternal truth is objective, it can be grasped only within the contingency of a tradition of rational inquiry.

Objectivity, however, attempts to overcome our actual present situation in the world by situating the thinker in abstract thought. Objectivity regards the prejudices and conceptualizations acquired from tradition as obstacles to understanding truth that must be overcome rather than as necessary conditions for understanding truth.[6] Here Kierkegaard *undoes* Hegel's translation of subjectivity into objectivity in the same way that an inverse function undoes the operation performed on a function. In the case of truth in science, subjectivity presents an obstacle to objectivity.[7] But in the case of truth in Christianity, it is precisely the inverse. Objectivity presents an obstacle to subjectivity or faith. As Paul L. Holmer argues, there is something subtle about the objective approach to knowledge. It is as if thought induces a self-forgetfulness which the thinking is being undertaken to undo. Consequently, the self is betrayed by its own effort! So, real nonsense is being perpetrated.[8]

In the grip of the illusion of scientific objectivity, the religious believer forgets that he is a subject that must become what he already in a sense is, namely, a Christian. Kierkegaard argues that the problem itself is a problem of reflection.[9] As David F. Swenson explains, "the Truth is, not to know the Truth, but to be the Truth; to know the Truth only, is to be enmeshed in

6. Kierkegaard, *Postscript*, 116.

7. More accurately, as I argued in chapter 5, subjectivity as at once a condition of and obstacle to scientific knowledge.

8. I owe this to Paul L. Holmer in discussion.

9. Kierkegaard, *Point of View*, 43.

error."[10] Thus, induced by objective thinking, the illusion of scientific objectivity ensnares the thinker in a self-deception in which he believes that he can solve the objective problem by undertaking more objective thinking. The greater the effort, the more objectivity interferes with the project of selfhood. The more compelling a person finds the illusion, the more he needs the remedy that only the truth can supply. Thus, as Wittgenstein writes, "a man is capable of infinite torment therefore, and so too he can stand in need of infinite help."[11]

Kierkegaard's philosophical pseudonym Climacus argues that there is another way in which the relationship between a person and the truth in Christianity may be misrepresented. In the case of the historical-critical method, the question is whether it is possible to base an eternal happiness on historical knowledge or evidence.[12] If the historical-critical method can objectively verify the truth of historical testimony through evidence, a person will prove ready and willing to accept it. Here Climacus attacks the transition from the scientific objectivity of historical knowledge to subjectivity or faith. Appealing to G. E. Lessing's argument that accidental historical truths can never serve as proofs of eternal truths of reason, Climacus argues that the transition from the reliability of historical testimony to the acceptance of the truth in Christianity is a leap.[13] As Climacus writes, "Lessing opposes what I would call an attempt to create a quantitative transition to a qualitative decision. He attacks the direct transition from historical trustworthiness to the determination of an eternal happiness . . . It is always the transition, the simple and direct transition, from the reliability of an historical account to an eternal decision, against which Lessing opposes himself."[14]

The historical-critical method dodges the difficulty of accepting the truth through faith by attempting to make a direct transition from the objective knowledge of the reliability of an historical account to the subjective decision to accept it. As in the case of speculative philosophy, this method circumvents the critical role of the will in making the decision. But since historical knowledge is always an approximation, historical truths can never be objectively verified. As Climacus argues:

10. Swenson, *Something about Kierkegaard*, 29.

11. Wittgenstein, *Culture and Value*, 45.

12. See Kierkegaard, *Fragments*.

13. Kierkegaard, *Postscript*, 86.

14. Ibid., 88.

> Suppose a man who wishes to acquire faith; let the comedy begin. He wishes to have faith, but he wishes also to safeguard himself by means of an objective inquiry and its approximation-process. What happens? With the help of the approximation-process the absurd [the God-man] becomes something different; it becomes probable . . . Now he is ready to believe it, and he ventures to claim for himself that he does not believe as shoemakers and tailors and simple folk believe, but only after long deliberation . . . and lo, now it has become precisely impossible to believe it. Anything that is almost probable . . . is something he can almost know . . . but it is impossible to believe. For the absurd is the object of faith, and the only object that can be believed.[15]

Thus, instead of grasping the truth within subjectivity, objectivity ensnares the biblical scholar in an endless approximation process of truth or correctness ascertainings. Because these ascertainings are always provisional, they are incapable of yielding the determinate knowledge that is characteristic of the eternal truths of reason. If one earnestly seeks God, Climacus argues that the dialectical difficulty becomes acute, since every moment is wasted in which one does not have God.[16]

In the case of Reformed epistemology, a person is led astray from God in immediacy rather than objectivity. Instead of situating the thinker in abstract thought, the thinker is situated in the familiar elements of his religious knowledge. Unlike objectivity, the transition from knowledge to faith in Reformed epistemology does not occur after long deliberation. Rather, it takes place in a direct and immediate manner through the epistemic conception of faith as a belief-forming process at a first-order level of basic doxastic ascent. As in the cases of speculative philosophy and the historical-critical method, this approach circumvents the critical role of the will in making the decision. Thus, like the speculative and historical approaches to eternal truth, the epistemic conception of faith misrepresents the relationship between a person and the truth in Christianity as something that happens *automatically*. Because the will is circumvented by an immediate belief-forming process, the act of faith becomes fideistic and arbitrary, something over which we have no control.

In contrast to both objectivity and immediacy, Kierkegaard argues that the truth itself tells us how we may know it through the category of the "leap." Salvation comes by faith alone, by the act of believing or accepting

15. Ibid., 189.

16. Ibid., 178–79.

something as coming from God in a way that depends critically on the will. Whether faith is conceived as a relationship between a subject and an object of abstract thought as in objectivity, or as an immediate belief-forming process with justification-conferring conditions that make it a case of knowledge just in case the belief is true, the act of faith is translated into a matter of believing or knowing something rather than doing something. Against this objective tendency, Christianity posits the leap as a full stop. The translation of the subjective approach of faith into the objective approach of knowledge does not hold. Hence the transition from knowledge to faith, or objectivity to subjectivity, cannot be direct or immediate. The logic or grammar of faith is different from the grammar of knowledge. Thus, the leap, Climacus tells us, is a protest against the inverse procedure of objectivity.[17] This protest may be extended to Reformed epistemology in its immediate conception of faith. Here, contrary to a popular misunderstanding of Kierkegaard, faith itself is not a leap. Nor is the leap a decision as some scholars have argued.[18] Rather, as Holmer explains, the leap precedes faith and the decision that brings faith into existence as a kind of grammatical remark or reminder about how we may approach the truth in Christianity. The leap tells us how we may establish a relationship with the truth in existence through faith, and clarifies and maximizes the qualitative decision confronting the will in the act of faith.[19] Faith itself is a passion. For, as I will argue in the next chapter, there can be no personal relationship with God without *pathos*.

Recall the distinction drawn in the previous chapter between two cases of knowledge or believing something as coming from God. Although both cases involve an ungrounded reaction characterized by certainty, they correspond to different levels of doxastic ascent. In the first case of knowledge, believing something as coming from God refers to the *acquisition* of a system of religious belief by trusting the authority of the Christian tradition. Like all formative beliefs acquired from a tradition of rational inquiry, religious beliefs are acquired in a spontaneous, involuntary, and epistemically innocent manner through a credulity disposition. Belief acquisition corresponds to a first-order level of basic doxastic ascent that is independent of the will. In the second case of knowledge, believing something as coming from God refers to the *acceptance* of a system of religious belief

17. Ibid., 96.

18. See Evans, *Kierkegaard's "Fragments" and "Postscript,"* 274–76.

19. I owe this to Paul L. Holmer in discussion.

in whole or in part in a critical manner. Belief acceptance corresponds to a second-order level of doxastic ascent that is critically dependent on the will. In contrast to a credulity disposition, which is a natural reaction implanted by nature, faith is a supernatural disposition implanted by grace. The transmutation of religious belief into knowledge depends on belief acquisition and belief acceptance. Because both faith and the transmutation of what is believed or accepted through faith into knowledge depend on the will, faith and knowledge correspond to a second-order level of doxastic ascent characterized by critical belief.

Wittgenstein argues that there is a kind of certainty in believing something as coming from God at the first-order level of basic doxastic ascent that is lacking in knowing at the second-order level of doxastic ascent. Knowledge and certainty, Wittgenstein tells us, belong to different categories. They are not two mental states like, say, surmising and being sure.[20] Certainty is a characteristic of an ungrounded reaction that lies at the foundation of the language game, including the language games of knowing and doubting. Whereas believing is a natural reaction or an ungrounded way of acting according to a system of belief with assurance, knowing and doubting are learned reactions that depend on our instinct to trust what we apprehend other people as telling us as true. Thus, knowing and doubting are deeper ways of believing that are refinements at the second-order level of doxastic ascent or critical belief of the more primitive language game of believing at the first-order level of basic doxastic ascent.

But the philosophical tradition assumes that certainty is a product of reflection. This assumption has led to a pathology of thought in the case of rational justification. On one hand, Wittgenstein argues that we must give justifying reasons for our believings in the face of skeptical challenges. Otherwise we cannot learn to believe in a deeper way. On the other hand, there are limits to rational justification.[21] The rational justification of our religious beliefs is appropriate at a second-order level of doxastic ascent. As we become aware of incoherence in the system of religious belief we have acquired from the Christian tradition, we become epistemically responsible for continuing to hold doubtful beliefs in light of counterevidence. But the pressure to justify our religious beliefs prematurely at the first-order level of basic doxastic assent leads to an infinite regress of justification-conferring conditions. Here, like Reformed epistemology, Wittgenstein

20. Wittgenstein, *On Certainty*, ¶ 308.

21. Ibid., ¶ 192.

argues that we are *prima facie* justified in relying on these beliefs as a trustworthy foundation for rational inquiry until there is evidence in particular cases to believe that some of these beliefs are unreliable or false. Unlike Reformed epistemology, however, Wittgenstein argues that the pathology of thought involves misapplying the standards of rational justification, which are appropriate at a second-order level of doxastic ascent, at the first-order level of basic doxastic ascent. The difficulty, Wittgenstein tells us, is to realize the groundlessness of our believing at this basic level.[22] In the words of Thomas S. Kuhn, the infinite regress problem in epistemology is a symptom of crisis. Reformed epistemology attempts to avoid this problem by substituting *prima facie* justification-conferring conditions for the *ultima facie* notion of the directly evident. Here, analogous to the case of objectivity, thought induces a forgetfulness about the certainty of our ungrounded ways of acting which the process of rational justification is being undertaken to undo. Consequently, the self is betrayed by its own effort! So, again, real nonsense is being perpetrated.[23]

The transmutation of what is believed or accepted through faith into knowledge at a second-order level of doxastic ascent is necessary for faith seeking understanding. A rational faith or reasoned trust is the mark of a mature Christian. The emergence of responsible doubt marks a dissatisfaction that drives us to a more adequate form of believing called knowing. But the pressure to justify our most basic religious beliefs prematurely accumulates doubt in place of initial certainty, making the acceptance of the truth through faith more difficult in proportion to our effort and passion as a thinker. As Wittgenstein writes, "one says 'I know' when one is ready to give compelling grounds. 'I know' relates to a possibility of demonstrating the truth. Whether someone knows something can come to light, assuming that he is convinced of it. But if what he believes is of such a kind that the grounds that he can give are no surer than his assertion, then he cannot say that he knows what he believes."[24] When we attempt to ground our most basic beliefs in justification-conferring conditions, the conditions are always less certain than the ungrounded reaction of believing. As Barry Stroud argues, "we find ourselves with questions about knowledge that lead either to an unsatisfactory sceptical conclusion or to this or that 'theory' of knowledge which on reflection turns out to offer no more genuine satisfac-

22. Ibid., ¶¶ 166, 204.

23. I owe this to Paul L. Holmer in discussion.

24. Wittgenstein, *On Certainty*, ¶ 243.

tion than the original sceptical conclusion it was meant to avoid."[25] Further, as Kierkegaard argues, to believe something as coming from God until such time as there is evidence not to believe is incompatible with the absolute faith stance of Christianity. Unlike knowledge, which seeks to become more objective and disinterested, faith is a relationship with the truth that seeks to become more subjective and personal. The movements of knowledge and the movements of faith are in opposite directions relative to the truth in Christianity. Thus, Kierkegaard argues that evidence is irrelevant to faith. Evidence for or against religious belief has significance only in the epistemic process of transmuting what is believed or accepted through faith into knowledge.

Like Kierkegaard, Wittgenstein argues that the logic or grammar of truth in Christianity is not inherently difficult to understand. It becomes difficult because of what we *want* to see instead. The Christian tradition claims that the will is closed to truth in its natural state. The will has blinded our natural powers of conception with prejudices that impede our understanding of the truth. Thus, Wittgenstein argues that "the very things which are most obvious may become the hardest of all to understand. What has to be overcome is a difficulty having to do with the will rather than with the intellect."[26] This suggests that the difficulty of accepting the truth in Christianity has to do with the will and our being closed to what the Bible has to say to us rather than with the intellect, our epistemic mechanisms, or natural powers of conception. But the solution is not to minimize the influences of the will, for without the will there can be no freedom, autonomy, knowledge, or faith. Rather, the will must be converted so that a new relationship with the truth becomes possible.

The Truth Self-defined as Faith

If the truth in Christianity cannot be known objectively, or immediately, how may we know it? The answer is suggested by Wittgenstein's response to a statement made by the mathematician G. H. Hardy about the problem of the infinite in calculus: "Hardy: 'That the finite cannot understand the infinite should surely be a theological and not a mathematical war-cry'. True, the expression is inept. But what people are using it to try and say

25. Stroud, *Philosophical Scepticism*, 168.

26. Wittgenstein, *Culture and Value*, 17, 31–32.

is: 'We mustn't have any juggling! How comes this leap from the finite to the infinite?' Nor is the expression all that nonsensical—only the 'finite' that can't conceive the infinite is not 'man' or 'our understanding', but the calculus. And *how* this conceives the infinite is well worth an investigation . . . 'The finite cannot understand the infinite' means here: It cannot work *in the way* you, with characteristic superficiality, are presenting it."[27] Similarly, understanding the truth in Christianity cannot work *in the way* objectivity and immediacy present it. Therefore *how* the truth itself conceives the infinite is well worth an investigation. Climacus calls this the subjective problem of the truth in Christianity.

If one is concerned for an eternal happiness, Kierkegaard argues that objectivity leads to despair rather than the acceptance of the truth. When a person despairs of the possibility of objectively verifying the truth in Christianity, the truth itself reveals another approach. Through despair, one is pressed to abandon the objective question, What is its verification?, so that another kind of question can be asked, How can one know it? The subjective question investigates how the eternal truth can be understood within a contingent tradition of rational inquiry rather than in abstract thought. Unable to make a transition from objective knowledge about the truth to the subjective decision to accept it, one is pressed to choose between different ways of relating to the truth. Either one continues to pose the problem of understanding the truth in the form of the objective question, What is its verification? Or one makes a new start by posing the problem in the form of the subjective question, How may a person who exists within a contingent tradition of rational inquiry establish a relationship to the eternal truth that exists outside any tradition of rational inquiry?[28] Whereas the objective question assumes that a person will accept the truth if it can be objectively verified through reason or evidence, the subjective question assumes that the truth will reveal itself to a person if he is first concerned for an eternal happiness.

Here a person is faced with a skeptical challenge to his own approach that Kierkegaard argues is a necessary consequence of objectivity. In light of the dialectical difficulty of objectively verifying the truth in Christianity, one is pressured to reexamine the nature of the relationship between the self and the truth. At this point, the singular and unique nature of truth in Christianity begins to emerge. Earlier we saw that Kierkegaard argues

27. Wittgenstein, *Zettel*, ¶ 273.

28. Kierkegaard, *Postscript*, 181.

that the absurd is the object of faith because it is the only object that can be believed. Similarly, we saw that Wittgenstein argues that one had to say that one believed in the existence of God, and that if one did not believe, this was regarded as something bad. Thus, the absurd—the eternal truth revealed in the absolute paradox of the God-man—is the only object that is related to faith rather than knowledge. For in ordinary contexts, we do not say that we believe in an object. Rather, we say that we know it or can know it. But in the case of the truth in Christianity, because we cannot know the absurd through abstract thought, we must believe it through an act of faith. Thus, Kierkegaard argues that a person's relationship to truth in Christianity is different from their relationship to truth in other areas of knowledge.

Reflection is not thereby abandoned or downplayed in the act of faith. The nature of faith is critical rather than immediate because it depends on an act of the human will. Given the logic or grammar of the truth as to how we may know it, reflection must become less objective and outward, and more subjective and inward. Reflection must map the concepts of repentance, faith, hope, and love onto a person's way of living. For, unlike the beliefs of the Christian tradition, the Christian concepts seek their locus in a person's existence rather than intellect. As Wittgenstein argues, it is the soul with its passions, as it were with its flesh and blood, that has to be saved, not the abstract mind.[29] As Holmer argues, whereas the language "about" faith describes the surface grammar of the Christian faith comprised of the beliefs and practices found in the Bible, creeds, confessions, and doctrines of the Christian tradition, the language "of" faith describes the depth grammar of the Christian faith as a form of life shaped by the Christian concepts.[30] Whereas religious beliefs may be acquired passively through a credulity disposition, the Christian concepts must be actively acquired. These concepts provide the rational norms or criteria of meaning and intelligibility according to which the self is shaped into a concrete identity of thought and being in the image of God. Here reflection must become less objective in turning away from the truth as an ordinary object of abstract thought, and more subjective in concentrating on the ethical task of becoming the truth. Because no one is born with a ready made identity, subjectivity is not an option but an ethical requirement of the whole human race, shoemakers and tailors and professors alike.

29. Wittgenstein, *Culture and Value*, 33.

30. I owe this to Paul L. Holmer in discussion.

Thus, in the case of Christianity, the truth does not require us to abandon or downplay reflection in favor of a blind and irrational faith. On the contrary, faith or subjectivity requires us to double reflection. For unlike knowledge in other areas, there are two movements of reflection in faith. In the first movement, one reflects on the beliefs deposited in the Christian tradition, including the Bible, creeds, confessions, doctrines, and liturgical practices of the Christian community. These beliefs provide a cognitively meaningful description of the possibility of a religious subjectivity or way of living. In the second movement, one reflects on how to establish a personal relationship with the person about whom these beliefs speak by actualizing or becoming this possibility.[31] The possibility in thought must be actualized in the everyday experience of the subject. These movements of reflection are in parallel. For Kierkegaard, we cannot separate Christian experience into a cognitive part and an emotive part without distorting the form of life whose logic or grammar is described by the Christian concepts. The life of faith involves the reflective appropriation of the Christian concepts in the making of a substantial Christian identity. One understands the truth, not merely in proportion to one's objective knowledge "about" the Christian teachings, but in proportion to one's subjective and critical appropriation "of" these teachings in the making of new emotional dispositions that change the form of one's way of living. Christianity commands us to be the truth, not to know the truth only. This command does not ask us to renounce our reason, but to redirect our reason to the ethical task of becoming a Christian.

This ethical task is suggested by Wittgenstein when he argues that formidable concepts such as those found in the Christian teachings cannot be acquired cheaply like beliefs. Faith, hope, and love are not beliefs that are produced spontaneously or immediately in us. They are emotional capacities or abilities that a person may or may not acquire with the beliefs. In order to acquire them, one must pay the same price it cost the teacher.[32] Whereas the beliefs of the Christian tradition are easily acquired like milk, the Christian concepts must be slowly acquired or assimilated as they comprise the meat of the Christian tradition. This means that the truth is known in proportion to our transformation or qualification as subjects by these concepts rather than in proportion to the strength of the evidence for our beliefs. Thus, in the case of Christianity, the truth impinges on us in a

31. Holmer, "Religious Propositions," 212.

32. Wittgenstein, *Culture and Value*, 13.

way that ordinary objects of thought do not. To know the truth only, even if it were objectively possible, is not sufficient. Acquaintance with the truth requires more than a familiarity with holy things. It requires the subject to become the truth. This kind of knowledge requires more than intellectual effort. It requires a modification of human subjectivity or personality. One has to change the way one lives as well as the beliefs one holds. To exist in the truth means that both our religious beliefs and our form of life must correspond with the truth.

Whereas a person's talent as a thinker varies, Kierkegaard claims that the ethical task of subjectivity is the same for the whole human race. It is the great equalizer that is just as difficult for the professor as for the shoemaker and tailor. Here, unlike other areas of knowledge, the learned have no advantage in understanding the truth in Christianity. On the contrary, Kierkegaard argues that scholarship and learning may create intellectual obstacles and confusions on the path to full truth. For in order to overcome the illusion of scientific objectivity, what is needed is not more objective thinking, but an action of the will to change one's mode of reflection. But since the will is closed to the truth in its natural state, a person remains ensnared in the objective approach. Thus, objectivity does not lead to the acceptance of the truth through faith, but to despair, the opposite of faith.

According to Kierkegaard, faith is an emotional disposition or passion that shapes the subjectivity of a person into a form of life that corresponds with the truth. In contrast, despair involves a form of life that fails to correspond with the truth. Life becomes problematic because its logical shape does not fit into the mould God created for human life in his image. Christianity in this sense describes the logic or grammar of a form of life into which human subjectivity is moulded by the inward work of grace. Thus, Kierkegaard describes faith as a happy passion because a person is related to the truth in the right way. In contrast, despair is described as an unhappy passion because a person is related to the truth in the wrong way. Similarly, Wittgenstein draws a distinction between the world of the happy person and the world of the unhappy person. The world of the happy person corresponds with the meaning of the world which Wittgenstein identifies as the mystical or God.[33] In contrast, the world of the unhappy person fails to correspond with this meaning. Because the truth defines itself as subjectivity, the more objective one's thinking, the more the self fails to

33. Wittgenstein, *Tractatus*, 10. See *Notebooks*, 74–75.

correspond with the truth. Thus, despair increases in proportion to the lack of correspondence.

For Kierkegaard, despair gives rise to real doubt or Socratic doubt that drives the personality toward the Absolute and makes decisiveness possible, in contrast to philosophic doubt or skeptical doubt that immobilizes the individual in indifference. The Danish words for doubt (*tvivl*) and for despair (*fortvivlelse*) correspond to the German words *Zweifel* and *Verzweifelung*. In an intended play on these terms, Reidar Thomte argues that the ethical pseudonym Judge William "looks forward to the time when the philosophical point of departure in search for the Absolute is no longer [Cartesian] doubt (*Zweifel*) but despair (*Verzweifelung*). Such a philosophy would find its starting point not in thought but in existence, that is, in life itself."[34] Despair expresses two kinds of Socratic doubt. On one hand, it expresses doubt about whether our thoughts or beliefs about God are adequate. On the other hand, it expresses doubt about whether our form of life is adequate in relation to the one who created us in his image. Through despair, which Wittgenstein describes as the voice of God, a person becomes conscious of the fact that neither her beliefs nor way of living correspond with the truth. Thus, just as Kuhn argues that the emergence of an epistemological crisis precipitates a scientific revolution, Kierkegaard and Wittgenstein argue that the emergence of the consciousness of sin precipitates a religious conversion experience.

Kierkegaard describes this consequence of objectivity as an existential dialectic because it resituates the thinker from abstract thought back into existence. The existential dialectic of despair is Christianity's antidote to the intellectual dialectic of objectivity. Working against the objective tendency, despair resituates the thinker back into a contingent tradition of rational inquiry. Here a new point of departure for reflection becomes possible, namely, subjective thinking. The truth enters a person's consciousness through subjective reflection rather than through either objectivity or immediacy. The mode of acceptance is faith rather than knowledge. As Kierkegaard's religious pseudonym Anti-Climacus writes, "God in heaven, I thank Thee that Thou hast not required it of man that he should comprehend Christianity; for if that were required, I should be of all men the most miserable. The more I seek to comprehend it [objectively], the more incomprehensible [absurd] it appears to me, and the more I discover merely the possibility of offense [despair]. Therefore I thank Thee that Thou dost only

34. Thomte, *Kierkegaard's Philosophy of Religion*, 36–37.

require faith [subjectivity], and I pray Thee to increase it more and more."[35] The transition from objectivity to subjectivity, as well as the transition from immediacy to subjectivity, involves a conscious and deliberate change in a person's relationship to the truth. Thus, the transition between knowledge and faith cannot be direct or immediate. A person is related to the truth objectively so long as she is disposed to it in a purely intellectual manner in the way a subject is related to an ordinary object of abstract thought. In contrast, a person is related to the truth subjectively when she chooses to have a personal relationship with the truth in the way one person is related to another person. For, once again, the truth is a concrete reality or person rather than an abstract object of thought.

Although objectivity and subjectivity both involve reflection and interpretation, Holmer argues that they involve divergent modes of reflection and interpretation relative to the truth in Christianity. Whereas objectivity is directed outwardly away from the self, subjectivity is directed inwardly toward the self. For in the case of scientific truth objectivity requires a person to become detached from the object of study and to minimize personal interestedness and passion, the very qualities that are needed in subjectivity to move the self closer to the truth in Christianity. Although objectivity can provide a cognitively meaningful description of an ethico-religious way of living, it is powerless to produce moral responsibility and faith in a person. This is the goal and purpose of subjectivity. Kierkegaard argues that there is a leap between these modes of interpretation. As Holmer explains, "it is only by shifting the mode, shall we say even the mood, and the attitude (the subject's weight?), that the religious may begin to appear. But when it appears, everything is again subject to the new mode of interpretation."[36] Holmer describes these modes of interpretation as moods because they involve a general way of taking in or intending the world. Here meaning is a function of how a person addresses or intends the things around him.[37]

Notice that this shift in mode or mood does not involve a change in belief systems, but a change in *attitudes* which I argued in chapter 4 lie at the foundations of belief systems. Thus, a change in point of view requires a more fundamental change in a person's emotions, attitudes, and dispositions underlying his or her belief system. Also notice that although these modes may be regarded as complementary interpretations of our experience of

35. Kierkegaard, *Sickness unto Death*, 260.

36. Holmer, *Kierkegaard and the Truth*, 73.

37. Holmer, *Grammar of Faith*, 23. See *Kierkegaard and the Truth*, 76.

the world according to the hermeneutical model of rationality developed in earlier chapters—one scientific and the other religious—there is no correspondence between them. Although some of the beliefs that grow out of these different modes of interpretation may correspond as I argued in chapters 4 and 5, the attitudes themselves do not. Consistent with Wilhelm Dilthey's theory of worldviews, unlike the beliefs that grow out of them, these attitudes toward life are basic in the sense that the religious mode of interpretation cannot be reduced to the scientific mode of interpretation or vice versa. These attitudes toward life correspond to different activities of mental life or ways of intending the things around us.

This shift in attitudes toward life emphasizes the disposition, inclination, or orientation of the will in its relation to the truth in Christianity. Whereas the "about" mood expresses the natural disposition of the will to the knowledge of God when reflexivity is enclosed in itself, the "of" mood expresses the receptivity of the will to this godly knowledge through the inward work of grace which breaks open reflexivity to a wider truth outside the self. In the act of believing or accepting something as coming from God through faith, reason acknowledges its dependence on God for knowledge of the truth. Although the thinker cannot storm the truth by force by building a ladder of syllogisms to God, he receives it as a gift from the God-man himself. Although the subject cannot know this truth as an ordinary object of abstract thought, or immediately by examining the contents of his own consciousness or the foundations of his noetic structure, he can know it through faith. Whereas despair increases in proportion to one's intellectual relation to the truth as an ordinary object of abstract thought, faith increases in proportion to one's personal relationship with the truth as a living reality or person. The leap describes the logic or grammar of this truth. Although the leap tells us how we may approach the truth through faith, it does not lead to the acceptance of the truth any more than the illusion of scientific objectivity. For the acceptance of the truth through faith depends critically on an act or decision of the will. Whereas the leap clarifies and maximizes the qualitative decision confronting the will, the illusion obscures and minimizes the critical role of the will in accepting the truth through faith. According to Holmer, this is why the leap cannot be conceived as a decision.[38]

Whereas despair qualifies the subjectivity of the individual gradually so that he is prepared to hear the words of faith, the shift from objectivity to subjectivity or faith as a new mode of interpretation is abrupt like

38. I owe this to Paul L. Holmer in discussion.

a gestalt switch as in Kuhn's analogy between a scientific revolution and a religious conversion experience. The shift occurs at the moment when the will chooses to submit to the authority of the truth in regard to how we may approach it. This analogy emphasizes the psychological aspect of the shift in terms of being able to "see" the world differently through faith as a new mode of interpretation.

But there is another aspect of the shift that may be brought out with an analogy from classical physics. As we have seen, Kierkegaard argues that the moment of decision signifies a leap in human consciousness. Although the leap itself is not a decision, it may be visualized as a step discontinuity between natural consciousness and Christian consciousness, or objectivity and subjectivity, that may be interpreted as a potential barrier. This interpretation is consistent with our definition of the leap as a category that tells us how we may approach the truth. Thus, just as a particle cannot surmount the barrier if it lacks sufficient energy, human consciousness is incapable of making the shift from objectivity to subjectivity without supernatural intervention.[39] In order to surmount the barrier, a person's mode of reflection must be changed qualitatively. In the moment when a person chooses to realize the possibility of subjective thinking, the God-man comes to his assistance in a breaking through of eternity into time. Here, as Reidar Thomte argues, a person becomes the truth through repetition in a progressive attitude toward the eternal, in contrast to the regressive attitude in Socratic thought in which the truth is immanental and recollected.[40] We may interpret this assistance as the particle being given just enough energy, but not more, to surmount the barrier. This analogy emphasizes the ethical aspect of the shift in terms of what we are capable of in relation to God.

Kierkegaard argues that in the moment of decision a person receives the condition of faith from the God-man necessary for the acceptance of the truth. As the truth enters human consciousness through faith, the will is converted and a person's actual present situation is changed. Whereas despair resituates a person, whether in abstract thought or in immediacy, into

39. This analogy does not hold in the quantum mechanical case. Because the uncertainty principle allows the laws of classical physics to be violated for very short periods or very small distances, there is a small probability that the particle may tunnel through the barrier into a classically forbidden region if the width of the barrier is small enough. This may occur even if the potential is infinite in the case of a delta-function barrier. See Thornton and Rex, *Modern Physics*, 210–11; and Griffiths, *Quantum Mechanics*, 76.

40. Thomte, *Kierkegaard's Philosophy of Religion*, 71.

a contingent tradition of rational inquiry where faith or subjective thinking becomes possible, faith resituates a person from error into the truth by reorienting the will to the knowledge of God. Thus, although despair and faith are two opposite passions, one unhappy and the other happy, they are also complementary epistemic mechanisms, one natural and the other supernatural, that cooperate in disposing the will to the truth in the right way according to the leap.

Just as most epistemologists find Wittgenstein's account of the groundlessness of belief unsatisfactory, most metaphysicians find Kierkegaard's account of truth as subjectivity unsatisfactory. Thus, Nicholas Wolterstorff and Alvin Plantinga argue that the truth-conditions for our beliefs must be determined by facts independent of any epistemic practice of justification. Only a non-epistemic theory of truth can provide the objective touchstone necessary for a non-alienated view of the world. For if the anti-realist's epistemic theory of truth degenerates into a vicious regress of truth or correctness ascertainings, the result is a radical form of skepticism that one must go to extreme lengths to undo. This eschatological conception of truth only intensifies our sense of alienation from the world. To avoid this dilemma, Wolterstorff argues that we must reject Hilary Putnam's internal realism in favor of metaphysical realism. Although Wolterstorff agrees with Putnam that Kant combined a correspondence theory of truth with the theory that we are the constitutors of our world, Wolterstorff argues that we are the constitutors of our world in the strong realist sense of recognizing or "seeing" the structure inherent in reality prior to our conceptualization of it. According to Wolterstorff, not all inputs to knowledge are contaminated by conceptualization as they are for Putnam.[41] This strong version of realism implies that our view of the world is not always biased. It suggests that there is a simple, one-way coupling between the observer and his object of study which I argued in chapter 5 is untenable on both philosophical and scientific grounds.

Wolterstorff's skeptical conclusion is influenced by the exclusive disjunction of objectivism or relativism discussed in the first part of the book. Either we must adopt a correspondence theory of truth, or we cannot avoid skepticism about the connection between rationality and truth. But as Paul Horwich points out, "the ancient idea that truth is some sort of 'correspondence with reality' has still never been articulated satisfactorily: the nature of the alleged 'correspondence' and the alleged 'reality' remain

41. Wolterstorff, "Realism vs. Anti-Realism," 201.

objectionably obscure."[42] A correspondence theory of truth depends on the availability of an objective perspective uncontaminated by any conceptualization. But if an unsituated rationality is an untenable ideal, as Wolterstorff claims, it is difficult to see how we can make any correspondence theory of truth intelligible without falling into the conundrums of objectivism. As I argued in previous chapters, it is a mistake to suppose that there is a way of being in the world in which we can bracket our prejudices in order to understand an object without bias. If we reject classical realism, we need not abandon the goal of increasing our stock of true beliefs any more than we need abandon our obligations to rationality if we reject the classical picture of knowledge. If a more epistemically humble theory of knowledge is plausible, why not a more alethiologically humble theory of truth? If we cannot make the strong version of realism intelligible, why must we slide into a radical form of skepticism? For, as Wolterstorff himself suggests, whether we slide depends on how we use our epistemic mechanisms in a given situation. Although we cannot adjudicate the veracity of our beliefs or interpretations relative to a perspective that stands outside all traditions of rational inquiry, Putnam argues that there are still better and worse interpretations within a tradition of rational inquiry. Some interpretations are more truth-preserving than others.[43]

In the case of truth in Christianity, Kierkegaard reminds us that the truth is not an abstract metaphysical object but a concrete reality or person. Through the unrest of faith, which functions as an epistemic mechanism in a sense quite different from the one proposed by Reformed epistemology, God leads the believer into the truth through the ultimately guiding beacon of the Holy Spirit. Ethically understood, the unrest of faith corresponds to the natural urge to know. This natural urge is expressed in the ethics of belief tradition that affirms the epistemic duty to do our best in forming beliefs that put us in touch with reality. Thus, as the ethical pseudonym Judge William argues, "if you will understand me aright, I should like to say that in making a choice it is not so much a question of choosing the right as of the energy, the earnestness, the pathos with which one chooses. Thereby the personality announces its inner infinity, and thereby, in turn, the personality is consolidated. Therefore, even if a man were to choose the wrong, he will nevertheless discover, precisely by reason of the energy

42. Horwich, "Truth," 510.

43. Putnam, *Realism with a Human Face*, 19–21.

with which he chose, that he had chosen the wrong."[44] Religiously understood, the unrest of faith corresponds to the spiritual urge to find rest in the truth, that is, in the person of Jesus of Nazareth. Thus, as the philosophical pseudonym Climacus argues, "for he who with quiet introspection is honest before God and concerned for himself, the Deity saves from being in error, though he be never so simple, him the Deity leads by the suffering of inwardness [faith] to the truth."[45] Similarly, John Locke argues that God has promised his assistance in this matter: "if we do what we can, he will give us his Spirit to help us to do what, and how we should."[46]

Judge William and Climacus express differing points of view about how a person is related to the truth, either ethically or religiously. Although there is a movement in Kierkegaard's literature from the aesthetic through the ethical and into the religious, the religious does not automatically follow from the aesthetic and ethical in the way a conclusion follows straightway from its premises in a formally valid syllogism. That the ethical finds its highest expression in the religious is not a necessary conclusion, but a *telos* that guides the movement which may or may not be realized by the individual. Contrary to Hegel, Kierkegaard allows these points of view to co-exist without a final resolution in order to make the movement depend solely on the individual's choice between an "either/or," in contrast to an artifact of the logical or formal character of a metaphysical system.[47] In light of the hermeneutical model of rationality developed in earlier chapters, we may regard these differing points of view as complementary interpretations of a person's relationship with the truth that correspond in the limit where the individual has done all that he can and requires divine assistance to do what and how he should. Thus, a "leap" is involved here. Just as George Mavrodes has argued that Kant's moral enterprise needs the postulate of a God who can, and will, make happiness correspond to virtue, we may argue that these differing points of view need the postulate of a God who can, and will, make truth correspond to the ethics of belief.[48] Therefore, these differing points of view suggest that God can, and will, make rationality correspond to truth through the passion of faith. This is the only type of correspondence theory of truth that makes sense in Christianity.

44. Kierkegaard, *Either/Or*, 171.

45. Kierkegaard, *Postscript*, 543–44.

46. Locke, *Reasonableness of Christianity*, 70.

47. Holmer, *Kierkegaard and the Truth*, 39.

48. Mavrodes, "Religion and Morality," 220.

Today, however, many theologians have appealed to critical realism in order to articulate a sufficiently non-skeptical connection between rationality and truth that is less centered on the subjective element. Although critical realism may be applied to empirical and scientific knowledge where subjectivity is an obstacle to objectivity, it cannot be applied to the knowledge of God where objectivity is an obstacle to subjectivity or faith. For according to most versions of critical realism, truth is conceived as an objective certainty that must be approached through the subjective uncertainty of an infinite *approximation* process of truth- or correctness-ascertainings. Although critical realism provides a more epistemically humble alternative between a correspondence theory of truth and an epistemic theory of truth, it misrepresents the relationship between a person and the truth in Christianity. For, according to Kierkegaard, this relationship is precisely the inverse of *the way* it is presented by critical realism. Climacus argues that truth is an objective uncertainty that must be approached through the subjective certainty of an infinite *appropriation* process of faith.[49]

Here the movements of knowledge and the movements of faith are in opposite directions relative to the truth in Christianity. Whereas knowledge searches for the truth outside the self as an ordinary object of abstract thought, faith searches for the truth inside the self as a concrete reality or person who has promised to enter our hearts through the door of human consciousness at the invitation of our act of trust. Whereas the truth eludes the infinite approximation process of knowledge, it is grasped in the infinite appropriation process of faith. Whereas the truth remains a stranger to both objectivity and immediacy, it becomes a friend to subjectivity. Thus, Kierkegaard describes the infinite appropriation process of faith as the certainty of the ethical. To exist in the ethical yields the only certain knowledge of God because it is the only knowledge that may not transform itself into a *hypothesis*.[50] This certainty, as Wittgenstein tells us, is not akin to hastiness or superficiality because it lacks grounds of rational justification. Rather, it is an ethical or religious form of life.[51]

If Kierkegaard and Wittgenstein are right, the objective problem of the truth in Christianity is like a knot in our thinking.[52] In the grip of the illusion of scientific objectivity, a person believes that the knot can be undone

49. Kierkegaard, *Postscript*, 182.

50. Ibid., 136.

51. Wittgenstein, *On Certainty*, ¶ 358.

52. Wittgenstein, *Zettel*, ¶ 452.

by undertaking more of the same kind of reflection that created it. The truth itself, however, tells us how we may approach it through the category of the leap. Reflection is not thereby abandoned in favor of a blind and irrational faith. Rather, a different kind of reflection is needed to undo the knot, lest a person betray herself by her own effort. This shift in mode of reflection corresponds to a change in questions. The objective question, What is its verification?, is replaced with the subjective question, How can one know it? Here, as Wittgenstein suggests, the way to solve the objective problem is "to live [not merely believe] in a way that will make what is problematic disappear. The fact that life is problematic shows that the shape of your life does not fit into life's mould. So you must change the way you live and, once your life does fit into the mould, what is problematic will disappear."[53] Unlike truth in other areas of knowledge, a person is related to the truth in Christianity through faith rather than knowledge. Thus, the problem of understanding the truth has to do with more than the intellectual virtues. It has to do with a theological virtue that enables our lives, as well as beliefs, to correspond with the truth.

53. Wittgenstein, *Culture and Value*, 27.

8

Faith, Knowledge, and Suffering

ALTHOUGH SOME PERSPECTIVES ON religious knowledge have downplayed the rational aspect of our nature, other perspectives have downplayed the emotional aspect of our nature. The narrow emphasis in Reformed epistemology on warranted Christian belief is a case in point. Although Alvin Plantinga has briefly discussed the redemptive aspect of suffering and evil, he is primarily concerned with these issues as potential defeaters to warranted Christian belief.[1] Although Nicholas Wolterstorff has eloquently discussed suffering in relation to the endurance of faith, he has not integrated these insights into a theory of religious knowledge that takes more into account than authentic Christian belief. According to the Christian tradition, however, suffering is not only an unavoidable element of religious experience, it is necessary for religious knowledge. Thus, the Reformer Martin Luther emphasizes the theology of the cross. The Danish philosopher Søren Kierkegaard speaks ironically of the gospel of suffering. The apostle Paul tells us that we must bear the cross of Christ crucified if we are to follow Jesus of Nazareth.

The regulative or normative conception of epistemology as a doxastic practice may help us form more truth-preserving beliefs. But we must also address the question of how suffering may soften the hardened attitudes of alienation at the foundation of our system of belief in order to prepare a place for faith in the human heart. Contrary to the central thesis of Reformed epistemology, I have argued that faith cannot be properly conceived as a new cognitive disposition that produces beliefs immediately in a way that justifies the rationality of their acceptance. Rather, as we saw in the previous chapter, faith is an emotional disposition implanted by grace that

1. Plantinga, *Warranted Christian Belief*, 499.

reorients the will to the knowledge of God, thereby making a new relationship between the self and the truth in Christianity possible. For the truth does not exist as an ordinary object of abstract thought but as a concrete person, namely, Jesus of Nazareth. As such, faith constitutes a new beginning or mediated immediacy for natural consciousness. This relationship must be sustained by a continuing action of the will in opposition to the attitudes of alienation rooted in our common human nature. Thus, the knowledge which comes from God is not immediate, but is acquired in proportion to overcoming our natural attitudes and dispositions with the supernatural disposition of faith. Here I will argue that the endurance of suffering is essentially related to the endurance of faith.

The Unrest of Faith vs. Feeling at Home in the World

Wolterstorff tells us that the story of epistemology is the story of our quest to feel at home in the world. Through epistemology, we seek to attain a non-alienated view of the world. At the heart of the skeptical spirit is a deep sense of alienation from the world and from God that is rooted in our common human nature. The Christian tradition describes this natural fact with the doctrine of original sin. In the case of our empirical beliefs about the world, there appears to be no direct or immediate connection between rationality and truth, or rather between truth and its knowability. Similarly, in the case of our religious beliefs about God, there appears to be no immediate or ready access to God. Skepticism arises from the question of whether there is a higher source of truth outside the self, apart from our conceptualizations and interpretations of reality, and whether we can know this truth if it exists. In an effort to avert skepticism, Wolterstorff claims that there is a mode of being at home with something that consists of *recognizing* it, in contrast to finding ourselves mirrored back in something we have made. This recognition involves grasping something of an object's character and hence no longer finding it strange, mysterious, and alien.[2] In his book on Thomas Reid, however, Wolterstorff claims that Reid is right in arguing that we live in deep impenetrable darkness concerning the things that most satisfy the desires of our rational nature. Our avidity to know

2. Wolterstorff, "Realism vs. Anti-Realism," 203.

the true causes of things cannot be satisfied.[3] Thus, it would appear that Wolterstorff has embraced the very skeptical conclusion he was combating with Reid's naturalist response to skepticism.

It would be a mistake, however, to conclude that these claims express a contradiction. Rather, what appears to be a contradiction that tells us nothing is really a veridical paradox that tells us something deep about our actual present situation. For, unlike Plantinga, Wolterstorff grapples with the most profound issue in Reid's epistemology: the things that we take for granted in the living of life in the everyday are rationally ungrounded. Other than a description of the epistemic mechanism that leads us to believe these things, we have no insight into its causal nature. Thus, quoting Reid, Wolterstorff writes that "upon the theatre of nature we see innumerable effects, which require an agent endowed with active power; but the agent is behind the scene."[4] The deepest aspect of Reid's epistemology, Wolterstorff argues, is his pietistic acknowledgement of ungrounded trust, trust without any reasons for trusting. This acknowledgement involves accepting and opening ourselves to the mystery of reality with humility and gratitude, rather than railing against it with a skeptical attitude. Although the aim of Reid's epistemology may be to help us feel at home in the world, it suggests that we are in fact pilgrims, strangers, and aliens in the world. Although the creator has endowed us with powers of conception, Reid argues that God has placed appropriate constraints on our avidity to know the true causes of things in order to make room for faith. Whereas the way of knowledge is by sight, the way of faith is by believing or trusting in what cannot be seen. In addition to sharing a common human nature that leads us to believe the principles of Common Sense, Reid argues that we also share a common noetic situation that constrains our avidity to know the true causes of things. Hence no human being bears a special connection between rationality and truth.

Although we live in the world, the Bible claims that we are not of the world because we are essentially spiritual beings. Thus, from a religious point of view, to feel at home in the world is to belong to the world rather than to God. In contrast to the aim of epistemology, Kierkegaard argues that to be a believer means that "what I seek is not here, which is precisely the reason I believe it. Faith signifies precisely the deep, strong, blessed unrest which urges on the believer, so that he cannot find rest in this world, so

3. Wolterstorff, *Thomas Reid*, 256.

4. Ibid., 260.

the one who does find complete rest here, would also cease to be a believer; for a believer cannot sit still, as one sits with a walking-stick in his hand; a believer pushes forward."[5] Like Reid, Kierkegaard claims that what is most important to know is not what can be seen, but what cannot be seen. Contrary to Wolterstorff's interpretation, Reid's epistemology leads us from the rational pretensions of a non-alienated view of the world back to the simple piety of faith. For faith, precisely because it signifies a deep, strong, blessed unrest, is incompatible with the epistemological aim of feeling at home in the world.

The Reorientation of the Will through Sufferings

In presuming the possibility of ready access to God through an immediate and familiar acquaintance with holy things, Reformed epistemology appears to overlook the Christian doctrine of original sin. Just as scientific claims are limited in scope by the fundamental constants of nature, so theological claims are limited in scope by the fundamental constraints of human nature. According to Reid, the creator has limited our powers of conception in order to make room for faith. For the creator could not give the creature all without making it a god. As the Schoolmen argued from Plato and Aristotle, this implies that there are different degrees in the perfection of created substances or things, and hence also of limitations that arise in relation to these degrees of perfection. The imperfection of the creature arises from this original limitation. Because the possibility of evil and suffering is rooted in the imperfection of the creature, the question occurs whether God is not in some sense the cause of evil and suffering. Further, if God permits evil and suffering, the question occurs whether he does not participate in some sense in the existence of evil.

These questions have presented a skeptical obstacle to belief in the justice and goodness of God called theodicy. I will address these questions in turn, arguing that God neither causes evil and suffering, nor participates in its existence. Rather, evil is due to the privation of good and the lack of receptivity in the creature. Further, contrary to participating in the existence of evil, God overcomes evil with good in bringing about the salvation of the creature. Of course this argument is by no means original. But it is

5. Kierkegaard, *Gospel of Suffering*, 5–6.

necessary to restate the teachings of the Christian tradition on the reality of sin, which seem to be marginalized when we philosophize about the nature of religious knowledge and what we are capable of in relation to God. We must therefore keep the doctrine of original sin before us in order to avert the egregious error of a philosophical anthropology that ignores the biblical account of our actual present situation.

Although God did not create sin or cause it in the creature, Augustine argues that it is inherent in human nature and is imputed to the whole human race before the individual will has even participated in it. This hereditary vice impels the will to commit actual sins. Although God created the creature innocent, guilt entered the world through the Fall of Adam. Augustine's doctrine of original sin is based on the Pauline teaching that through one man sin entered the world so that by the disobedience of the one the many died. God designed the rational aspect of our nature so that it could reach beyond sensory data to the true cause of all things. But, as John Paul II argues, God diminished this ready access because of the disobedience by which our first parents set themselves in absolute autonomy in relation to the one who had created them:

> This is the human condition vividly described by the Book of Genesis when it tells us that God placed the human being in the Garden of Eden, in the middle of which there stood "the tree of knowledge of good and evil" (Gen. 2:17). The symbol is clear: man was in no position to discern and decide for himself what was good and what was evil, but was constrained to appeal to a higher source. The blindness of pride deceived our first parents into thinking themselves sovereign and autonomous, and into thinking that they could ignore the knowledge which comes from God. All men and women were caught up in this primal disobedience, which so wounded reason that from then on its path to full truth would be strewn with obstacles. From that time onwards the human capacity to know the truth was impaired by an aversion to the One who is the source and origin of truth.[6]

This account of our actual present situation describes the noetic effects of sin. As the will became more autonomous and enclosed in itself, it refused to acknowledge its dependence on God for knowledge of the truth, and reason became more and more a prisoner to itself. When Adam and Eve opened their eyes to the knowledge of good and evil, pride blinded them

6. John Paul II, *Fides et ratio*, § 2.

to the knowledge which comes from God. The knowledge of good and evil disturbed their natural and immediate relationship with God. Ready access to God became limited. As the Reformed theologian Karl Barth argues, the Fall occurred when Adam became "ethical man." Since that time, the apostle Paul argues that the wise have regarded the knowledge which comes from God as foolishness.

At the same time, John Paul II argues that the point of the gospel is that the weakness of reason has been redeemed as a result of Christ coming into the world: "the coming of Christ was the saving event which redeemed reason from its weakness, setting it free from the shackles in which it had imprisoned itself."[7] As the apostle Paul argues, the law revealed Adam's disobedience, for guilt is not imputed when there is no law. Here the law drives a person to the gospel, in the same way despair drives a person to faith. Although disobedience brought deception and guilt into the world, the Son of God also came into the world to make peace between God and the human race. Thus, as the apostle Paul writes, "for as through the one man's disobedience the many were made sinners, even so through the obedience of the One the many will be made righteous" (Rom 6:19). Through the creature's obedient act of faith, the obedient actions of the one are imputed to him as righteousness. Through the obedient actions of the one, the possibility of ready access to God is restored. But, as the apostle Paul makes clear, the creature's access to God is now by trust rather than by sight. The possibility of a new relationship with God is based on faith rather than knowledge.

Instead of liberating reason from its constraints, John Paul II argues that absolute autonomy has placed reason in shackles. Similarly, Luther argues that "free choice without the grace of God is not free at all, but immutably the captive and slave of evil, since it cannot of itself turn to the good."[8] Without the knowledge which comes from God, the rational aspect of our nature becomes more and more a prisoner to its own prejudices. The more objective we try to become, the more these prejudices blind us to the truth that we seek to understand. The more we try to comprehend the mysterious ways of God, the more weary and despairing of our own ability we become. Thus, despair is a necessary consequence of objectivity. The problem is not that subjectivity presents an epistemic obstacle to objectivity by limiting the rational aspect of our nature. As John Paul II suggests, this is precisely the illusion that ensnared our first parents, that we must first overcome our

7. Ibid.

8. Luther, *Bondage of the Will*, 67.

limited essence in order to acquire the knowledge which comes from God. Rather, objectivity presents an epistemic obstacle to subjectivity or faith. The path of reason to full truth is strewn with skeptical obstacles created by disobedience to God.

Whereas objectivity or the knowledge of good and evil leads only to condemnation and death under the law, the apostle Paul tells us that subjectivity or justification by faith alone leads to the forgiveness of sins and eternal life under grace. For only grace can liberate reason from the shackles in which it has imprisoned itself. Like Kierkegaard, John Paul II argues that grace opens up the possibility of a new relationship between the creator and the creature through a theonomous autonomy. Reason is truly liberated when it discovers its dependence on God for knowledge of the truth. Thus, as John Paul II argues, "the truth of Christian revelation, found in Jesus of Nazareth, enables all men and women to embrace the 'mystery' of their own life. As absolute truth, it summons human beings to be open to the transcendent, whilst respecting both their autonomy as creatures and their freedom. At this point the relationship between freedom and truth is complete, and we understand the full meaning of the Lord's words: 'You will know the truth, and the truth will make you free' (Jn. 8:32)."[9]

Similarly, the German mathematician and philosopher G. W. Leibniz argues that grace opens up the possibility of a new relationship between the creator and the creature. As Leibniz explains, the same reason that has made God create Adam innocent, but liable to fall, makes him recreate Adam when he falls.[10] Because God has made his son take human nature upon him to expiate our sins, so that all who believe in him shall be saved, faith is a gift of God. In our natural state of original sin, we are dead to all good works and even our will must be aroused by grace. But God gives us the will and power to do it. Whether this is done through a divine inward motion that wholly determines our will to good, or through a sufficient grace that does not fail to attain its end, God is the final reason of salvation, grace, faith, and election in Jesus Christ.[11] Leibniz describes the human soul as a spiritual automaton with divine laws that govern its proper function. Because God has designed a perfect theonomous autonomy for the creature, Leibniz argues that God did not correct any defects in the creature when he recreated Adam after he fell. Although the imperfection of the

9. John Paul II, *Fides et ratio*, § 1.

10. Leibniz, *Theodicy*, 140.

11. Ibid., 125–26.

creature arises from the limitation of its essence, the failure of the creature to act in accordance with these divine laws is not caused by this limitation. Although God has limited the creature's essence, it does not follow that God is the cause of the creature's disobedience.

Leibniz defends this claim with an analogy from nature. Whereas the natural imperfection of creatures is analogous to the natural inertia of matter, the divine inward motion is analogous to the force of a river current moving a boat down a river. Suppose that the force of the river current is constant like the perpetual divine inward motion that moves the will to good. Then Newton's second law of motion tells us that the more massive the boat, the more slowly it moves down the river. That is, if $F = ma$ is constant, then a decreases as m increases. Moreover, if the mass of the boat is doubled, experiments confirm that twice as much force must be used to give the boat the same speed. That is, if we let $F_1 = ma$ and $F_2 = 2ma$, then $F_1/F_2 = 1/2$, or $F_2 = 2F_1$. Thus, the mass of the boat is inclined to slowness or privation of speed. Mass has a natural resistance to being moved analogous to the will. Although the force of the river current is the cause of the boat's motion down the river, the retardation or lack of receptivity of the boat to this motion is caused by its mass. Similarly, although the divine inward motion is the cause of perfection in the nature and actions of the creature, the defects or retardation in the actions of the creature are caused by the creature's lack of receptivity. Leibniz concludes that "God is no more the cause of sin than the river's current is the cause of the retardation of the boat. Force also in relation to matter is as the spirit in relation to the flesh; the spirit is willing and the flesh is weak."[12] Hence the divine inward motion that moves the will to good is realized in proportion to the receptivity of the creature.

According to this analogy from nature, the source and cause of defects in the creature's actions are located in the will of the creature rather than in God's design of the creature. Defects in the creature's actions do not arise from defects in God's design, but from the creature's freedom to choose. The creature may choose to be receptive to the divine inward motion that determines the will to good, or it may choose to resist God's determination through self-determination. Whereas the first choice preserves the creature's life, the second choice leads to self-destruction. The question occurs whether God could have designed the creature with an infallible theonomous autonomy so that it was not liable to fall. This is equivalent

12. Ibid., 141.

to the question of whether God could have created a better world without evil and suffering. On the contrary, Leibniz argues that "if the smallest evil that comes to pass in the world were missing in it, it would no longer be this world; which, with nothing omitted and all allowance made, was found the best by the Creator who chose it. It is true that one may imagine possible worlds without sin and without unhappiness . . . but these same worlds again would be very inferior to ours in goodness."[13] Just as God has designed the best possible world, with nothing omitted and all allowance made, so he has designed the best possible theonomous autonomy for the creature. Like the mass of a boat that resists the force of a river current, the lack of receptivity of the will resists the divine inward motion in determining the will to good.

The question still occurs whether God participates in the existence of evil by permitting it. Although moral evil is the cause of physical evil or suffering, Leibniz argues that moral evil itself has no efficient cause. Like Augustine, Leibniz argues that moral evil consists in privation, in that which the efficient cause does not bring about, in deference to the autonomy and freedom of the creature. Thus, as Leibniz tells us, the Schoolmen describe the cause of evil as deficient. Since moral evil exists only as a privation of good, and God wills antecedently the good and consequently the best, it follows that God does not will or permit moral evil at all. Leibniz, however, argues that God sometimes permits physical evil or suffering in the sense of a hypothetical necessity that connects it with the best. For unlike absolute necessity, whose contrary is impossible, hypothetical necessity is contingent as it may or may not occur. Thus, Leibniz argues that "one may say of physical evil, that God wills it often as a penalty owing to guilt, and often also as a means to an end, that is, to prevent greater evils or to obtain greater good. The penalty serves also for amendment and example. Evil often serves to make us savour good the more; sometimes too it contributes to a greater perfection in him who suffers it, as the seed that one sows is subject to a kind of corruption before it can germinate."[14]

In another analogy from nature, Leibniz compares the orientation of the will to the orientation of a magnetic compass needle. Leibniz argues that suffering is a force that can change the orientation or direction of the will, aligning it with the divine inward motion, like the magnetic material of a compass needle is aligned with an external magnetic field. Contrary to

13. Ibid., 128–29.

14. Ibid., 137.

Descartes, Leibniz argues that we are not always aware of the causes that move the will as they are often imperceptible. When a magnetic needle changes its direction toward north, it does not do so independently of any other cause, but as the bulk effect of imperceptible movements of the magnetic matter.[15] Today, in light of quantum theory, we know that the change in direction of the compass needle is caused by the unpaired magnetic spins of the electrons in the ferromagnetic material of the needle aligning themselves with the external magnetic field of the earth.[16] Thus, the net magnetization or change in direction of the material is indeed caused by imperceptible though measurable movements of the magnetic matter.[17] Similarly, when the will changes its orientation or direction in moral space, the causes are often imperceptible as in the case of despair. The bulk effect of redemptive sufferings can align the will with the divine inward motion in the same way as a magnetic force aligns the unpaired magnetic spins of the electrons in the compass needle with the earth's magnetic field. Thus, suffering may overcome the natural inertia of the will or its lack of receptivity to the divine inward motion.

Like Kierkegaard, Leibniz argues that objectivity is an illusion in the case of the human will. The Cartesian assumption of a perfect equipoise between two courses of action is impossible. Like Augustine, Leibniz argues that the will cannot be indifferent, where all is completely even on both sides of a choice. Although the reasons for this disparity are not evident to the senses, they incline or dispose the will toward one action or the other. Thus, in the natural state of original sin, the will is already inclined toward disobedience. This inclination is identical with the natural inertia or resistance of the will to the divine inward motion. By permitting the physical consequence of moral evil to arise without permitting moral evil itself, however, God gives the creature a means of changing the natural inclination of the will. By permitting suffering as a penalty for guilt, God gives the creature the opportunity for repentance and salvation. In this way, suffering may lead to another possibility for the creature. One may become either more skeptical and enclosed, or more trusting and open in response to grace in the form of redemptive sufferings.

15. Ibid., 150–51.

16. Thornton and Rex, *Modern Physics*, 333–36.

17. Paramagnetism is extremely weak and takes a delicate experiment and powerful magnet to detect. See Griffiths, *Electrodynamics*, 262.

Philosophers have argued that the problem of evil raises the question of whether a life laced with suffering and punctuated by death can have any positive meaning.[18] Leibniz's defense of the justice and goodness of God suggests that suffering has a positive meaning. Although evil in itself, suffering may bring about the greater good of the redemption of the human soul. As Ludwig Wittgenstein writes, "life can educate one to a belief in God. And *experiences* too are what bring this about; but I don't mean visions and other forms of sense experience which show us the 'existence of this being', but, e.g., sufferings of various sorts. These neither show us God in the way a sense impression shows us an object, nor do they give rise to *conjectures* about him. Experiences, thoughts,—life can force this concept on us."[19] Thus, far from presenting a skeptical obstacle to belief in God, suffering may educate one to belief in God by changing the orientation or direction of the will. The various sorts of sufferings experienced in life make us painfully aware of the inadequate sources within ourselves to cope. This may lead to a search for a moral source outside ourselves to help bear the burden.

Just as a physical force can change the direction of an object in nature, Leibniz suggests that suffering is an existential force or dialectic that can change the direction of the human will in moral space. The hardened attitudes of alienation underlying conflicting systems of belief are held in place, not by carefully considered arguments, but by the natural inertia of the will which is resistant to change. Analogous to Newton's first law, Leibniz argues that the will tends to remain at rest or maintain its original orientation unless acted on by a force. Unlike purely intellectual argument, which is powerless to move us, suffering can provide the force necessary to change the orientation of the will. Thus, as Wittgenstein observes, "one of the things Christianity says is that sound doctrines are all useless. That you have to change your *life*. Or the *direction* of your life . . . a sound doctrine need not *take hold* of you; you can follow it as you would a doctor's prescription.—But here you need something to move you and turn you in a new direction . . . Once you have been turned around, you must *stay* turned around."[20] Although theological methods and doctrines are important in elucidating our creeds and confessions of faith, they are powerless to change the orientation of the will. As Leibniz suggests, in order to move the

18. See, e.g., Adams and Adams, "Introduction."

19. Wittgenstein, *Culture and Value*, 86.

20. Ibid., 53.

will in a new direction, the force must be greater than the natural inertia of the will. Further, as Wittgenstein suggests, the natural inertia of the will has a tendency to restore its original orientation, analogous to a restoring force in nature. Thus, this reorientation must be maintained by a continuing action of the will. Perhaps this is why the spiritual fathers speak of the dark night of suffering of the soul as a constant in their journey to God, something that they hope to transcend in an eternal happiness, yet something that they require as an expedient to move them closer to God.

Therefore, although God does not cause physical evil or sufferings he brings good from them. For, as the apostle Paul tells us, "we know that God causes all things, whether good or evil, to work together for good to those who love God" (Rom 8:28). By permitting suffering, God shows forth his power in overcoming evil with good. If, on the contrary, suffering were not permitted, there would be no penalty for guilt. Consequently, the creature would have no opportunity to turn away from evil and seek good. Then the creature's fate would be iron-clad before it could act to change it. Further, although God does not cause moral evil or participate in the existence of physical evil, he freely chooses to identify with the physical evil or suffering of the creature in order to overcome both moral and physical evil with good. Here the divine will does not compel the human will to good through suffering. Rather, the divine will draws the human will to good through God's participation in the suffering of the creature and the love that this arouses in the heart of the creature.

The Movements of Faith vs. the Movements of Knowledge

We cannot speak properly about the knowledge of God without speaking about the reality of sin and the problem of disobedience. The disobedience of the creature has separated it from its natural and immediate relationship with God. As John Paul II makes clear, the creature no longer has ready access to God. Thus, far from being caused by God, the suffering of the creature originates from its disobedient and skeptical reactions to God. Because this suffering is too heavy for the creature to bear alone, however, the Son of God freely chooses to condescend to the creature in the form of a suffering servant. In this way, God the Father identifies with the suffering of the creature through the suffering of Jesus of Nazareth, his only begotten

Son. The creator takes the burden of the creature's suffering upon himself to make the load easy for the creature to bear. As John Paul II argues, this is the meaning of the biblical text: "Come to me, all who are weary and heavy-laden, and I will give you rest. Take my yoke upon you, and learn from me, for I am gentle and humble in heart; and you shall find rest for your souls. For my yoke is easy, and my load is light" (Matt 11:28–30). Here God the Father leads the creature back to himself through the example and amendment of Christ's suffering.

Luther argues that it is in the identification of our own suffering with the suffering Christ that God most fully reveals himself. Thus, the center of Lutheran theology is the cross. As Paul Althaus argues, when Luther claims that God is known only in suffering, this claim "points to the deep correlation between the suffering Christ, in whom God makes himself known, and the suffering man, who is the only man able to enter into community with God."[21] After the Fall of Adam, Luther argues that the visible and manifest things of God can only be seen through suffering and the cross. True theology and knowledge of God are in the crucified Christ. The wisdom of God is paradoxically hidden in the folly of the cross.[22] Althaus argues that the theology of the cross knows God from his suffering rather than from his works. Whereas natural theology provides a superficial knowledge of God through reason, the theology of the cross provides an intimate knowledge of God through faith.[23] Luther argues that we cannot know God objectively apart from the theology of the cross because God does not allow us to find him in our abstract thoughts. For "if we could do this, we would not need God; but because we need him, he has designated a place and a person—showing us where and in what way he ought to be found."[24] Similarly, Kierkegaard argues that we find God in the sufferings of our actual present situation in the world rather than in abstract thought, and that the way we find God is through faith rather than knowledge.

For both Luther and Kierkegaard, God has paradoxically hidden his wisdom in the folly of the cross to safeguard it from the learned and proud. Therefore, in order to know the things of Christ crucified, a person must humble himself as Christ humbled himself in the world. A person must acknowledge the mystery of God hidden in the cross with the humility and gratitude of faith, rather than railing against this mystery with a skeptical

21. Althaus, *Theology of Martin Luther*, 28.

22. Luther, *Heidelberg Disputation*, 52–53.

23. Althaus, *Theology of Martin Luther*, 26.

24. Quoted in Althaus, *Theology of Martin Luther*, 21.

spirit. Kierkegaard argues that when knowledge entered the world, grief also entered the world. Reflection disturbed the creature's natural and immediate relationship with God. Adam's disobedience made him skeptical of the knowledge which comes from God. Thus, Kierkegaard writes that "the doubt that had come along with the knowledge coiled itself alarmingly around his heart, and the serpent that had seduced him with the delectable now squeezed him in its coils . . . doubt became more inward, and the knowledge, which should have guided him, fettered him in distress and contradiction."[25]

When our first parents chose to eat from the tree of knowledge of good and evil, the serpent sowed the seed of skepticism deep in the human heart. In choosing absolute autonomy in relation to the one who created us, the will became more and more enclosed in itself, ignoring the knowledge which comes from God. Kierkegaard argues that "the stratagem of skeptical doubt is to make a person believe that he by himself can overcome himself, as if he were able to perform the marvel unheard of in heaven or on earth or under the earth—that something that is in conflict with itself can in this conflict be stronger than itself!"[26] The illusion of objectivity, which promised to free human thought from its constraints, placed the will in bondage instead. Thus, as the apostle Paul despairs, "the good that I will, I do not do; but I practice the very evil that I do not will" (Rom 7:19). Thus, like Kierkegaard, Luther argues that the necessary consequence of objectivity is despair. For "it is certain that man must ultimately despair of his own ability before he is prepared to receive the grace of Christ."[27]

Luther and Kierkegaard both argue that God has given us powers of conception so that we may know his perfections. But reason cannot fully perceive God's perfections without grace. For only grace can remove the shackles of skeptical doubt that bind and contract the human heart. In contrast to the seed of skepticism sown by the serpent, grace sows the seed of faith in the human heart which opens the will to the knowledge which comes from God. Thus, Kierkegaard argues that faith is a new immediacy implanted by grace that is mediated through the hearing of the Word of God. Because the human being originally exists in error, the will is closed to the knowledge which comes from God, and must be reoriented to God through faith in order to exist in the truth. When the will acknowledges

25. Kierkegaard, "Every Good Gift," 127.

26. Ibid., 128.

27. Luther, *Heidelberg Disputation*, 51.

its dependence on God for knowledge of the truth, the immediacy of faith establishes a new point of departure for reflection in the truth. In this way, the act of faith creates a new form of life, the possibility of a theonomous autonomy in which the creature is determined by the knowledge which comes from God in a way that respects the autonomy and freedom of the creature.

Kierkegaard argues that suffering is necessary to break down the old self in order to build a new self. The utter barrenness and emptiness of absolute autonomy must be experienced before a theonomous autonomy can be established. Here two reactions to suffering are possible, repentance or defiance, owing to the autonomy and freedom of the creature. The will may choose to become either more receptive, or more enclosed, in relation to the one who created us. As Kierkegaard writes:

> Your words were powerless, as powerless as your thought, as powerless as your arm, and heaven did not hear your prayer; but when you then humbled yourself under God's mighty hand and, crushed in spirit, sighed: My God, my God, great is my sin, too great to be forgiven—then heaven opened again, then God, as a prophet writes, looked down from his window at you and said: Yet a little while; yet a little while and I shall renew the countenance of the earth—and see, your countenance was renewed, and God's compassionate grace had loved forth in your barren mind the meekness that is receptive to the words. Then you humbly confessed before God that God tempts no one, but that everyone is tempted when he is beguiled and drawn by his own cravings, just as you were tempted by proud, presumptuous, and defiant thoughts.[28]

Similarly, Luther argues that "it is impossible for a person not to be puffed up by his good works unless he has first been deflated and destroyed by suffering and evil until he knows that he is worthless and that his works are not his but God's."[29] At the same time, the Bible assures us that whoever humbles himself will be exalted (Matt 23:12). Whereas the law and the knowledge of good and evil humbles us, grace and the knowledge which comes from God through suffering exalts us.

Thus, contrary to Barth, suffering may educate one to belief in God by creating a *neediness* for a moral source outside the self that only grace may satisfy. According to Kierkegaard, this neediness is the human being's

28. Kierkegaard, "Every Good and Every Perfect Gift," 38.

29. Luther, *Heidelberg Disputation*, 53.

highest perfection.[30] As Luther argues, "through the law comes knowledge of sin (Rom. 3:20), through knowledge of sin, however, comes humility, and through humility grace is acquired."[31] Although grace restores ready access to God through faith, however, the access is not direct or immediate but critical. Luther argues that Christ opens our hearts so that we may understand the scriptures using our own reason. Without the knowledge which comes from God, however, the scriptures appear dark and obscure because the hearts of men are dark and obscure apart from grace.[32]

Contrary to fideistic interpretations of Luther and Kierkegaard, the transition from absolute autonomy to a theonomous autonomy does not correspond to the transition from reason to a blind and irrational faith. Rather, it corresponds to the transition from a self-determined rationality to a rationality that is determined by the knowledge which comes from God in a way that respects the autonomy and freedom of the creature. This transition corresponds to the transition from objectivity to subjectivity discussed in the previous chapter. Objectivity arises from the benevolent desire to acquire wisdom and the avidity to know the true causes of things. But, as Luther argues, without the theology of the cross we misuse the best in the worst manner.[33]

Although we cannot know the things that most satisfy the desires of our rational nature, Jesus tells us that whoever drinks of the water he gives will never thirst. Because we thirst for the knowledge which comes from God, Augustine argues that our hearts our restless until they find rest in God.[34] Kierkegaard describes this restlessness as the unrest of faith. According to Kierkegaard, Christ shows us the way in which we may satisfy our restlessness. Between heaven and earth there is only one way, namely, to follow Christ. But, as Gregory of Nyssa argues, he who follows God sees the back of God rather than the face of God. Thus, Moses is taught that he may behold God by following him wherever he might lead.[35] To follow Christ, as Kierkegaard explains, "means denying one's self, and hence it means *walking the same way* as Christ walked in the humble form of a servant—needy, forsaken, mocked, not loving worldliness and not loved

30. Kierkegaard, "To Need God," 303.

31. Luther, *Heidelberg Disputation*, 51.

32. Luther, *Bondage of the Will*, 27.

33. Luther, *Heidelberg Disputation*, 55.

34. Augustine, *Confessions*, 45.

35. Gregory of Nyssa, *Life of Moses*, 119.

by the worldly-minded. Consequently, it means to *walk alone*, for he who in self-abnegation renounces the world and all that is the world's, forsakes every relationship which otherwise tempts and holds captive."[36]

In the struggle between two opponents, Kierkegaard argues that one is naturally stronger than the other. But it is also natural that no one is stronger than himself. Thus, there is one enemy a person cannot conquer by himself, and that is himself.[37] When the human soul struggles to overcome the world, it struggles to conquer itself by overcoming the desires that bind it to the world. For the soul, Kierkegaard argues, is "the contradiction of the temporal and the eternal, and here, therefore, the same thing can be possessed and the same thing gained and at the same time."[38] From the perspective of eternity, the soul is a possession that is given to us by the creator. From the perspective of space-time, however, the soul is not yet what it was created to be, namely, a self. A person must make a self by gaining his soul in patience. Therefore, the soul is a possession that is to be gained. The alternative, Kierkegaard argues, is to lose one's soul. For what one does not preserve in patience one can indeed lose.[39]

Just as the one who desires to gain the world gradually gives away his soul in exchange for the world, so the one who desires to gain his soul in patience must give up the world.[40] Thus, Kierkegaard argues that to possess the world is really to be possessed by the world. In contrast, to gain one's soul in patience one must follow Christ and resist the world. Just as Christ emptied himself of his divine subjectivity in order to become in space-time what he already was from eternity, so the disciple must empty himself by denying himself in order to become what he is created to be, a self in the likeness of the teacher (Phil 2:5–9). Through faith, which strengthens the inner being, God gives the disciple the power to overcome the world as Christ overcame the world. Whereas knowledge aims to make us feel at home in the world, faith produces a sense of resistance to the movements of the world's life. To overcome the world, the believer must allow this resistance to become more and more pronounced.[41] Thus, the movements of faith and the movements of knowledge are in opposite directions relative

36. Kierkegaard, *Gospel of Suffering*, 10–12.
37. Kierkegaard, "Expectancy of Faith," 18.
38. Kierkegaard, "To Gain One's Soul," 163.
39. Kierkegaard, "To Preserve One's Soul," 185.
40. Kierkegaard, "To Gain One's Soul," 164.
41. Ibid., 165.

to the movements of the world's life. When unimpeded by faith, the movements of the world's life induce a self-forgetfulness. One forgets that the soul is a possession that is to be gained, and that the soul is able to gain itself only by losing or denying itself.[42]

Like worldliness, Kierkegaard argues that knowledge induces self-forgetfulness. Thus, the straying thought must be turned toward a saving obedience. In contrast, Plantinga argues that faith is a matter of believing something rather than doing something.[43] Although knowledge may have its significance, it deceives a person in the same way the world does. For in believing that one possesses knowledge, it is really the knowledge that possesses the believer. Thus, contrary to Plantinga, this is why all knowing that is unrelated to a gaining or doing is deficient, for knowing is not the gaining. Unlike other areas of knowledge, the knowledge which comes from God cannot be possessed.[44] For as soon as the believer gives up the gaining of the knowledge, he gives up the acquisition. Thus, as Kierkegaard argues, "the knower does just what the hiker does—he puts aside his patience [or the endurance of faith] when he has won knowledge. But the person who wants to be patient only in order to know his soul will not gain his soul in patience."[45]

To follow Christ, therefore, means to gain one's soul from God, away from the world, and in patience. Whereas faith is the deep, strong, blessed unrest which urges on the believer, patience is the endurance of faith. Kierkegaard argues that this invisible assistance is identical with learning to go alone, which means "learning to transform the mind into a likeness with that of the teacher, who nevertheless is not visibly present."[46] For the teacher must conceal himself so that it may become evident whether his disciple will follow him. This means that we must remain in the world to do the work God has given us. Thus, contrary to any claim that the disciple is to be spared from trial and tribulation, Kierkegaard argues that it was not Christ's intention to take men and women out of the world and into Paradise, where there is neither any need nor any wretchedness, or to transform the earthly life into a world of peace and prosperity. A person's lot here on earth is not different because Christianity has come into the

42. Ibid., 172.

43. Plantinga, *Warranted Christian Belief*, 249.

44. Kierkegaard, "To Gain One's Soul," 173.

45. Ibid., 174.

46. Kierkegaard, *Gospel of Suffering*, 8–9.

world. A believer may suffer in the same way as before, yet the heavy burden becomes light for the believer because Christ helps him carry it.[47] The burden becomes light by the aid of the thought that the suffering is profitable or easy.

But "that the suffering *is* easy, that must be *believed*, it cannot be seen . . . when one sees perpetual wretchedness about him, then, believing, to see the joy: aye, that is fitting. It is fitting with respect to the use of that word faith, for faith always has to do with that which is not seen, be it the *invisible* or the *improbable*; and it is fitting that a man should be a believer."[48] Through faith, the believer not only hopes for things unseen, but hopes to overcome the world as Christ overcame the world. The world, Kierkegaard argues, cannot take this hope away because it is acquired in tribulation and becomes strong through tribulation. Adversity helps a person gain strengthening in the inner being. For "the person who learned what he learned from what he suffered, gained not only the best learning but what is much more—the best instructor—and the person who learns from God is strengthened in the inner being. Then even if he lost everything, he would still gain everything, and Abraham possessed nothing but a burial place in Canaan, and yet he was God's chosen one."[49]

Just as Abraham is the father of faith, Job is the example of the endurance of faith or patience through trial and tribulation. When Job lost everything, Kierkegaard tells us that his heart was not squeezed into silent subjection to the sorrow by skeptical doubt. On the contrary, Job's heart expanded in thankfulness to the Lord because he had given him all the blessings that he now took away.[50] When Job learned of his great misfortune, he immediately understood the terrible thought that it was God who had taken everything away, just as it was God who had given everything to him. Job did not risk his soul to worldliness by blaming other people or God. He did not imperil his soul with deliberations and speculations that only foster skeptical doubt about God's justice and goodness. Instead, Job withdrew himself in quiet resignation. He responded to God with childlike trust and awaited God's explanation which, as Kierkegaard tells us, "found his mind, like good earth, well cultivated in patience."[51] Through trial and

47. Ibid., 25.

48. Ibid., 26–28.

49. Kierkegaard, "Strengthening in the Inner Being," 95.

50. Kierkegaard, "The Lord Gave, the Lord Took Away," 115–16.

51. Ibid., 118–19.

tribulation, Job learned that God loved him because the one God tests he loves. Despite his unimaginable loss, Job maintained intimacy with the Lord which became more inward than ever. In the words of Kierkegaard, Job's thanksgiving is quiet in humility, his pain so deep that the peace of God is not far away, his trust so childlike that he does not need to go far in order to live once again, to be moved, and to have his being in God.[52]

Because Job saw the Lord through faith, Kierkegaard argues that he did not see despair. For the one who sees God through faith in the dark night of tribulation has overcome the world.[53] For such a person, prosperity and adversity equally serve for strengthening in the inner being. The story of Job is an example of patience or the endurance of faith in the face of suffering and perplexity. At the same time, it serves as an amendment to skepticism, which is the opposite of patience. Because Job's heart was not contracted by skeptical doubt, it was able to expand in thankfulness to God through faith. Thus, Job is the definition of patience. By his lights, we see that intimacy with God depends on ungrounded trust rather than knowledge, trust without any reasons for trusting. For if intelligence can perceive the benefit of suffering, faith cannot see God. But, as Kierkegaard argues, "when human knowledge cannot see a hand's breadth before it in the dark night of suffering, then faith can see God, for faith sees best in the dark."[54]

To know God means to follow Christ, which involves transforming the mind into a likeness with that of the teacher. This transformation includes developing new emotions as well as new beliefs. Without substantial religious affections, the Christian identity is shallow and formless. Unlike the beliefs of the Christian tradition, which may be acquired passively through a credulity disposition, the Christian concepts of faith, hope, and love describe emotions that must be actively acquired through a *gaining* or *doing*. For the believer must actively learn to trust the justice and goodness of God in the face of adversity and perplexity, to hope that she will overcome the world as Christ overcame the world, and to love God for making the heavy burden of suffering light. Since abilities are always actively acquired, it follows that the Christian concepts are abilities or capacities that a person may or may not acquire. Kierkegaard defines and analyzes these concepts with an objectivity made possible only through a complex pseudonymous authorship. The Christian concepts are placed in dialectical relation to

52. Kierkegaard, "Think about Your Creator," 244.

53. Ibid., 121.

54. Kierkegaard, *Gospel of Suffering*, 32.

concepts in other regions of language and domains of knowledge that bear a family resemblance in order to show how the aesthetic, ethical, and religious aspects of our nature may be structured in a form of life that leads to our highest perfection—to need God. The Christian concepts are the substance or meat of the Christian faith that the apostle Paul admonishes us to digest. These concepts cannot be acquired cheaply like beliefs. As Paul's life bears testimony, they may be acquired only at the cost of discipleship through a gaining or doing that involves suffering with Christ.

Thus, to know God also means to have intimacy with God through the experience of suffering, which is nevertheless made profitable through faith. For, according to Luther's theology of the cross, the knowledge of God is impossible apart from suffering. According to Kierkegaard's gospel of suffering, there is good news and even joy in the pain of suffering. As the apostle Paul tells us, "the spirit himself bears witness with our spirit that we are children of God, and if children, heirs also, heirs of God and fellow heirs with Christ, if indeed we suffer with him in order that we may also be glorified with him" (Rom 8:16–17). Through the pathos of faith, God shows us the way back to full intimacy with him. Since pathos can mean both emotion and suffering, faith may be defined as an emotional disposition that establishes a new relationship with God, not only by reorienting and opening the will to the knowledge of God, but by enabling us to empathize and identify with Christ's sufferings through the experience of our own sufferings. Here the endurance of suffering is essentially related to the endurance of faith. Whereas suffering proves the endurance of faith or patience, faith makes the endurance of suffering profitable or easy.

Conclusion

LUDWIG WITTGENSTEIN ONCE SAID that elucidating philosophical problems is like untying knots in our understanding. Although the result of philosophy is simple, the process of philosophizing must be as complicated as the knots it unties.[1] The philosophical problems of skepticism and relativism are like knots in our understanding that have made it difficult to believe in God. In the process of untying one knot, sometimes another knot is created. As Wittgenstein argues, philosophical concepts may alleviate mischief or they may make it worse.[2] Despite the well intentioned responses to skepticism and relativism from within the Reformed tradition, I have questioned whether these responses have alleviated mischief or made it worse. Although Karl Barth quite rightly insists on the transcendence of God in response to the problem of immediacy in liberal theology, I have argued that he proposes a more objective way of understanding God through Christology that cannot be defended with critical realism. Although Reformed epistemology quite rightly insists that belief in God is rational as it stands in response to the problem of evidentialism in modern philosophy, I have argued that its attempt to ground belief in God in an immediate belief-forming disposition is fideistic. Both of these responses to skepticism and relativism misrepresent the relationship of a person to the truth in Christianity as either too objective and exclusive or too immediate and enclosed, respectively.

My criticism has been mostly directed at Reformed epistemology in light of its dominant influence on current discussions of faith and reason. One problem has to do with the appeal to the metaphysical tradition to provide a more objective perspective in religion and theology to avoid skepticism about our truth-ascertainings. Wolterstorff argues that there is a deep hostility among all Wittgensteinians toward the metaphysical

1. Wittgenstein, *Philosophical Remarks*, 52.

2. Wittgenstein, *Culture and Value*, 55.

tradition.[3] Although Wittgenstein is critical of the obscure nature of the alleged "correspondence with reality" in metaphysical realism, I have argued that he has deep respect and admiration for the fundamental human need for meaning and intelligibility that leads us to want to transcend our experience of the world. Unlike the logical positivists, who sought to emancipate philosophy from metaphysics, Wittgenstein incorporated metaphysics into his philosophy through the category of the mystical. What shows itself cannot be expressed as facts. This includes, among other things, the problems of life with which ethics and religion deal. The "mystical" in Wittgenstein's philosophy is analogous in some respects to the "leap" in Søren Kierkegaard's philosophy. Both categories draw a distinction between essential truth in ethics and religion and truth in matters of fact in science.

This distinction, while intended to prevent the radical reduction of the sphere of the mystical to the sphere of science as in naturalism, imposes limits on the classical realist or propositional interpretation of religious language. The issue is not whether religious language is cognitive, but whether it is cognitive in the sense required by logical positivism of picturing facts in the world. Religious language does not describe the reality of what is spoken about as a "fact" in the world. Rather, as Paul L. Holmer argues, it provides a cognitively meaningful description of an ethico-religious way of living that *shows* the reality of what is spoken about.[4] Thus, the nature of the "correspondence with reality" in theology is different from science. As John E. Smith argues, while the abstraction of a "fact" is well founded within theoretical science and has admirably served the purposes for which it was made, it is absolutely illegitimate to suppose that this abstraction is the fundamental and final expression of the nature of reality. Science, ethics, and religion are different dimensions of experience, each of which has its part to play in the disclosure of reality. One should not suppose that the conditions governing the acquisition of theoretical knowledge are appropriate for every dimension of experience. Like Wilhelm Dilthey, Smith argues that the relative autonomy of the various dimensions of experience requires appropriate critical principles for each one. But, contrary to the presupposition of the science-religion dialogue, one should not suppose that there is a single set of conditions governing any one dimension of experience that can be made universal and legislative for all dimensions. Unless the scope of the abstraction of a "fact" is acknowledged, the inevitable consequence

3. Wolterstorff, *Philosophical Review*, 455.

4. Holmer, *Kierkegaard and the Truth*, 8.

is the reduction of experience to but one of its dimensions.[5] This raises the question of the wisdom of applying critical realism to theology. If Smith is right, the more we try to accommodate theology to science, the more we may be inadvertently aiding its reduction to naturalism.

Another problem in Reformed epistemology has to do with its epistemic conception of faith as an immediate belief-forming disposition. Based on a distinction between two different levels of doxastic ascent, I have argued that the acquisition of a system of religious belief takes place at a first-order level of basic doxastic ascent in an uncritical, spontaneous, and epistemically innocent manner through a credulity disposition implanted by nature. In contrast, the acceptance of this system of belief, in whole or in part, takes place at a second-order level of doxastic ascent in a critical, deliberate, and epistemically responsible manner through the supernatural disposition of faith implanted by grace. Faith, therefore, cannot be properly conceived at a level of basic doxastic ascent as a new cognitive disposition that produces religious belief immediately without circumventing the critical role of the will. Rather, faith is a new emotional disposition that reorients the will to God, opening the mind to the knowledge of God, rather than implanting or infusing this knowledge in the foundations of human consciousness in an immediate manner such that the rationality of its acceptance is justified. Although faith is implanted by grace, it must be actively acquired or developed by bringing our natural belief-forming processes to bear on the interior life. Unlike the acquisition of religious belief, which occurs spontaneously or automatically through immersion in the Christian tradition, the acquisition of faith depends critically on a qualitative decision confronting the will, which must be made time and again rather than once and for all. The acquisition of faith not only involves the formation of justified true beliefs "about" God through the competent exercise of intellectual virtues. It involves the establishment of a personal relationship with the truth such that the Christian identity or self becomes an expression "of" the truth through the competent exercise of theological virtues. The problem of accepting the truth in Christianity through faith has to do with the will and our being closed to the knowledge which comes from God. The problem of acceptance is rooted in our disobedience to God, not in the improper functioning of our epistemic mechanisms.

I have also argued that suffering, although in many cases abominable to moral sensibility and inscrutable to human thought, has a positive

5. Smith, *Experience and God*, 39–41.

meaning in Christian experience. According to the Christian tradition, the experience of suffering is necessary for the conversion of the will. Whereas self-pride contracts the human heart, suffering may open the heart to accept the Christian message of hope. As Wittgenstein writes, "anyone who receives the gift of opening his heart, rather than contracting it, accepts the means of salvation."[6] This reorientation of the will to the things of Christ crucified is accomplished through a change in attitudes rather than beliefs. Wittgenstein argues that "if life becomes hard to bear we think of a change in our circumstances. But the most important and effective change, a change in our own attitude, hardly even occurs to us, and the resolution to take such a step is very difficult for us."[7] As Dilthey suggests, this step is difficult for us because our beliefs are rooted in reactions to life, in attitudes toward life and to its problems. Thus, a qualitative change in one's belief system requires a more fundamental change in one's attitude. Since the experience of suffering may influence the attitudes of alienation that underlie our belief systems in a way that intellectual argument cannot, suffering may become a belief-forming process that can educate one to belief in God. This account of the formation of belief in God is diametrically opposed to the account given in Reformed epistemology, according to which belief in God is produced immediately like a natural birthright without decisiveness and independently of life's experiences. For the believer, this account makes belief in God appear too easy. For the agnostic or atheist, the account does little to help clarify the intellectual obstacles and confusions on the path to full truth strewn by disobedience.

According to Kierkegaard, despair is an epistemic mechanism that reorients the will to the truth in Christianity. That despair is a redemptive form of suffering is perhaps Kierkegaard's deepest psychological insight. Despair expresses the natural skeptical disposition of the will or attitude of alienation toward the one who created us in his image. As such, despair reveals a lack of correspondence between the self and the truth. Because despair expresses doubt about whether our thoughts and lives are adequate in relation to the one who created us, despair can become a belief-forming process that can open the heart to accept something as coming from God. Kierkegaard's religious pseudonym, Anti-Climacus, draws a distinction between two forms of despair—the despair of infinitude due to the lack of

6. Wittgenstein, *Culture and Value*, 46.

7. Ibid., 53.

finitude, and its inverse, the despair of finitude due to the lack of infinitude.[8] Whereas Kierkegaard associates the first form of despair with objectivity, the second form of despair is associated with immediacy. Objectivity and immediacy represent extreme forms of life or ways of living that distort the intended form or logical shape of Christian experience. Although both forms of despair lead us astray from God, whether in our abstract thoughts, a natural religiousness devoid of the inward reflection of faith, or in an aesthetic life of enjoyment in which our attitude toward life and its problems remains indifferent, they may also lead to a deep dissatisfaction with ourselves that can reorient the will to the knowledge of God. Thus, contrary to Barth, despair may create a neediness for a moral source outside the self that only grace may satisfy. Kierkegaard calls this neediness the human being's highest perfection. As Kierkegaard argues, "Christianity assumes that there inheres in the subjectivity of the individual, as being the potentiality of the appropriation of the good, the possibility of its acceptance . . ."[9]

Reformed epistemology has admirably addressed the lack of reflection or critical belief in the Christian life by stressing the importance of the intellectual virtues. In this sense, Reformed epistemology is quite undeserving of the charge of fideism. Its emphasis on the rational aspect of our nature at the expense of our emotional nature, however, distorts Christian experience in another way. On one hand, the adult Christian who fails to transmute what is believed or accepted through faith into knowledge according to her ability falls short of making a substantial Christian identity. For Christianity requires us to form more truth-preserving beliefs about God, and to develop a new point of view. Thus, the apostle Paul admonishes us to put on the mind of Christ. Although the child or the new adult believer is naturally fideistic in trusting the authority of the Christian tradition, he must go on to develop a rational faith or reasoned trust concerning the familiar elements of his religious knowledge and experience. Like Wittgenstein, Anti-Climacus argues that the adult Christian who acquiesces in a familiar acquaintance with holy things, or who longs to return to such a state of natural religiousness, is in despair. The ethical task of becoming a Christian, on the other hand, cannot be reduced to a matter of believing something as Plantinga claims. A substantial Christian identity requires new emotions, attitudes, and dispositions, as well as new beliefs. Not only must one's mind be renewed; one's life must be changed. The problem of

8. Kierkegaard, *Sickness unto Death*, 163–68.

9. Quoted in Holmer, *Kierkegaard and the Truth*, 77.

becoming a Christian involves more than acquiring a set of basic beliefs that are true. It involves learning and practicing a set of theological virtues or competences such as faith, hope, and love that modify the form of a human life. Thus, the apostle Paul also admonishes us to walk in the world as Christ walked. Whereas the basic beliefs of the Christian tradition may be acquired passively through a credulity disposition, the theological virtues can only be acquired actively through a gaining or doing. Therefore, one may acquire the basic beliefs without acquiring the emotions, attitudes, and dispositions that make the beliefs meaningful.

For this reason, objectivity and immediacy represent one-sided forms of Christianity that are equally distortive of Christian experience. The emphasis in Reformed epistemology on the beliefs we hold at the expense of the lives we lead overlooks the ultimate end of the Christian teachings. It is not one's abstract mind that needs saving, but one's soul with its passions. Thus, the epistemic conception of faith as a belief-forming disposition is too narrow. Faith is a new emotional disposition implanted by grace that allows us to apply our natural belief-forming processes in the development of new emotions, attitudes, and dispositions, as well as more truth-preserving beliefs. The cognitive and emotive aspects of our nature cannot be separated without distorting the form of life God has created in his image. As Wolterstorff quite rightly argues, knowing God is part of a more complex process of becoming a Christian that cannot be reduced to a matter of believing something. Knowing God also depends on doing something, namely, becoming the cognitively meaningful possibility described by the language of faith. Here, knowing God, as the story of Abraham and Isaac illustrates, involves learning to trust God in an obedient act of faith without any reasons for trusting him in situations that make it possible to doubt the religious beliefs whose knowledge we have taken for granted. Although our doubts may lead us to discover that some of our beliefs about God are unreliable or false, they may also lead us to discover that we lack the appropriate emotions, attitudes, and dispositions that make the beliefs meaningful. Knowing God requires more than the rational aspect of our nature. It requires the participation of our whole human nature in the divine nature.

There is an intellectual or cognitive view of religion that appeals to many educated people which Kierkegaard calls aesthetic. Although learning and scholarship have their importance in religion and theology, they also have their limitations. In the case of ethics and religion, Kierkegaard argues that learning and scholarship cannot produce a sense of moral responsibility or religiousness in a person. To believe otherwise is an illusion. The assumption that ethical and religious problems can be treated in an objective or disinterested manner that leads to moral and religious self-concern continues to guide most scholarship in these areas of knowledge. But, as Holmer argues, "Kierkegaard was quick to see that if one takes away this interest in the 'objective truth,' or what we are here calling the cognitive view of religion, religion is dissipated for many people. For the tantalizing edge of a kind of scientific religious research was and is that certainly religious results will follow."[10] The cognitive view of religion assumes that the ordinary language of the Bible can be translated into a more objective, precise, and factual language like science. This assumption lies at the heart of the scientific model for academic theology. But, like Hegel's idealistic philosophy, this translation creates the illusion that the truth of religious statements can be tested like the truth of scientific statements by determining whether they are verified or confuted by the "facts." This illusion will persist so long as theology must justify its place in the university as a science, based on an evidentialist model of rational inquiry that not even the scientist can satisfy. For, as I have argued, the ideal model of rational inquiry in science that motivates the project of rational justification in theology is an abstraction that misrepresents the everyday activities of scientists. Although the scientific approach to religious knowledge has its place in the life of faith, it must be careful not to claim too much for its kind of learning.

Like Barth, Reformed epistemology has rightly criticized the limitations of this evidentialist approach to religious knowledge. It is doubtful, however, whether the analytic definition of knowledge as justified true belief can be applied across every domain of knowledge. Reformed epistemology has repeated the very mistake of the evidentialist model of rationality it was meant to avoid by inventing special and technical meanings for faith, belief, knowledge, and truth in light of a certain conception of knowledge, which make the ordinary meanings of these terms as they are used in the Bible look imprecise and epistemically below par. In fairness, I have argued that the same mistake may also be seen in Barth's invention of a special and technical meaning of obedience, which allegedly provides a more direct and objective way of interpreting the Bible that minimizes the distracting influences of the will. In contrast to both of these approaches, I have argued that Kierkegaard and Wittgenstein suggest that theology should concern itself with the task of discriminating the meanings of religious terms as they

10. Ibid., 70.

are actually used in the Bible. Indeed, this is the dialectical task of Kierkegaard's literature. The ordinary meanings of faith, belief, knowledge, truth, sin, repentance, and more, are valid as they stand without a philosophical interpretation. These terms provide a cognitively meaningful description of the possibility of a form of life that must be actualized through self-concern rather than merely described in a detached, scientific mood. Indeed, this is the religious task and genius of Kierkegaard's literature—to provide the conditions for activating the very emotions, attitudes, and dispositions in a person that make these terms meaningful.

That skepticism and relativism are ancient problems suggests that they are part of the human condition. For Kierkegaard and Wittgenstein, learning to live with doubt is part of our humanity. Similarly, Hilary Putnam argues that one of Stanley Cavell's points is that to wish to be free of skepticism is to wish to be free of one's humanity. Being alienated is part of the human condition. The problem is to learn to live with both alienation and acknowledgment of the world and other people without guarantees.[11] Whereas skepticism doubts whether we can know truth, I have argued that relativism doubts whether we can find a sufficiently objective perspective to adjudicate strong disagreement about truth. Thus, relativism involves skepticism about rationality or our ability to produce rational consensus. To combat both forms of skeptical doubt, we must learn once again to trust our capacity to know, and to trust the rational norms already available to us in a tradition of rational inquiry as a way to rationally proceed in the face of disagreement about rationality. Although doubt is necessary to produce more truth-preserving beliefs that put us in touch with reality, we must adopt the doxastic practice of interrogating our doubts as well as beliefs to prevent doubt from degenerating into a general mood of skepticism. This requires the competent exercise of intellectual virtues.

More fundamentally, we must recognize that skepticism and relativism are attitudes of alienation. Thus, as Kierkegaard argues, the skeptical spirit of modern criticism does not point to defects in the Bible, but in us. Revelation is not something we are to test like a scientific theory, but is that according to which we are tested.[12] Whereas Augustine's doctrine of original sin diagnoses the source of these attitudes of alienation in our disobedience to God, the Reformation doctrine of justification by faith alone prescribes their remedy. To address how these attitudes of alienation have made us

11. Putnam, *Renewing Philosophy*, 178.

12. Kierkegaard, *Authority and Revelation*, 59.

strangers to the truth, and how faith can make us friends with God once again, we need to recover the virtue tradition in ethics and in epistemology. Whereas Reformed epistemology aims only at a non-alienated view of the world, Christianity aims at a non-alienated way of living through the theological virtue of faith that enables both our lives and beliefs to correspond with the truth. This emphasis in Christianity not only on the beliefs we hold but on the lives we lead hearkens back to the virtue tradition in Plato and Aristotle, in which the intellectual and moral virtues are seen as necessary and complementary skills or competences in the quest for the good life.

Bibliography

Adams, Marilyn McCord, and Robert Merrihew Adams. "Introduction." In *The Problem of Evil*, edited by Marilyn McCord Adams and Robert Merrihew Adams, 1–24. Oxford: Oxford University Press, 1990.

Althaus, Paul. *The Theology of Martin Luther*. Translated by Robert C. Schultz. Philadelphia: Fortress, 1966.

Anselm of Canterbury. "An Address (Proslogion)." In *A Scholastic Miscellany: Anselm to Ockham*, edited and translated by Eugene R. Fairweather, 69–93. Library of Christian Classics 10. Philadelphia: Westminster, 1956.

Arnold, Matthew. "Literature and Science." In *Cultures in Conflict: Perspectives on the Snow-Leavis Controversy*, edited by David K. Cornelius and Edwin St. Vincent, 78–87. Chicago: Scott, Foresman, 1964.

Augustine. *The Confessions*. In vol. 1 of *The Nicene and Post-Nicene Fathers*, Series 1, edited by Philip Schaff, 45–207. Grand Rapids: Eerdmans, 1994.

Ayer, A. J. "Editor's Introduction." In *Logical Positivism*, edited by A. J. Ayer, 3–28. New York: Free Press, 1959.

———. *Language, Truth, and Logic*. New York: Dover, 1952.

Bambrough, Renford. "Introduction." In *Reason and Religion*, edited by Stuart C. Brown, 13–19. Ithaca, NY: Cornell University Press, 1977.

Barth, Karl. *Church Dogmatics*. 1/2: *The Doctrine of the Word of God*. Edited by G. W. Bromiley and T. F. Torrance. Translated by G. T. Thomson and Harold Knight. Edinburgh: T. & T. Clark, 1956.

———. *Church Dogmatics*. 2/1: *The Doctrine of God*. Edited by G. W. Bromiley and T. F. Torrance. Translated by T. H. L. Parker et al. Edinburgh: T. & T. Clark, 1956.

———. *Church Dogmatics*. 2/2: *The Doctrine of God*. Edited by G. W. Bromiley and T. F. Torrance. Translated by G. W. Bromiley et al. Edinburgh: T. & T. Clark, 1957.

———. *The Epistle to the Romans*. Translated by Edwyn C. Hoskyns. London: Oxford University Press, 1933.

———. *Evangelical Theology: An Introduction*. Translated by Grover Foley. New York: Holt, Rinehart, and Winston, 1963.

Bartley, W. W. *The Retreat to Commitment*. 2nd ed. La Salle, IL: Open Court, 1984.

Bernstein, Richard J. *Beyond Objectivism and Relativism: Science, Hermeneutics, and Praxis*. Philadelphia: University of Pennsylvania Press, 1991.

Bohr, Niels. *Atomic Physics and Human Knowledge*. New York: Science Editions, 1958.

Burtt, E. A. *The Metaphysical Foundations of Modern Science*. Rev. ed. Atlantic Highlands, NJ: Humanities, 1952.

Calvin, John. *Institutes of the Christian Religion*. Vol. 1. Library of Christian Classics 20. Edited by John T. McNeill. Translated by Ford Lewis Battles. Philadelphia: Westminster, 1960.

Carroll, Bradley W., and Dale A. Ostlie. *An Introduction to Modern Astrophysics.* 2nd ed. San Francisco: Addison-Wesley, 2007.

Cassirer, Ernst. *The Philosophy of the Enlightenment.* Princeton: Princeton University Press, 1968.

Chisholm, Roderick M. *The First Person: An Essay on Reference and Intentionality.* Minneapolis: University of Minnesota Press, 1981.

———. *Theory of Knowledge.* 2nd ed. Englewood Cliffs, NJ: Prentice-Hall, 1977.

Clark, Kelly James. *Return to Reason: A Critique of Enlightenment Evidentialism and a Defense of Reason and Belief in God.* Grand Rapids: Eerdmans, 1990.

Clifford, W. K. *The Ethics of Belief and Other Essays.* New York: Prometheus, 1999.

Davidson, Donald. "On the Very Idea of a Conceptual Scheme." In *Inquiries into Truth and Interpretation,* 183–98. Oxford: Clarendon, 1984.

Descartes, René. *The Passions of the Soul.* In *The Philosophical Writings of Descartes.* Vol. 1, translated by John Cottingham, Robert Stoothoff, and Dugald Murdock, 325-404. Cambridge: Cambridge University Press, 1985.

Dilthey, Wilhelm. "The Construction of the Historical World in the Human Studies." In *W. Dilthey: Selected Writings,* edited by H. P. Rickman, 170–245. Cambridge: Cambridge University Press, 1976.

———. "Ideas about a Descriptive and Analytical Psychology." In *W. Dilthey: Selected Writings,* edited by H. P. Rickman, 88–97. Cambridge: Cambridge University Press, 1976.

———. "The Nature of Philosophy." In *W. Dilthey: Selected Writings,* edited by H. P. Rickman, 122–32. Cambridge: Cambridge University Press, 1976.

———. "The Types of World-view and Their Development in the Metaphysical Systems." In *W. Dilthey: Selected Writings,* edited by H. P. Rickman, 133–54. Cambridge: Cambridge University Press, 1976.

Drury, M. O'C. "Some Notes on Conversations with Wittgenstein." In *Recollections of Wittgenstein,* edited by Rush Rhees, 76–171. Oxford: Oxford University Press, 1984.

Einstein, Albert. *Ideas and Opinions.* Edited by Carl Seelig. Translated by Sonja Bargmann. New York: Crown Publishers, 1954.

Einstein, Albert, and Leopold Infeld. *The Evolution of Physics: From Early Concepts to Relativity and Quanta.* New York: Simon & Schuster, 1961.

Evans, C. Stephen. *Kierkegaard's "Fragments" and "Postscript": The Religious Philosophy of Johannes Climacus.* Atlantic Highlands, NJ: Humanities, 1983.

Evans, C. Stephen, and Merold Westphal. "Introduction." In *Christian Perspectives on Religious Knowledge,* edited by C. Stephen Evans and Merold Westphal. Grand Rapids: Eerdmans, 1993.

Forde, Gerhard O. *Justification by Faith: A Matter of Death and Life.* Mifflintown, PA: Sigler, 1990.

Gadamer, Hans-Georg. *Philosophical Hermeneutics.* Translated by David E. Linge. Berkeley: University of California Press, 1976.

———. *Truth and Method.* 2nd ed. Translated by Joel Weinsheimer and Donald G. Marshall. New York: Continuum, 1993.

Geertz, Clifford. *The Interpretation of Cultures: Selected Essays.* New York: Basic Books, 1973.

Gregory of Nyssa. *Gregory of Nyssa: The Life of Moses.* Translated by Abraham J. Malherbe and Everett Ferguson. Classics of Western Spirituality. New York: Paulist, 1978.

Griffiths, David J. *Introduction to Electrodynamics*. 3rd ed. Upper Saddle River, NJ: Prentice-Hall, 1999.

———. *Introduction to Quantum Mechanics*. 2nd ed. Upper Saddle River, NJ: Prentice-Hall, 2005.

Gutting, Gary. *Religious Belief and Religious Skepticism*. Notre Dame: University of Notre Dame Press, 1982.

Hanson, N. R. *Patterns of Discovery: An Inquiry into the Conceptual Foundations of Science*. Cambridge: Cambridge University Press, 1958.

Heidegger, Martin. *Being and Time*. Translated by John Macquarrie and Edward Robinson. San Francisco: HarperSanFrancisco, 1962.

Holmer, Paul L. *The Grammar of Faith*. San Francisco: Harper & Row, 1978.

———. *Making Christian Sense: Spirituality and the Christian Life*. Edited by Richard H. Bell. Philadelphia: Westminster, 1984.

———. "The Nature of Religious Propositions." In *Thinking the Faith with Passion: Selected Essays*. Edited by David J. Gouwens and Lee C. Barrett III, 203–17. Paul L. Holmer Papers 2. Eugene, OR: Cascade, 2012.

———. *On Kierkegaard and the Truth*. Edited by David J. Gouwens and Lee C. Barrett III. Paul L. Holmer Papers 1. Eugene, OR: Cascade, 2012.

Horwich, Paul. "Theories of Truth." In *A Companion to Epistemology*, edited by Jonathan Dancy and Ernest Sosa, 509–15. Oxford: Blackwell, 1993.

Hunsinger, George. *How to Read Karl Barth: The Shape of His Theology*. New York: Oxford University Press, 1991.

Jackson, Timothy P. "Against Grammar." *Religious Studies Review* 11 (1985) 240–45.

John Paul II. *Encyclical Letter* Fides et Ratio *of the Supreme Pontiff John Paul II to the Bishops of the Catholic Church on the Relationship between Faith and Reason*. Vatican: Libreria Editrice Vaticana, 1998. Online: http://www.vatican.va/holy_father/john_paul_ii/encyclicals/documents/hf_jp-ii_enc_15101998_fides-et-ratio_en.html.

Kaufman, Gordon D. *An Essay on Theological Method*. Rev. ed. Atlanta: Scholars, 1979.

———. *In Face of Mystery: A Constructive Theology*. Cambridge: Harvard University Press, 1993.

———. *The Theological Imagination: Constructing the Concept of God*. Philadelphia: Westminster, 1981.

Kierkegaard, Søren. *Concluding Unscientific Postscript*. Translated by David F. Swenson and Walter Lowrie. Princeton: Princeton University Press, 1974.

———. *Either/Or*. Vol. II. Translated by Walter Lowrie. Princeton: Princeton University Press, 1944.

———. "Every Good and Every Perfect Gift Is from Above." In *Eighteen Upbuilding Discourses*, edited and translated by Howard V. Hong and Edna H. Hong, 31–48. Kierkegaard's Writings 5. Princeton: Princeton University Press, 1990.

———. "Every Good Gift and Every Perfect Gift Is from Above." In *Eighteen Upbuilding Discourses*, Kierkegaard's Writings 5, edited and translated by Howard V. Hong and Edna H. Hong, 125–58. Princeton: Princeton University Press, 1990.

———. "The Expectancy of Faith." In *Eighteen Upbuilding Discourses*, Kierkegaard's Writings 5, edited and translated by Howard V. Hong and Edna H. Hong, 7–29. Princeton: Princeton University Press, 1990.

———. *Fear and Trembling*; and *The Sickness unto Death*. Translated by Walter Lowrie. Princeton: Princeton University Press, 1954.

———. *The Gospel of Suffering;* and *The Lilies of the Field.* Translated by David F. Swenson and Lillian Marvin Swenson. Minneapolis: Augsburg, 1948.

———. *Johannes Climacus, or, De Omnibus Dubitandum Est;* and *A Sermon.* Translated by T. H. Croxall. Stanford: Stanford University Press, 1958.

———. "The Lord Gave, and the Lord Took Away; Blessed Be the Name of the Lord." In *Eighteen Upbuilding Discourses,* edited and translated by Howard V. Hong and Edna H. Hong, 109–24. Kierkegaard's Writings 5. Princeton: Princeton University Press, 1990.

———. *On Authority and Revelation.* Translated by Walter Lowrie. New York: Harper Torchbooks, 1966.

———. *Philosophical Fragments.* Translated by David F. Swenson. Rev. trans. by Howard V. Hong. Princeton: Princeton University Press, 1974.

———. *The Point of View.* Translated by Walter Lowrie. London: Oxford University Press, 1939.

———. "Strengthening in the Inner Being." In *Eighteen Upbuilding Discourses,* Kierkegaard's Writings 5, edited and translated by Howard V. Hong and Edna H. Hong, 79–101. Princeton: Princeton University Press, 1990.

———. "Think about Your Creator in the Days of Your Youth." In *Eighteen Upbuilding Discourses,* Kierkegaard's Writings 5, edited and translated by Howard V. Hong and Edna H. Hong, 233–51. Princeton: Princeton University Press, 1990.

———. "Three Upbuilding Discourses." In *Eighteen Upbuilding Discourses,* Kierkegaard's Writings 5, edited and translated by Howard V. Hong and Edna H. Hong, 227–90. Princeton: Princeton University Press, 1990.

———. "To Gain One's Soul in Patience." In *Eighteen Upbuilding Discourses,* Kierkegaard's Writings 5, edited and translated by Howard V. Hong and Edna H. Hong, 159–75. Princeton: Princeton University Press, 1990.

———. "To Need God Is a Human Being's Highest Perfection." In *Eighteen Upbuilding Discourses,* Kierkegaard's Writings 5, edited and translated by Howard V. Hong and Edna H. Hong, 297–326. Princeton: Princeton University Press, 1990.

———. "To Preserve One's Soul in Patience." In *Eighteen Upbuilding Discourses,* Kierkegaard's Writings 5, edited and translated by Howard V. Hong and Edna H. Hong, 181–203. Princeton: Princeton University Press, 1990.

Kuhn, Thomas S. *Black-Body Theory and the Quantum Discontinuity,* 1894–1912. Chicago: University of Chicago Press, 1987.

———. "Reflections on My Critics." In *Criticism and the Growth of Knowledge,* edited by Imre Lakatos and Alan Musgrave, 231–77. Cambridge: Cambridge University Press, 1970.

———. *The Structure of Scientific Revolutions.* 2nd ed. Chicago: University of Chicago Press, 1970.

Lehrer, Keith, and Stewart Cohen. "Justification, Truth, and Coherence." *Synthese* 55 (1983) 191–207.

Leibniz, G. W. *Theodicy: Essays on the Goodness of God, the Freedom of Man, and the Origin of Evil.* Edited by Austin Farrer. Translated by E. M. Huggard. La Salle, IL: Open Court, 1985.

Locke, John. *The Reasonableness of Christianity;* with *A Discourse of Miracles,* and part of *A Third Letter Concerning Toleration.* Edited by I. T. Ramsey. Library of Modern Religious Thought. Stanford: Stanford University Press, 1958.

Luther, Martin. *The Bondage of the Will.* In *Luther's Works.* Vol. 33, *Career of the Reformer III*, edited by Philip S. Watson and Helmut T. Lehmann, 15–295. Philadelphia: Fortress, 1972.

———. *Heidelberg Disputation.* In *Luther's Works.* Vol. 31, *Career of the Reformer I*, edited by Harold J. Grimm and Helmut T. Lehmann, 39–70. Philadelphia: Fortress, 1957.

MacIntyre, Alasdair. *Whose Justice? Which Rationality?* Notre Dame: University of Notre Dame Press, 1988.

Malcolm, Norman. *Nothing Is Hidden: Wittgenstein's Criticism of His Early Thought.* Oxford: Blackwell, 1986.

———. *Thought and Knowledge: Essays.* Ithaca, NY: Cornell University Press, 1977.

Marshall, Bruce D. *Trinity and Truth.* Cambridge Studies in Christian Doctrine. Cambridge: Cambridge University Press, 2000.

Mavrodes, George I. "Religion and the Queerness of Morality." In *Rationality, Religious Belief, and Moral Commitment: New Essays in the Philosophy of Religion*, edited by Robert Audi and William J. Wainwright, 213–26. Ithaca, NY: Cornell University Press, 1986.

McCormack, Bruce L. "Divine Revelation and Human Imagination: Must We Choose between the Two?" *Scottish Journal of Theology* 37 (1984) 431–55.

———. *Karl Barth's Critically Realistic Dialectical Theology: Its Genesis and Development, 1909–1936.* Oxford: Clarendon, 1995.

McInerny, Ralph. "Reflections on Christian Philosophy." In *Rational Faith: Catholic Responses to Reformed Epistemology*, edited by Linda Zagzebski, 63–73. Notre Dame: University of Notre Dame Press, 1993.

Meiland, Jack W., and Michael Krausz. "Introduction." In *Relativism: Cognitive and Moral*, edited by Jack W. Meiland and Michael Krausz, 1–9. Notre Dame: University of Notre Dame Press, 1982.

Mill, John Stuart. *On Liberty.* Edited by Currin V. Shields. New York: Macmillan, 1956.

Nielsen, Kai. "Religion and Groundless Believing." In *The Autonomy of Religious Belief: A Critical Inquiry*, edited by Frederick J. Crosson, 93–107. Notre Dame: University of Notre Dame Press, 1981.

Pelikan, Jaroslav. *Jesus through the Centuries: His Place in the History of Culture.* New York: Harper & Row, 1985.

Peters, Ted. *God as Trinity: Relationality and Temporality in Divine Life.* Louisville: Westminster John Knox, 1993.

Phillips, D. Z. "Belief, Change, and Forms of Life: The Confusions of Externalism and Internalism." In *The Autonomy of Religious Belief: A Critical Inquiry*, edited by Frederick J. Crosson, 60–92. Notre Dame: University of Notre Dame Press, 1981.

Plantinga, Alvin. "Justification in the Twentieth Century." In *The Theory of Knowledge: Classic and Contemporary Readings*, edited by Louis P. Pojman, 351–68. Belmont, CA: Wadsworth, 1993.

———. "Reason and Belief in God." In *Faith and Rationality: Reason and Belief in God*, edited by Alvin Plantinga and Nicholas Wolterstorff, 16–93. Notre Dame: University of Notre Dame Press, 1983.

———. *Warranted Christian Belief.* New York: Oxford University Press, 2000.

———. *Where the Conflict Really Lies: Science, Religion, and Naturalism.* New York: Oxford University Press, 2011.

Polanyi, Michael. *Science, Faith, and Society.* Chicago: University of Chicago Press, 1964.

Putnam, Hilary. *Realism with a Human Face*. Edited by James Conant. Cambridge, MA: Harvard University Press, 1990.

———. *Reason, Truth, and History*. Cambridge: Cambridge University Press, 1981.

———. *Renewing Philosophy*. Cambridge, MA: Harvard University Press, 1992.

Reid, Thomas. *Thomas Reid's Inquiry and Essays*. Edited by Ronald E. Beanblossom and Keith Lehrer. Indianapolis: Hackett, 1983.

Rescher, Nicholas. *A System of Pragmatic Idealism*. Vol. 1, *Human Knowledge in Idealistic Perspective*. Princeton: Princeton University Press, 1992.

Schroeder, Daniel V. *An Introduction to Thermal Physics*. San Francisco: Addison-Wesley, 2000.

Smith, John E. "The Critique of Abstractions and the Scope of Reason." In *Process and Divinity: The Hartshorne Festschrift*, edited by William L. Reese and Eugene Freeman, 19–35. La Salle, IL: Open Court, 1964.

———. *Experience and God*. New York: Oxford University Press, 1968.

———. "Mediation, Conflict, and Creative Diversity." In *Harmony and Strife: Contemporary Perspectives, East & West*, edited by Shu-hsien Liu and Robert E. Allinson, 31–48. Hong Kong: Chinese University Press, 1988.

Snow, C. P. *The Two Cultures*. Cambridge: Cambridge University Press, 1993.

Sosa, Ernest. "The Raft and the Pyramid: Coherence versus Foundations in the Theory of Knowledge." In *Empirical Knowledge: Readings in Contemporary Epistemology*, edited by Paul K. Moser, 145–70. Totowa, NJ: Rowman & Littlefield, 1986.

———. *A Virtue Epistemology: Apt Belief and Reflective Knowledge*. Vol. 1. New York: Oxford University Press, 2007.

Stroud, Barry. *The Significance of Philosophical Scepticism*. Oxford: Clarendon, 1984.

Stump, Eleonore. "Introduction." In *Reasoned Faith: Essays in Philosophical Theology in Honor of Norman Kretzmann*, edited by Eleonore Stump, 1–11. Ithaca, NY: Cornell University Press, 1993.

Swenson, David F. "Objective Uncertainty and Human Faith." In *Kierkegaardian Philosophy in the Faith of a Scholar*, edited by Lillian M. Swenson, 96–130. Philadelphia: Westminster, 1949.

———. *Something about Kierkegaard*. Edited by Lillian M. Swenson. Macon, GA: Mercer University Press, 1983.

Taylor, Charles. *The Ethics of Authenticity*. Cambridge, MA: Harvard University Press, 1991.

———. *Sources of the Self: The Making of the Modern Identity*. Cambridge, MA: Harvard University Press, 1989.

Thomte, Reidar. *Kierkegaard's Philosophy of Religion*. Princeton: Princeton University Press, 1948.

Thornton, Stephen T., and Jerry B. Marion. *Classical Dynamics of Particles and Systems*. 5th ed. Ft. Worth, TX: Brooks/Cole, 2004.

Thornton, Stephen T., and Andrew Rex. *Modern Physics for Scientists and Engineers*. 2nd ed. Ft. Worth, TX: Brooks/Cole, 2002.

Toulmin, Stephen. *The Return to Cosmology: Postmodern Science and the Theology of Nature*. Berkeley: University of California Press, 1982.

Winch, Peter. "Meaning and Religious Language." In *Reason and Religion*, edited by Stuart C. Brown, 193–221. Ithaca, NY: Cornell University Press, 1977.

Wittgenstein, Ludwig. *Culture and Value*. Edited by G. H. von Wright and Heikki Nyman. Translated by Peter Winch. Chicago: University of Chicago Press, 1980.

———. "A Lecture on Ethics." *The Philosophical Review* 74 (1965) 3–12.

———. *Lectures & Conversations on Aesthetics, Psychology, and Religious Belief.* Edited by Cyril Barrett. Berkeley: University of California Press, 1966.

———. *Notebooks* 1914–1916. 2nd ed. Edited by G. H. von Wright and G. E. M. Anscombe. Translated by G. E. M. Anscombe. Chicago: University of Chicago Press, 1979.

———. *On Certainty*. Edited by G. E. M. Anscombe and G. H. von Wright. Translated by Denis Paul and G. E. M. Anscombe. New York: Harper Torchbooks, 1969.

———. *Philosophical Grammar*. Edited by Rush Rhees. Translated by Anthony Kenny. Berkeley: University of California Press, 1974.

———. *Philosophical Investigations*. 3rd ed. Translated by G. E. M. Anscombe. New York: Macmillan, 1958.

———. *Philosophical Remarks*. Edited by Rush Rhees. Translated by Raymond Hargreaves and Roger White. Chicago: University of Chicago Press, 1975.

———. *Tractatus Logico-Philosophicus*. Translated by D. F. Pears and B. F. McGuinness. Atlantic Highlands, NJ: Humanities, 1974.

———. *Wittgenstein's Lectures, Cambridge*, 1932–1935. Edited by Alice Ambrose. Chicago: University of Chicago Press, 1979.

———. *Zettel*. Edited by G. E. M. Anscombe and G. H. von Wright. Translated by G. E. M. Anscombe. Berkeley: University of California Press, 1967.

Wolterstorff, Nicholas. "Can Belief in God Be Rational if It Has No Foundations?" In *Faith and Rationality: Reason and Belief in God*, edited by Alvin Plantinga and Nicholas Wolterstorff, 135–86. Notre Dame: University of Notre Dame Press, 1983.

———. "Introduction." In *Faith and Rationality: Reason and Belief in God*, edited by Alvin Plantinga and Nicholas Wolterstorff, 1–15. Notre Dame: University of Notre Dame Press, 1983.

———. *John Locke and the Ethics of Belief*. Cambridge: Cambridge University Press, 1996.

———. "Realism vs. Anti-Realism: How to Feel at Home in the World." *Proceedings of the American Catholic Philosophical Association* (1985) 182–205.

———. *Reason within the Bounds of Religion*. 2nd ed. Grand Rapids: Eerdmans, 1984.

———. Review of *Faith after Foundationalism*, by D. Z. Phillips. *The Philosophical Review* 101 (1992) 452–55.

———. *Thomas Reid and the Story of Epistemology*. Cambridge: Cambridge University Press, 2001.

Zagzebski, Linda. *Epistemic Authority: A Theory of Trust, Authority, and Autonomy in Belief*. New York: Oxford University Press, 2012.

Name Index

Subject Index

www.ingramcontent.com/pod-product-compliance
Lightning Source LLC
LaVergne TN
LVHW010936100826
845153LV00001B/66
9781498264068